The Politics of Identity and Education

Madeleine R. Grumet and Peter M. Taubman

SERIES EDITORS

Sex, Death, and the Education of Children

Our Passion for Ignorance in the Age of AIDS

Jonathan G. Silin

FOREWORD BY
Madeleine R. Grumet

Teachers College, Columbia University
New York and London

Published by Teachers College Press, 1234 Amsterdam Avenue, New York, NY 10027

Grateful acknowledgment is made for permission to adapt and reprint the author's previously published material in the following chapters:

Portions of Chapter 2, adapted from "What AIDS Teaches Us About the Education of Children," *Educational Theory*, 42(3), 253–269 (1992).

Portions of Chapter 3, adapted from "Children, Teachers, and the Human Immunodeficiency Virus: Authorizing AIDS Education in the Curriculum, *Journal of Education*, Boston University School of Education (1992), Vol. 174 #1, pp. 52–69, with permission from the Trustees of Boston University.

Portions of Chapter 4, adapted from "The Early Childhood Educator's Knowledge Base: A Reconsideration," *Current Topics in Early Childhood Education*, Vol. 7, edited by Lilian Katz, reprinted by permission of Ablex Publishing Corp.

Portions of Chapter 4, adapted from "New Subjects, Familiar Roles: Progressive Legacies in the Postmodern World," in Frank Pignatelli and Susanna W. Pflaum, eds., *Celebrating Diverse Voices: Progressive Education and Equity*, pp. 221–243 (Newbury Park, CA: Corwin Press, 1992).

Portions of Chapter 6, adapted from "Standing for Michael," *Kerem*, 1994 (Winter), pp. 88–94.

Library of Congress Cataloging-in-Publication Data

Silin, Jonathan G.
   Sex, death, and the education of children : our passion for
ignorance in the age of AIDS / Jonathan G. Silin ; foreword by
Madeleine R. Grumet.
      p.   cm. — (The politics of identity and education series)
   Includes bibliographical references.
   ISBN 0-8077-3406-3 (cloth : acid-free paper). —
ISBN 0-8077-3405-5 (paper : acid-free paper)
   1. AIDS (Disease)—Study and teaching (Early childhood)—United
States. 2. AIDS (Disease)—Social aspects—United States.
3. Children and adults—United States. 4. Gender identity—United
States. 5. Feminist theory—United States. 6. Educational
sociology—United States. I. Title. II. Series.
LB3418.A35S55   1995
372.3'7—dc20   94-39771

ISBN 0-8077-3405-5 (paper)
ISBN 0-8077-3406-3 (cloth)

Printed on acid-free paper

Manufactured in the United States of America

02 01 00 99 98 97 96 95 8 7 6 5 4 3 2 1

The capacity and worth of writing and speaking in protest or lament are not, therefore, to be undervalued; they are something, after all, other than tears writ large.

Timothy F. Murphy, "Testimony"

Contents

Foreword

A child scrambles off his chair, wiping the milk from his mouth, his cereal half finished. His big brother has already left, allowed to walk with the other bigger boys. The baby sitter, still in her coat, takes the baby from his mother, who turns to the child, roughly wiping his face with a piece of wet toweling paper. She zips up his jacket, reminding him not to forget his lunch, and he squirms away, rushing to catch the bus at the corner.

A man pours coffee into the covered mug for his ride to the school. He leaves the coffee maker on for his lover, still asleep after working late, and, checking his watch, gathers the newspaper into his briefcase. The frost will have to be scraped off the front and back car windows before he leaves, so he hurries. He wants to be there in time to get things in order before the kids come piling out of the busses.

The child and the man meet at school.

How do they speak of the lives they left at home, of the lives they pass as they move through the streets to the school? What portion of what is said— as coats and boots are taken off and stories read, as questions are asked and paint brushes are washed—will they take home with them again?

Barriers that block us, sieves that strain us, veils that blur us, lines that define us, and songs that celebrate us can all be found in the curriculum that passes between the man and the child.

Anyone, big or small, who enters a school brings along a life. In this series, *The Politics of Identity and Education*, we ask how those hours and days and years in school affect the ways we think about our lives. In schools some things are studied and reviewed and tested, over and over and over again, and some things are never mentioned. In schools the jumble of thoughts is sorted into conversations, separating what one says to another kid from what one says to the teacher; what the teacher says to the kids from what the teachers say to each other. And then there's all the stuff nobody says to anybody. The parts of the world that are not spoken do not disappear. They are still there in the streets, on TV, and at home when school is over, and things both said and unsaid whisper in our minds even when the school has been boarded up and sold for condominiums and we can name hardly anyone in the faded class picture.

In *Sex, Death, and the Education of Children*, Jonathan Silin brings what he knows from his life to his ideas about education. In a simpler world this continuity would not be remarkable, but our lives are plotted and pieced together in intricate designs that separate what we know from what we do. Foucault has argued that these interruptions are not accidental but the relentless project of the modern state to frustrate and inhibit individual praxis, and Silin is not naive about his achievement. He writes his life together, clearly naming the discourses that he is linking as well as the rules of separation and silence that he is ignoring. In *Sex, Death, and the Education of Children* Silin has created a generous literary register that can comprehend the many languages of his life: language for what he has learned about the education of young children, language for what he has learned about love and sexuality as a gay man, language for what he has learned about life and death in the age of AIDS.

With careful and brilliant patience Silin has found the language that joins these knowledges to each other and to the curriculum of our schools. Refusing what he calls "our passion for ignorance," Silin wrenches what he knows out of the categories of discretion and avoidance that confine knowledge. He shows us how the early childhood curriculum deploys a false altruism, pretending to protect children from what adults are afraid to think about. He shows us how we culture ignorance in children and in each other by refusing to hear and respond to what they and we already know.

Most important, however, is that Jonathan Silin shows us that the path to what we should teach to children originates in what we are willing to know about our own lives. Silin brings coherence to the relation of identity and education that acknowledges the diversity of the postmodernist self without becoming mesmerized by its elusive multiplicities. Nor is the coherence that he offers us tethered to fundamentalist certainties.

Because the coherence that binds this book together embraces the contradictions and specificity of individual experience, it also acknowledges the diversity and complexity of social experience. Although the coherence that is the achievement of this particular book integrates the author's experience of the AIDS epidemic and his work as an early childhood educator, it also comprehends the issues of coherence that all educators confront as we struggle to do meaningful work. And because this coherence is mapped on the coordinates that frame human existence, it brings courage and compassion to curriculum theory.

This is a book about sex and death. It is also a book about love and life. Sex and death are connected to life and to the love that generates and sustains life. In this book Silin challenges us to face our fears of mortality, of difference, and danger, and to find the information that our children need to face their own lives with confidence and understading.

Madeleine R. Grumet
Series Editor

Acknowledgments

In a foundational way, all books about education are books about the teachers in our lives. At work on this project, I have often thought about the sixth-grade teacher who encouraged my first attempts at "creative writing," the high school teacher who opened a new world of ideas, and the graduate school professor who welcomed me as a colleague, initiating a subtle transfer of power across the academic generations. Subscribing to the belief that parents are our first teachers, I am ever grateful for the love and unflagging support of my own family, even as we traversed some rocky terrain together.

In these acknowledgments I want to publicly cite those who have most directly contributed to the work that follows. Foremost among these are the people with HIV/AIDS in my life—many long dead, others alive and healthy. Friends, lovers, and colleagues, they have taught me the most profound lessons about living and dying, caring for the self and caring for each other. They have led me to ask the questions about my life and commitments that frame this book. They are alive in my every thought and action, embodied in every page of this text.

Over the years Harriet Cuffaro has been most mindful of my desire to take flight and soar as well as of the need to land and come to rest in an intellectually honest place. She has given time and provided insight without measure. From my first course at Teachers College to the most recent meeting of the American Educational Research Association, Maxine Greene has always been there. Our encounters are brief, but the rewards long lasting. Others, too—Ken Corbett, Jo Anne Pagano, Michael Piore, Karen Weiss— have read these chapters in their various incarnations, have sat through conference sessions, terminable and interminable, in which I first presented many of them, and have provided the emotional sustenance required for productive labor. I am also thankful for the ongoing conversations with Therese Bertsch, John Haigney, Dolores Klaich, and Pat Maravel; Rob Caramella, Virginia Casper, Steven Schultz, Eileen Wasow, and Elaine Wickens; Muriel Dimen, Reuben Dworsky, Allen Ellenzweig, Cindy Jurow, Harvey Makadon, Eric Rofes, and Leslie Williams. I include Carole Saltz and the staff of Teachers College Press among these provocative questioners and the librarians at Bank Street College among those who effectively responded to endless queries.

Without the disciplined nurture offered by Madeleine Grumet, who seemed to understand this project clearly, even when my own vision grew fuzzy, this work would not have seen the light of day. Nor would it have been possible without the loving, patient, and good-humored assistance of Robert Giard to whom it is fondly dedicated.

Sex, Death, and the Education of Children

Our Passion for Ignorance in the Age of AIDS

Introduction

I don't feel it is necessary to know exactly what I am. The main interest in life and work is to become someone else you were not in the beginning. If you knew when you began a book what you would say at the end, do you think you would have the courage to write it?

Michel Foucault, "Truth, Power, Self"

Over the last decade I have become obsessed with remembering and forgetting, a response to the multiplicity of AIDS-related deaths that have come to frame my life world. Even now as I write these words, individual images emerge from my unconscious to struggle with one another for the primacy of memory. At first I tried to manage this profusion of names by imposing an order, arranging them in rational categories—former lovers, close friends, more distanced acquaintances, co-workers, clients, famous people. But the lists were a failure. They did not help to make sense of a senseless reality. And so I found myself writing small scraps of narrative, not yet whole stories, that reflected the fragmented nature of my experience. In these scraps of narrative can be found the genesis of *Sex, Death, and the Education of Children*. With time I integrated the narratives into more coherent expository essays, hopefully creating meaningful contexts, places where they might be at home. I have wanted to bridge the gap between the personal and theoretical, between my world and yours.

I like to believe I write for myself. I know better. Writing is an essentially social project that assumes a reader, a reason for repeating the story. Perhaps this is why I found those initial scraps of narrative comforting. They brought me into relation with others, into a dialogue. My lists were comprehensive and linear, while narrative is selective and thematic. Storytelling, like teaching, requires the author to make choices that highlight some themes and allow others to remain in the background. No doubt I was reassured by claiming this familiar role of teacher. Narrative also instructs us about what to

1

remember and what to forget. Through narrative the canon, and that which lies just outside its margins, become part of the same regime of truth, the same understanding of the moral and the problematic. It may be said that the hours spent writing at my desk, squinting at the computer screen while adding, deleting, and relocating blocks of text; the pages of notes penciled on buses between work in New York and home on the East End of Long Island; the critical thoughts half remembered on airplanes between distant conference sites—all have been in the service of assuring that my life might find a place in the official story of the last years of the twentieth century.

Just as I tell several stories in this book, so do I speak with several voices and from within different communities. I write in turn as the early childhood educator concerned with the future of childhood; the political activist angered by the failure of an effective governmental response to HIV/AIDS; the gay man enduring personal losses too frequent to calculate. At different moments and in different contexts one voice takes precedence over the others. Postmodern theorists have taught us to deconstruct the unified, coherent subject, the Cartesian cogito. In its place they offer an understanding of subjectivity as contradictory and splintered, the effect of our historical positioning in a variety of discursive practices. This means that I occupy positions of social privilege as a white, male academic as well as positions of less certain social value as a Jewish, gay early childhood educator. I am both oppressor and oppressed. My aim here is to explore how these multiple identities might inform and transform one another.

In this project I have felt especially welcomed by the feminist discourse that insists on the polyvocal nature of thinking, on the possibilities of learning from the conflicting and overlapping identities that give shape to our lives (Young-Bruehl, 1989). Resisting the hegemonic patriarchy, feminists have actively sought the strategies through which to name and re-present their experience in all its richness and integrity. They have also been mindful of the limitations of social categories. Butler (1990) summarizes:

> If one "is" a woman, that is surely not all one is; the term fails to be exhaustive, not because a pregendered "person" transcends the specific paraphernalia of its gender, but because gender is not always constituted coherently or consistently in different historical context, and because gender intersects with racial, class, ethnic, sexual and regional modalities of discursively constituted identities. As a result, it becomes impossible to separate out "gender" from the political and cultural interactions in which it is invariably produced and maintained. (p. 3)

Despite this embeddedness of identity, gay and lesbian theorists also affirm the power of social categories for expanding personal experience:

Identity may well be a historical fiction, a controlling myth, a limiting burden. But it is at the same time a necessary means of weaving our way through a hazard-strewn world and a complex web of social relations. Without it, it seems, the possibilities of sexual choice are not increased but diminished. (Weeks, 1991, p. 85)

This book reflects my own struggle to find an authentic voice with which to name the passion for ignorance that informs our approach to questions of identity and other pressing social issues in schools. Admittedly it was the silence surrounding AIDS in early childhood classrooms that first set me to investigate the negotiation of knowing/not knowing so fundamental to our curricular efforts. In one respect, then, this is very much a book about the human immunodeficiency virus (HIV). Several chapters address the immediate issue of AIDS education; others attempt to unpack the wider pedagogical implications of HIV in our world. I have tried to re-present the disease in such a way that the lessons it teaches us extend beyond the important but closely focused topic of health education to other domains of curriculum. This journey has led me to explore questions of gender and sexuality, epistemology and psychology, identity and ethics in childhood education.

In another respect however, this could as easily be a book about substance use, homelessness, violence, or racism as about HIV/AIDS. The unprecedented growth of these and other problems challenges those of us involved in the lives of children to reassess the fundamental purposes of schooling. What role can or will the school play in curtailing social ills? Who bears responsibility for welcoming the newcomer into the world? How do the taken-for-granted definitions of our social roles—teacher, parent, administrator, or child—facilitate or stifle change? These questions have been asked before. They take on a new urgency, however, as we face the critical realities of life in the 1990s.

But this is *not* a book about substance use, homelessness, violence, or racism, although these are themes that surface throughout the text. Rather it is a book that has grown out of my experiences as an AIDS educator, advocate, and caregiver, a book that looks at broad issues of social identity through the narrow lens of gay experience. Herein lies its potential to stimulate and provoke, to be particular and general. For no one can claim to be objective about HIV/AIDS, least of all those of us who have been a part of its history. Each of us builds a unique interpretive matrix, grounded in accumulated layers of past experience. It is this matrix that enables us to make sense of our experience and to process new information in a meaningful way. An exploration of my own interpretive framework becomes the background against which I hope to illumine the specific meanings that HIV/AIDS has acquired over time.

For me, the history of HIV/AIDS began in the winter of 1981, when a number of my friends and acquaintances experienced strange symptoms that did not fit any recognizable pattern. Others contracted bizarre infections that had never been seen before in human populations. That spring, a small article on the back page of the second section of *The New York Times* confirmed what a few of us already knew: A new and lethal disease had entered our world. Having just completed my doctoral work in education, I chose to become involved—disseminating what little information we had about safer sex and raising money for care and education.

These were confusing times, the times of the "gay cancer" and "GRID" (gay related immunodeficiency). We did not know what caused this mysterious disease, nor exactly how it was transmitted. The one thing we could be sure of was the lack of governmental response. As with so many others in the gay community, I found it unacceptable to sit passively by while our friends, lovers, and colleagues lost their lives. These were young men, men who were dying too soon, out of turn.

I remember speaking on a panel of underserved populations at Stony Brook University Medical School late one fall afternoon in 1982. At that time, there had been only 654 cases of AIDS, 325 deaths. I talked gingerly about the incipient health crisis. My information was not coming from academic medical journals or national media that would have legitimated my concerns. Instead it came from gay-oriented newspapers like *The New York Native*, from New York City doctors on the front lines, many of whom were themselves gay, and from their patients, my friends. Even as I spoke with increasing confidence in public about the need to understand that which was as yet incomprehensible to health officials and biomedical researchers, I would return home to search nervously for swollen lymph glands and the small, hard, purplish lumps that would indicate Kaposi's sarcoma, so often the first symptom of HIV infection in those days.

It was not until 1985 that I began to work full time for the fledgling community-based organization that was to become the Long Island Association for AIDS Care (LIAAC). Squeezed into a tiny office with two telephones for three people, a secretary who doubled as a hotline coordinator, and a growing client list, we learned to invent our program at every turn. For while plagues, infectious diseases, and critical illnesses have always been a part of human history, none in recent times has brought together quite the same confluence of meanings. We became instant experts in retrovirology, health financing, and social policy. Like many others, we created safer sex workshops and buddy systems, while offering services to whole new categories of people—worried well, HIV-positives, and PWAs (people with AIDS).

My assumption in joining the agency was that I would be leaving behind my knowledge of school systems as well as my understandings of parents, children, and teachers in order to educate health care professionals about infection control precautions and gay men about safer sex. I could not have anticipated the degree to which my life would continue to be bound up with the lives of families—elderly parents looking after adult children at home, new parents tending to the needs of young children, heterosexual and homosexual couples caring for one another. But AIDS had not only triggered crises for innumerable individual families, indeed in our very concept of the family itself. It had also triggered a crisis in the schools, a crisis that unfolded at the level of policy and at the level of curriculum development and implementation.

As I moved between the work of HIV/AIDS care and of education I came to recognize the mutual influence that these two ostensibly discrete worlds were beginning to have on each other. My background in education informed my concerns about AIDS. I had long ago learned to listen closely to those whom I wanted to help, to seek their active participation in creating a meaningful curriculum, and to respect the decision-making powers that reside in each of us. As an early childhood practitioner, I was sensitive to the scientism inherent in much of the psychological literature and the need to transcend the categorical, developmental schema so readily used by professionals to distance themselves from those with whom they work.

My emerging understanding of this new, chronic illness was in turn reflected in my approach to education. A growing sense of urgency imparted by daily contact with the disease was reinforced by the evident lack of governmental effort to reduce the suffering it was causing. I became impatient with the quick–fix mentality behind public health measures such as testing, quarantine, and contact tracing, and with educators who saw HIV/AIDS prevention as a matter of providing students with information about the disease process and the injunction to practice abstinence. At the same time, I had a new acceptance of the limits of technological interventions and respect for the human spirit in the face of intolerable circumstances. And I began to see that health care workers and teachers alike were being challenged by this disease to reconsider their authority as professionals, their understandings of those they intended to help, and their commitment to changing the bureaucratic systems of which they are a part.

I had become a teacher during the turbulent years of the late 1960s, when I rejected the promise of graduate school in England in order to work with young children. Idealism led me to believe that social change was only possible if it affected the lives of the youngest members of society, who, I assumed, presented educators with a blank slate on which to write their ideas. In practice, I thrived on the variety of activities and materials, from blocks and clay to reading and math, present in early childhood classrooms. Beyond the energy and movement of the children, it was the deeper questions they posed about human relationships and social structures that provided the stimulus for my own more formal researches into philosophy, psychology, and curriculum theory.

It was a 4-year-old in one of my first classes who summarized the discomfort that many experienced with my choice of traditional "women's work." Cathy saw me leaving school one afternoon wearing a necktie and carrying a briefcase, unusual attire for me in those days. She ran up to me, enthusiastically exclaiming, "Jonathan, are you going to work now?" I remember laughing and joking, thinking about how I was probably dressed like her father, a prominent psychotherapist, but also astounded by Cathy's insight into the conflict between the role of male and the role of caregiver in our society.

Not that being an outsider was a new theme in my life. As a gay man growing up in the 1950s, actively exploring his sexual orientation in the 1960s, I had many reasons to reflect on traditional sources of authority and codes of behavior. The messages given to me by my parents and society at large were clearly in conflict with my own sense of who I was and what I wanted. My determination to help set the agenda for the gay movement in the 1970s led to increasing involvement in community organizing. However, by the end of the decade, I had become disillusioned with the growing conservatism of mainstream gay politics that had transformed a broad personal and political liberation movement into a limited gay rights lobby. What had begun as resistance to the social order had turned into a demand for a bigger piece of the pie.

Being in the minority—a gay man in a straight world, a male in a predominantly female workplace, an early childhood educator in a society that placed little real value on the lives of young children and those who care for them—had been a source of strength and defining identity. It had also raised many questions about the nature of the political status quo. When I entered a doctoral program at Teachers College, Columbia, these questions motivated investigations into Marxism, phenomenology, and critical theory. Comfortable with the way that radical curriculum theorists applied these disciplines to understanding contemporary educational practices, I was still reluctant to name the interconnecting themes that fueled my own pedagogical passions. How could I talk about simultaneous commitments to gay liberation, young children, and the curriculum? As a gay man, the personification of corrupting evil in the eyes of some, what could I say about children, the apotheosis of innocence and vulnerability in our culture? If such words were to be found, what would be their theoretical or practical import?

By 1985 I had experienced enough of academic life to know that it did not satisfy my restless drive to be both a committed activist and a mindful theoretician. Teaching in a small, Ivy League college, where my greatest rewards came from sparsely attended Sunday night meetings with gay and lesbian students, did not compare with the multilevel stimulation of the early childhood classroom. Besides, the daughters and sons of the upper-middle class whom I taught too often reminded me of the isolation and harassment I had experienced as a teenager. I tried to break the irrational power they seemed to hold over me by coming out in class, pushing them and myself to grapple with the relationship between private and public acts, personal and social meanings. Coming out permitted me to talk about the way that being gay had shaped my political and pedagogical agenda. It was a step in the direction of greater authenticity that also shifted some of my discomfort onto the students. The situation had become less problematic for me, more disquieting for them.

That summer, before beginning work at LIAAC, I began to trace the outlines of a book that would look at what radical critics of schooling were saying about the unequal distribution of cultural and material capital, what gay and lesbian theorists wrote about sexual politics, and what I knew about the traditions of early childhood education. Steeped in these divergent bodies of literature, excited by the theoretical connections among them, I still lacked a specific focus. Nor had I found a voice that would allow all my interests to be heard at once. Fortunately, the press of immediate events saved me from a real confrontation with these inadequacies. They also provided critical time to do a more thorough assessment of the relevance of feminist perspectives to my own work.

In the 1970s, when tensions ran high between gay men and lesbians over many issues, including intergenerational sex, lesbian separatism, and "fringe" sexualities, I had struggled to come to terms with the practical implications of feminism. During the 1980s, I used authors such as Carol Gilligan (1982) and Nancy Chodorow (1978) in the courses I taught but had not yet understood the impact that a radical feminist pedagogy could have on my own thinking and writing. It was listening to Madeleine Grumet and Jo Anne Pagano at educational conferences, the rhythms of their voices and cadences of their speech, that suggested the possibility of a new way of working, a way that insisted on the centrality of the personal and on its connection to the political as expressed in the curriculum.

As a teacher and teacher educator, I had always recognized that the most exciting classrooms were those in which teachers had taken their own interests and translated them into age-appropriate curricular experiences. Now it appeared that an even more potent transformation of the curriculum might occur if teachers were to reflect upon the gendered nature of their extra-classroom lives and then turn to the curriculum with these reflections foremost in their minds. While the more sophisticated critics of the schools spoke of both material and cultural forms of hegemony, as well as moments of resistance, of incongruities between prescribed roles and sense of self, feminists spoke of subjectivity in concrete ways that seemed to allow me greater access to their conversations. Without denying the importance of the differential distributions of power embedded in our class, race, and gender relations, they valorized a new discourse of the body. They wrote of the dailiness of our lives, of coming to know the world through our connections to people and things, of trusting our own stories rather than the official versions of experience taught in schools. The school is a bastion of male knowledge, feminists claimed, and women collude in presenting this as the world of knowledge *tout court*, rather than investigating the forms and ways of knowing that are part of their gendered experience. I began to wonder how I might incorporate my own homoerotic history into explorations of curriculum for young children. More confident now than in 1985 about being personally present in the text, I was also buoyed by the increasing visibility of lesbian and gay scholarship. Although gays have been thrust into the media limelight and high-voltage political struggles by HIV/AIDS—the issues ranging from public health and multicultural curricula to same-sex marriage and participation in the military—they have also produced a steady stream of historical research and theoretical writings about social identity.

A fundamental theme of this work is the way in which socially transgressive behaviors, forms of otherness attributed to gays, women, and children, are inextricably linked to each other and to the norms they define. Michel Foucault (1973, 1977, 1978) teaches us that the nineteenth century produced new technologies of the self, discourses of surveillance, and institutions of control—hospitals, asylums, prisons, and schools—to identify and police threatening populations. Medical, pedagogical, and psychological disciplining replaced more visible forms of power as Charcot attended to subduing the hysterical woman, Binet and Simon to classifying the learning child, and Krafft-Ebing to naming heretofore unrecognized sexual perversions. I understand power to function through this proliferation of knowledge that allows us to "know" the individual with greater certainty. The more there is to be known, the more knowers there must be ensuring the growth of complex, professional hierarchies.

Throughout this book there is a consistent and insistent questioning of the dominance of psychological discourse in education. Whether looking at early education, health care, or safer sex programs, I am made uncomfortable by the power of professionals to shape our lives. Too often, in the fields with which I am familiar, professionals rationalize their choices using ideas borrowed from studies of human development. Masking a technical approach to solving ethical and value-laden questions with the trappings of humanistic sensitivities, they close down options for more democratic participation in decision making and for the investigation of different ways of knowing.

Today, gay and lesbian theorists (Abelove, Barale, & Halperin, 1993; Fuss, 1991a; Plummer, 1992), feminists, radical advocates for children, and AIDS activists all ask similar questions about what knowledge is most valued in our culture and whose interests it serves. The need to hide and the decision to announce one's sexual orientation, themes of the closet and coming out, make gays and lesbians especially interested in epistemological questions. I join the critical discussions about gendered forms of knowledge in the curriculum begun by feminist educators, with an additional concern for the social negotiation of ignorance in the classroom. This is the process through which we all work together, adults and children, homosexuals and heterosexuals, to deny the body and its desires. I believe that a better understanding of how we agree *not* to know will affect individual student–teacher interactions as well as our appreciation of the broader politics of knowledge. Undoubtedly my most immediate experiences with health care and HIV/AIDS education have drawn my attention to this concept. However, it clearly resonates with my own history of coming of age as a gay person.

Sex, Death, and the Education of Children has been a long time in the making. This is less an apology than an acknowledgment of the practical necessities that interfere with cultural production in our society and the personal struggles that have punctuated my efforts. Granting ourselves permission to explore the multiple identities that inform professional work is not the same as actually unraveling and reweaving the threads that form the woof and warp of our life tapestries. These essays are the first steps I have taken in pursuit of this goal. As such, they are not arranged to form a linear argument but rather fan out from an initial point, HIV/AIDS education, to suggest how consideration of one aspect of the curriculum can lead to rethinking childhood education more generally.

Chapter 1 establishes a rationale for HIV/AIDS education that expands traditional ideas about health education and disease prevention. Defining HIV/AIDS as an epidemic of signification, one whose mythological meanings have overshadowed its medical impact, this chapter explores the social and political construction of disease. Chapter 2 looks at the basic educational issues raised by HIV/AIDS and asks readers to examine how their understandings of human mortality impede or facilitate the creation of a socially relevant curriculum. Drawing on my experiences working with teachers as well as on an analysis of popular HIV/AIDS curricula, Chapter 3 discusses the reluctance of classroom teachers to talk about AIDS with younger students and the narrow, ineffective approaches taken with adolescents. The chapters that follow may be read as an extended meditation on themes raised in this initial critique. Chapters 4 and 5 examine how we think about children and childhood and how our thinking becomes a major barrier to discussing critical social issues in schools. Chapter 4 deconstructs the idea of developmentally appropriate practice, the dominant paradigm in early education, and suggests guidelines for re-visioning the field. Chapter 5 questions the distances we create between ourselves and children. Here I take up the historical creation of the innocent and ignorant child that allows us to play the role of the knowledgeable adult, protecting an all-too-easily-lost purity in the early years.

The final chapters address issues of identity and community from different perspectives. Chapter 6 focuses on language, the centrality of narrative knowing, the androcentric language of curriculum makers, and the ways that gay men may find to join in feminist conversations. In Chapter 7 I amplify my contribution to these conversations through exploring diverse experiences of the closet and what they teach about the ambiguity of knowledge. Chapter 8 peers more deeply into the closet, pulling out the stereotypes that link gay people and children in the popular imagination. Together these chapters describe how we construct disembodied identities that deny our sexuality, promote heterosexism and homophobia, and act as further obstacles to HIV/AIDS education.

This is an idiosyncratic book that defies easy categorization and might best be located in the territory that Clifford Geertz (1983) refers to as "blurred genres." It is by turn intensely subjective and rigorously objective, highly theoretical and concretely practical, focused on the lives of children and the experiences of adults. Seeking to understand how and why educators have failed to adequately address HIV/AIDS and other social issues in the classroom, it looks for answers in our taken-for-granted assumptions about children, childhood, and the curriculum through which they can best be served. It argues that an effective response to HIV requires that we learn from each other—adults from children, straights from gays, men from women, uninfected from infected. This means opening new pathways for communication, creating unexpected spaces for reflection, and forming strong action coalitions. For we are just beginning to understand the ramifications of the human immunodeficiency virus in our midst and the kinds of responses that will be required to deprive it of mortal power over us.

CHAPTER 1

HIV/AIDS: The Politics of an Epidemic

> . . . representations of AIDS have to be X-rayed for their fantasmatic logic; they document the comparative irrelevance of information in communication.
>
> Leo Bersani, "Is the rectum a grave?"

With the publication during the late 1980s of major reports by the Surgeon General (*Surgeon General's Report*, 1986), the National Academy of Sciences (1988), and the Presidential Commission on the Human Immunodeficiency Virus Epidemic (1988), HIV/AIDS increasingly and undeniably became a subject requiring the attention of school-based educators. No longer could we allow personal opinion alone to determine the ramifications of the disease for curriculum and policy. We were asked to prepare our students to live in a world in which 15 million people have already been infected—of whom 40% are women and over 80% live in developing countries—and where it is projected that as many as 100 million may be infected by the year 2000. In North America alone we may have up to 8 million cases of HIV infection and 3 million cases of AIDS among adults (Mann, Tarantola, & Netter, 1992). Whether or not our students will know or become someone with this disease, its economic, social, and political impact will be felt by them all.

At first, the questions raised by HIV/AIDS appeared to many educators to be new, the answers unavailable in existing literatures or classroom practices. Yet we are frequently asked to address perplexing events, events that may cause us discomfort or distress, from the Holocaust and terrorism to nuclear "accidents" and natural disasters. Hannah Arendt (1961) makes a critical distinction between the right to teach, which is grounded in love of the world, and the ability to teach, which is based in knowledge of the world and the skill to communicate it to others. From this perspective, pedagogic

11

authority ultimately rests on our willingness to take responsibility for a world that we neither have made nor approve of.

The immediate challenge for educators is to locate the traditions that permit us to understand the pedagogical significance of problems as they arise in society and impinge on our classrooms. We need to map the terrain in which to situate an HIV/AIDS discourse, a discourse that may be more familiar than generally expected. Describing such a discourse only begins the process, for then each one of us must find his or her own voice within it.

During the 1980s, critics of education employed the concept of technocratic-mindedness to explain the omnipresent belief that school problems are technical in nature and solvable through the application of scientific principles (Bullough, Goldstein, & Holt, 1984). This belief that science can provide an adequate knowledge base for describing all aspects of human experience is essential to highly rationalized school systems. The demand for certainty—for a safe, agreed-upon body of knowledge—has worked against the inclusion of controversial issues in the curriculum. Perhaps even more difficult to assess than the exclusion of subject matter is the way in which particular topics have been prepared for presentation. Jurgen Habermas (Dews, 1986) refers to the process in which human phenomena are abstracted from their naturally occurring contexts and submitted to intensive forms of rational analysis as the "colonization of life worlds." When this happens, basic life-sustaining activities such as child rearing, health care, and education become foci for administrative control rather than themes for communicative action.

Like most diseases, however, HIV/AIDS does not pose itself as a question of certainty but rather as a question of possibility versus probability. In schools, policy makers weigh the theoretical possibility of disease transmission in the classroom against the real probability of such an occurrence, and curriculum specialists make calculated judgments about the safest way to frame controversial subjects such as sex, death, and drugs. Outside of the school, everyone weighs the risks of contracting HIV in sexual encounters or exposure to blood and blood products, while PWAs face critical decisions about the use of experimental drugs and their families struggle with the potential social ostracism that can be the consequence of revealing an AIDS diagnosis to others. The complex social meanings engendered by this lethal virus cannot be controlled, predicted, and easily packaged for student consumption.

In this chapter I unpack these complex meanings as background against which to evaluate the adequacy of HIV/AIDS education in the schools. Relying more on critical social analysis and less on personal narrative than later chapters, I want to clarify the multilayered task this disease presents to teachers and the many disciplines it calls into play—biomedical fields, social sciences, and the humanities. Understanding the history of HIV/AIDS is essential to creating effective curricular responses for children of all ages.

DISEASE AS MORAL CONTAGION

The history of epidemics is the history of exclusions, panics, fears, and denials. Leprosy, plague, syphilis, cholera, and tuberculosis have evoked a common sense of powerlessness among us all. HIV/AIDS brings together the especially potent symbols of blood, sperm, and sex—summoning images of pollution and contamination in a culture obsessed with hygiene and risk control. Confronted by the unknown and uncontrollable, people seek to blame the strange and the stranger as identified by divine wrath, rumor, or conspiracy theory. Every historical period also has a unique *Zeitgeist* that informs its reading of disease. Elbaz and Murbach (1992) chart the unique social representations of evil as it is inscribed across the signed body of the diseased. In the case of HIV/AIDS, identity and behavior are confounded in the rush to designate specific populations—gay men, injection drug users, prostitutes, minorities—that might be isolated in a vain attempt to protect the "innocent." It is easier to blame the victims of an epidemic when they are conceived of as different, the space between self and other increased through stereotyping, misinformation, and innuendo. Public opinion becomes structured ignorance.

The fear of disease, and the psychological mechanisms employed to ensure distance from the epicenter of its spread, is shaped by the perceived status of the sick. In turn, this status is reflected in the allocation of resources and the public health measures employed. While the otherness of gay men may be predicated on their sexual orientation, now deemed physically as well as morally polluting, the otherness of the poor, today's stereotype of the injection drug user, has always been understood as the result of their own undisciplined slothfulness. Dirt and disorder have been associated with poverty and sin, both punishable by disease. Foreignness is both literal and figurative in the American experience. Patton (1985) writes:

> The simultaneous discovery of bacteria and the major immigrant movements into the U.S. in the late nineteenth and early twentieth centuries confused the ideas of sickness and foreignness. Even though scientists would argue that it was over-crowding and poor sanitation that led to tragic epidemics in congested urban ghettos, the general population believed that "foreigners" were dirty by nature, and that their dirt (and disease) was proof of inferiority. Dirt and germs serve an important symbolic role in the social organization of difference. (p. 11)

In the nineteenth century, venereal diseases especially came to be emblematic of evil, punishment for the transgressions against social convention and/or religious law. This was also a period when sexuality itself was coming under intense scrutiny by medical professionals and bourgeois moralists (Brandt, 1987). In Europe, sexologists were codifying sexual activities with increasing specificity, while in America feminists and social-purity activists worked to eradicate sexually transmitted diseases. The efforts of the latter were directed to protecting middle-class women from diseases theoretically spread from lower-class prostitutes via their own wayward husbands. To eliminate disease in the middle class, it was necessary to prevent poor young women from becoming prostitutes. Otherwise, the moral disorder of one group would lead to physical contamination of the other. The new discourse on sexuality and disease and the increased power this gave to professionals—legal, medical, psychological, penal—was part of the growing public articulation of what had once been considered private practices.

The threat of sexuality, a potential source of internal psychological and external social chaos, was paralleled by the fear of germs that could spread disorder by the unsanitary behaviors of the poor. To manage the anxieties stirred by fear of uncontrollable sexualities and polluting germs, bourgeois moralists relied on categorical certainties. Foucault (*CDC AIDS Weekly*, 1986) puts this process into historical perspective:

> Every society establishes a whole series of systems of oppositions between good and evil, permitted and prohibited, lawful and illicit, criminal and noncriminal, etc. All of these oppositions which are constitutive of society today . . . are being reduced to the simple opposition between normal and pathological. This opposition not only is simpler than others but also has the advantage of letting us believe there is a technique to bring the pathological back to the normal. (p. 9)

There are many examples in the Western literary tradition of the association of epidemics with moral corruption—from *Oedipus Rex* to *The Divine Comedy*, from *The Magic Mountain* to *The Plague*. In each, illness and/or plague not only brings deterioration of the body but also demoralization and collapse of the social fabric that holds communities together. A major factor in the initial fear and uncertainty surrounding HIV/AIDS was the inexact and at times confusing terminology of medical researchers. Until June 1986 three different names were used when referring to the virus now called the human immunodeficiency virus (HIV). By the late 1980s a narrow focus on AIDS had also been replaced by the concept of HIV-disease, a term that indicates the full range of the epidemic's impact by including those who are HIV-infected and asymptomatic, those who have less critical symptoms (once said to have AIDS-related complex [ARC]), and those with severely compromised immune systems and/or a major, AIDS-defining opportunistic infection.

However, even as the scientific language became more refined, popular accounts of the disease were still couched within a plague metaphor that made it appear to be a problem beyond human control. Emphasizing the mysterious and the unknown, this language fostered the belief that HIV is at least literally, if not morally, contagious. The physical disease is presented as having psychological correlates in those who have contracted it. HIV/AIDS has been defined as a metaphysical event, the modern social text for community sin.

In fact, HIV/AIDS is more genocide than plague, the latter idea only masking the failure of an effective governmental response, an individual sense of helplessness, and the oppressive marginalization of affected populations. The genocidal pattern of official duplicity was established early in the epidemic, when AIDS was declared the government's number-one health priority while a presidential directive required that no new funds be allocated for its cure, only money that could be diverted from other diseases. In 1984 only 2.3% of the minuscule AIDS budget was assigned to education, and in 1985 a report of the Federal Office of Technical Assessment confirmed that interagency competition, lack of funding, and bureaucratic red tape subverted initiation of HIV/AIDS research. To counter this neglect, activists called for a Manhattan Project to galvanize and rationalize government intervention. The image of a wartime mobilization emphasizes human causation and agency in contradistinction to images of natural disaster or plague. Unfortunately, it also brings to mind highly publicized but hastily conceived and underfunded efforts—the War on Poverty, War on Drugs, War on Cancer—to resolve complex problems requiring more sustained efforts (Sherry, 1993).

Although every disease elicits a different metaphoric language, in the postindustrial age the desired medical response is most often characterized by military terminology (Sontag, 1977). Scientists are expected to marshal their resources in an all-out offensive, educators to hearken to a battle call in order to avert a catastrophic defeat, health professionals to care for the victims of the struggle, and a few haggard survivors to emerge from among the decimated populations. Although the military vocabulary is used in both religious and medical discourse, within the latter it emphasizes the Western medical model, which portrays any disease agent as an invader requiring aggressive forms of assault—including radiation, chemotherapy, and drugs—to be rooted out.

The American Medical Association (Reuben, 1986) maintains quite simply that "the only real hope of success [in AIDS treatment] lies in attacking and destroying the virus itself" (p. 55). Solutions are to be found via external forces rather than by looking within the psychology of the human body or the body politic. Therefore the patient becomes a passive observer, his or her body the battlefield on which the invasive disease is fought with the latest magic bullet provided by modern science. In contrast, others would suggest a language that reinforces active participation in the healing process. Members of the People with AIDS Coalition eschew terms such as *victim*, *sufferer*, and *fatal*. This is not to deny the seriousness of HIV infection but rather to emphasize the role that persons with HIV can play in the management of the disease and in the quality of life they enjoy. Many who are affected also join community-based service agencies or direct-action groups, focusing their efforts on increasing the quantity and quality of resources being expended by government, industry, and private philanthropy (Kayal, 1993). They do not wait for the benevolence of others or miracles of science. An underlying theme of this approach is the willingness to differentiate between blame (passing negative judgments on ourselves for the results of past behaviors) and responsibility (holding ourselves accountable for behavior in the present).

Blame and Responsibility

The distinction between socially sanctioned blame and meaningful personal responsibility may be especially hard to maintain in a society that has used blame as an indicator of social worth. Three categories of PWAS were initially described in the press, including the innocent, the suspect, and the guilty (Albert, 1986). The first group included hemophiliacs, children, and recipients of blood transfusions. For example, in 1982 *The New York Times Magazine* referred to hemophiliacs as the "innocent bystanders caught in the path of a new disease" and their problems as "particularly poignant" (Henig, 1982, p. 36), while in 1985 a *Newsweek* caption under a picture of a baby and a hemophiliac read, "the most blameless victims" (August 12, 1985, p. 29). The second group, Haitians, were suspected of being closet homosexuals, drug users, or prostitutes, and were indicted for their assumed failure to cooperate with professional researchers. The third group, injection drug users, gay men, and prostitutes, were regarded as the truly guilty. Blame was attached to their involvement in non-normative behaviors that may have placed them at risk.

Within these socially constructed categories there have been subtle shifts and transformations (Treichler, 1988a). For example, although women were first portrayed as among the innocent, as the victims of promiscuous or closeted gay husbands, they have increasingly been represented as HIV "carriers," morally responsible for their own condition and a threat to others (Gagnon

& Folland, 1992). The automatic exclusion of women from many clinical trial protocols, for fear of potential risk to an unborn fetus, reflects this denial of the person with rights over her own body, as does the increasing use of court-mandated caesarean sections in cases of suspected "fetal abuse" by women who use illegal drugs (Hubbard, 1993). Women have most often been viewed as transparent vectors of transmission to others. It is not woman as woman that matters, but woman as commodity, her own interest subordinated, transformed into an object of circulation among men. Although a growing literature calls attention to the immediate impact of HIV/AIDS on women, it does not always honor the commitments to children that so often frame their lives (Woodruff, 1993). In theory and practice we must understand HIV/AIDS as a family disease.

In the contemporary world, blame is not only defined in theological or secular terms as the result of moral wrongdoing. A subtler but even more damaging form of blame is aroused by psychological interpretations indicating that character flaws may not only be expressed in specific diseases but may actually cause them. If people make themselves sick through mismanagement of stress or repression of desires, then they are presumed capable of curing themselves through strength of will or psychotherapy. The onus is still placed on the victim, the blame based on inability to correct the fatal disease-causing flaw. The effect of this slippage between psychoimmunology and moralistic judgment is compounded when disease is depicted as a private experience devoid of cultural and social determinants. For then the effective response is limited to interiorized self-transformation rather than political or scientific action.

The imposition of blame, whether it is imputed to moral failure or to weakness of psychological faculties, underlines the reality that healing does not occur only within the individual. It must also occur among people—an intersubjective process made possible by the abilities to forgive and to promise. Hannah Arendt (1958) points out that human action is characterized by irreversibility and unpredictability. We are not able to undo that which has been done, even though we may not have known what we were doing, except through forgiveness. Meanwhile, the chaotic uncertainty of the future can be confronted only through the promise. Neither forgiving nor promising occurs in isolation, but rather both emerge as possibilities out of our life with others:

> Both faculties, therefore, depend on plurality, on the presence and acting of others, for no one can forgive himself and no one can feel bound by a promise made only to himself; forgiving and promising enacted in solitude or isolation remain without reality and signify no more than a role played before one's self. (Arendt, 1958, p. 237)

Although some might place greater value on the possibilities of internal dialogue than Arendt, few would deny that the ability to forgive and to promise are part of every relationship and, indeed, lie at the core of the teaching–learning paradigm. As teachers, we seek to influence our students and in turn are influenced by them. Inherent in our attempts to persuade students to see the world as we do is the chance of error, of mistakes in judgment. Forgiveness provides the only way of freeing ourselves and others from irreversible mistakes of the past. Morally proffered influence assumes the ability to forgive and to be forgiven, thereby encouraging students to attempt the new and unrehearsed as well as to practice the old and familiar. It is an acknowledgment that teachers are not omniscient. Rather, they welcome children into the classroom with the promise of knowledge and in so doing offer them new ways of responding to themselves, to others, and to the world. Dwayne Huebner (1975a) explains:

> The various disciplines—mathematics, biology, physics, history, sociology, visual arts, drama and others—are not only bodies of principles, concepts, generalizations, and syntax to be learned. They are patterned forms of response-in-the-world, which carry with them the possibilities of the emergence of novelty and newness. Introducing the child to the language of symbols and methods of geography or chemistry or music or sculpture is not to introduce him to already existing forms of human existence which he must know in order to exist. Rather these disciplines increase his ability to respond to the world. (p. 230)

While each of the disciplines can be thought of as a unique language system, Heidegger suggests in a more fundamental way that speech itself is a basic form of the person's response-in-the-world. The unconditioned linguistic responses of children create new ways of expressing and evaluating experience. So, too, does the new vocabulary and syntax being formulated by people with HIV/AIDS. The increasing response-ability they show has led them into new as well as ancient forms of medicine. The present inability of science to provide anything but palliative care and limited-use medications for specific opportunistic infections has reinforced this search for alternative therapies. The proliferation of miracle drugs has been balanced by the reemergence of old healing arts. The HIV/AIDS lexicon not only includes AZT and pentamidine but also acupuncture and visualization.

For educators, too, HIV/AIDS may present a moment to increase response-ability by examining the knowledge base through which the issue is addressed. The first task given to us, the foundation on which our policies will be formulated and our curricula constructed, is to define the disease itself. What is HIV/AIDS? What exactly is the phenomenon under discussion?

HIV/AIDS: A Tear in the Social Fabric

There are some who claim that HIV/AIDS is just an illness, or more accurately, a medical condition whose consequences are a spectrum of illnesses. Sontag (1988) writes in order to reveal and criticize the metaphors in which we couch our references to HIV/AIDS and thus imbue it with meaning. She is particularly concerned with the military language positing the need for an all-out war on an invading agent that uses the body as a battlefield. Such metaphors not only have moral/ethical ramifications that contribute to the stigmatization of groups of people but also practical implications for individuals who may refuse to seek appropriate treatment or care. Language can be deadly when it fosters shame, embarrassment, and a sense of blame, turning people into passive victims rather than active participants in their own care. By freeing AIDS of its metaphors, Sontag hopes to disabuse us of the apocalyptic thinking that breeds irrational fears and programmatic paralysis. Ironically, however, her particular attention to language minimizes, even eliminates, the actual suffering that HIV infection imposes on the individual.

Others argue that there is no reality to be uncovered through critical, linguistic analysis but rather that HIV/AIDS is only known through its socially defined meanings (Crimp, 1988). This is not to deny the existence of viruses, opportunistic infections, or the all too real pain they have caused, but to seek control of the epidemic in new arenas. The most explicit statement of the relativist position was made by Delaporte (1986) in a study of the history of cholera when he argued "that 'disease' does not exist. It is therefore illusory to think that one can 'develop beliefs' about it or 'respond' to it. What does exist is not disease but practices" (p. 6). Medical knowledge is not discovered but constructed, not objectively out there, a reflection of physical reality, but socially negotiated to enhance an arbitrary set of economic arrangements and distribution of power.

This position has been used to create an incisive critique of the media and governmental response to HIV/AIDS. Treating the disease itself as a symptom, the counterdiscourse (Carter & Watney, 1989; Klusacek & Morrison, 1992) seeks to demystify HIV/AIDS and the apparatus through which the media produce their mythologies. The language of AIDS emerges from this analysis thick with political meanings. The counterdiscourse has also provided the theoretical underpinnings of much of the radical activist response to the disease. Familiarity with how the disease has been constructed has suggested opportunities for how it might be deconstructed. Often the small moments, specific representations of the disease and local programs, most clearly reveal the larger social interests at work. Those who are committed to changing immediate circumstances and, in many instances, also living with the disease are engaged by an analysis that balances the social and biological, the subjective and objective, the phenomenological and material.

Although the specific strategies of direct-action groups—playing to the media, deploying new technologies, street theater—may summon up very contemporary images of resistance (Crimp, 1990a), the assumptions in which they are rooted were articulated during the nineteenth century. British labor leaders, influenced by Engels's (1845/1971) research into the living conditions of the working class, declared that improvements in health could only be secured through the political and economic changes necessary to transforming oppressive social relationships. The realities of disease were the realities of poverty, deprivation, and economic hardships. Defining health as a sociopolitical phenomenon, achievable through a more equitable distribution of material resources, posed an unabashed threat to those with an interest in maintaining the status quo. Bourgeois apologists, including many in the newly emerging medical profession, countered that disease was solely the effect of a pathological change in the human body caused by an outside agent or agents. Such a mechanistic interpretation of disease allowed practitioners to claim scientific objectivity, to focus on the individual patient, and to ignore the socioeconomic conditions that hasten mortality and prevent health.

Reading disease as the product of relatively autonomous biologic processes or as constituted in and through dominant ideological perspectives is of more than just historical interest. For example, contemporary health policy analysts suggest that as a society we tend "to seek medical solutions to what are essentially tears in the social fabric. These tears can be in terms of violence, economic oppression and class ostracism, racism, sexism, a whole host of factors" ("The Demand Side," 1993, p. 32). High-tech medical care is not primarily responsible for health status. There is no direct correlation between the availability of medical care and health. Ultimately, people do not get sick because they lack medical care but rather because they live in substandard conditions that reflect various forms of social marginalization.

In reviewing recent charges of fetal abuse against individual women and the incidence of HIV transmission from mother to fetus, Hubbard (1993) highlights the connections between race and class, and health. She notes that in America the chances of vertical transmission of HIV was initially calculated at 60%, now closer to 30%, while European data place it at 13%. In another study, 70.9% of children born to lower-class, alcohol-addicted mothers exhibited fetal alcohol syndrome, while only 4.5% of children born to upper-middle-class, alcoholic mothers were born with the syndrome. Hubbard (1993) asks us to consider how the overall health of a woman affects her fetus, concluding:

Institutional neglect, not individual behavior, is responsible for the gross racial and economic disparities in HIV incidence, birth outcomes, and infant morbidity and mortality in this country. Federal, state and local government agencies—not pregnant women—should be charged with fetal abuse. (p. 14)

In a technology-driven medical system with proliferating specialties and radical interventions, we give far less attention to preventing disease from occurring than managing it once here. For example, in 1984, two years into the epidemic, the Public Health Service spent only $200,000 on HIV/AIDS education and reduced that amount to $120,000 the following year. During this same period, Polaroid spent $30 million to sell a new camera and Procter & Gamble spent $60 million to advertise a new liquid detergent. Health is more than a product to be purchased or service to be delivered by doctor to individual patient, and the effects of our neglect multiply yearly. Today, the World Health Organization estimates that improving prevention efforts in developing nations, through a 1.5% increase in health care budgets, would reduce the number of new HIV infections by 10 million—half the total number it expects by the year 2000 (Altman, 1993b).

The Contested Construction of Credibility

Questions about how to define HIV/AIDS and the role of social change in disease prevention lead to additional questions about how scientific knowledge itself is produced and legitimated in our society. Gay and lesbian activists were well prepared to raise these concerns, since it was only through their own efforts in 1974 that a reluctant medical profession (the American Psychiatric Association) erased homosexuality from the debit column of the health ledger. Preceded by cancer activists and the feminist health movement, HIV/AIDS advocates have challenged the hegemony of the medical establishment to speak authoritatively about disease. Important criticisms of double-blind testing, placebo controls, and university-based clinical trials have led to new drug protocols, the creation of "guerrilla" and community-based drug testing, and reevaluation of trial endpoints (Kahn, 1993; Kwitny, 1992; Sergios, 1993). Epstein (1990) refers to this process as the "contested construction of credibility." While prior challenges to medical authority targeted the monopoly of knowledge in which professional status is grounded and stressed a more democratic distribution of information, HIV/AIDS activists ask not only who controls scientific knowledge but also who creates it and to what ends.

The construction of knowledge about HIV/AIDS or any other disease does not take place in a vacuum by disinterested scientists. As Navarro (1988) suggests, it involves:

the collective set of beliefs, ideas, and knowledge in which the social thoughts of some classes, races, and genders are more dominant than those of others. It has a scientific element, owing in part to the relative autonomy of science, and an ideological element reproduced by the values, beliefs, and experiences of the scientists who work and operate in universities and social settings subject to a whole set of class, gender, race, and other forms of influences. Both elements—the scientific and the ideological—are not related in conditions of exteriority, i.e., scientific knowledge is not outside its ideological dimension. Rather, one is in the other. (p. 65)

It is just such an analysis of the way that scientific knowledge is socially constructed that is hidden in the media. Popular magazine covers portray that twentieth-century icon, the individual scientist, posed in white laboratory coat against a background of test tubes and research paraphernalia, staring hopefully into space. Newspapers offer discrete pieces of disconnected information devoid of any meaningful context, without space for cultural or subjective evaluation. HIV/AIDS is not meant to be assimilated into personal experience but to remain isolated, outside the self. Television news coverage of HIV/AIDS, which peaked in 1987 with stories about heterosexual transmission and the reassurance that the general population is still safe, has been largely reactive, presenting the most simplified formulations of a complex and often contradictory epidemic (Treichler, 1993). Although more time has been given to alternative views and critical, investigative reporting since 1990, the image of the scientist remains largely unscathed, conforming to a pre-HIV/AIDS ideal of the friendly, if distant, seer of the future.

Treichler (1988b) refers to AIDS as an epidemic of signification. Through an extensive analysis of the scientific and popular discourses on HIV/AIDS, she explores the ways in which these ostensibly discrete realms of language are in fact interactive and mutually determinative, thus undermining the once privileged position held by the scientific. It can no longer be assumed that science defines an objective base of information upon which we have built a symbolic superstructure that somehow distorts reality (Sontag, 1988). Rather, it is the scientific enterprise itself that comes under closest scrutiny, becoming one of many equally valid perspectives. Treichler's (1988b) perspective is theory-based but mindful of the needs of practice:

We must learn to live—indeed, *must* learn to live—as though there are such things as viruses. The virus—a constructed scientific object—is also a historical subject, a "human immunodeficiency virus," a real source of illness and death that can be passed from one person to another under certain conditions that we can apparently—individually and collectively—influence. The trick is to learn to live with this disjunction, but the lesson is imperative. Dr. Rieux, the physician-narrator of Camus's novel, acknowledges that by dealing medically with the plague he is allowing himself the luxury of "living in a world of abstractions." But not indefinitely; for "when abstraction sets to killing you, you've got to get busy with it." (p. 69)

Treichler's practical intent is clear. What HIV/AIDS signifies cannot be determined by the narratives of experts—scientific, religious, or political. A democratically structured discourse must be initiated that will encourage all those who have been directly affected by HIV to enter the dialogue and tell their stories. Hopefully this will serve to counter many of the mythical stories that have been generated by those who have attempted to control and explain the meaning of HIV/AIDS.

The original and perhaps most significant of these fictions arose from the attempt to read the story of AIDS from the text of the male, homosexual body, a text that has been largely unspoken in the public, if not the scientific, domain. This is a text that has been read simultaneously as absence and presence. Absent are the natural male drives that lead to reproduction and protection of the family. Present by implication are female characteristics and sensitivities, themselves read as void. Without family and children, the male homosexual is missing the requisite commitment to socially responsible behaviors that would lead him to repress his recalcitrant sexuality.

The first major television dramas about gay men with AIDS, NBC's "An Early Frost" broadcast in 1985 and ABC's "Our Sons" in 1991, exemplify the theme of absence. Focusing on the response of various family members to the AIDS diagnosis, the men themselves are barely present in comparison to their suffering, confused parents and siblings. As in much AIDS literature, we are not asked to immerse ourselves in the lives of those with the disease but rather in the lives of those who observe it from the outside (Cady, 1993).

In classic texts such as *The Picture of Dorian Gray* (Wilde, 1891/1985), being gay is less about absence than about a surfeit of sexual drive that leads to debauchery, self-absorption, and the need to recruit others into obsessive behavior. The contemporary tabloids reinforce this image with stories of HIV-positive gay men who knowingly put others at risk through a vindictive refusal to practice safer sex. Gay men are depicted as threatening rather than threatened, in need of control rather than support, part of a single culture, living a homogeneous "gay lifestyle." Prominent, too, are the images of the isolated and hapless victim, abandoned by family and friends, wasting away in a hospital bed—an image that cruelly deflects attention from the real abandonment by government and media (Watney, 1992).

In the gay world, we have often told a different story, but one with a similar moral (Silin, 1987a). This story takes the form of a developmental narrative of a community coming of age: The 1950s are seen as the infancy of the gay movement, the 1960s its childhood, the 1970s its adolescence, and the 1980s its adulthood. The culture of the 1970s, a reaction to years of life in the closet and relegation to sissidom, is interpreted as a time of youthful rebellion, sexual experimentation, and immaturity that was destined to play itself out. We have been appropriately chastened by a disease that has taught us the real lessons of sex and drugs. If we did not properly care for ourselves in the past, by implication bringing AIDS upon ourselves, now as mature adults we have the chance to redeem the community through personal sacrifice and love. We, too, can confuse blame and responsibility while creating a one-dimensional history that erases our differences.

These stories, as well as representations of heterosexually transmitted HIV, must be placed in the context of "a crisis of representation itself, a crisis over the entire framing of knowledge about the human body and its capacities for sexual pleasure" (Watney, 1987, p. 9). HIV/AIDS is embedded in a system of representations that is constituted by ideologically defined dichotomies—male/female, heterosexual/homosexual, adult/child. It does not represent a unique moment of moral panic but is part of an ongoing struggle by competing forces to define the meaning of the body that is reflected in debates over reproductive technologies, definitions of the family, abuse, and incest.

THE LANGUAGE OF CONTAINMENT

AIDS has been given as a disease of the "Other"—that is, a disease of people we do not know and in whose lives we are not implicated. Although the natural opacity of social life prevents us from knowing others in their totality, fragmentary and partial knowledge is embedded in the typifications we use to make sense of our interactions. Maurice Natanson (1972) explains:

> The actor constructs a world whose form and content are composed of the interpretation he gives both to his own acts and to the action of Others. To say that such interpretation is *situated* is to suggest that the "same" behavioral act is not at all necessarily the same social act. I understand the meaning of an act when I determine what it signifies to the actor. The Other understands my action when he determines what it means to me. That much determination is partial and faulty is precisely the truth of social existence, for the necessary reliance on typicality—the very construction of common-sense life—is a recognition that we know ourselves, let alone Others, in partial and hidden ways and yet are bound, if not condemned to find our way in the world within the restrictions of an opaque sociality. (p. 181)

Social reality is constructed through a spectrum of typifications, from those based on more complete, face-to-face meetings with others, to those created without any firsthand experience of the Other. The concreteness of face-to-face knowing, the multiplicity of stimuli in which we can ground our interpretations, makes it harder to generalize and to respond in stereotyped or alienating ways to the Other. Although it is neither possible nor desirable to make others known in their entirety, for the condition of our plurality is that which makes communication and action possible, it is feasible to conceive of the educator's function as one of helping students to become aware of the typifications on which they base their judgments of the Other. HIV/AIDS education can be the occasion to become conscious of how we are always the Other for someone else. Johnston (1987) comments:

> Close encounters with "The Other" usually tend to disorient us. But despite a possibly painful disorientation of our comfortable world view, an understanding of "The Other" can be an occasion for personal growth. It calls our self-centeredness into question and teaches us to take "The Other" into account. "The Other" confronts "me" with an appeal to take into account another center of meaning in my own understanding of the world. (p. 81)

When AIDS is viewed as a disease of the Other, it allows us to feel safe. The physical and emotional realities of the disease are not possibilities for our own lives and can be discounted. To give up this pose is to acknowledge that the possibility of the Other is also my possibility; the life of another presents itself as a theme for reconsideration of my own experience. We resist knowing the Other as if hoping that our ignorance will protect us, guaranteeing safety from infection.

A Risk-Group Vocabulary

This desire for safety impels us to use a language of containment rather than a language of community and belonging. On April 25, 1985, Margaret Heckler, then director of the Department of Health and Human Services, made official policy of the "us" versus "them" mentality by proclaiming: "We must conquer AIDS before it affects the heterosexual population . . . the general population. We have a very strong public interest in stopping AIDS before it spreads outside the risk groups, before it becomes an overwhelming problem" (quoted in Nunokawa, 1991, p. 311).

Initially referred to as the gay cancer or GRID (gay-related immunodeficiency), AIDS was viewed as a disease inherent in a particular sexual orientation, conveniently confirming what many wanted to believe: that gayness itself is unhealthy. Eventually, an expanded "risk-group" vocabulary, based on epidemiological evidence, was adopted by the federal Centers for Disease

Control (CDC). But this vocabulary was also a political vocabulary that has led to inaccurate information about HIV transmission and misleading prevention messages. Thus HIV-infected Haitians were initially described as constituting a separate risk group, then were later reclassified, mostly into the heterosexual transmission category (Farmer, 1992). Early in the epidemic, there was no category for men who have sex with men and also inject drugs. Men with both risk factors in their lives were placed in the male-to-male transmission group, confirming the assumption that AIDS was a gay disease and masking the realities of many lives.

At present there is no category for women who may have contracted the virus either through drug injection or sex, affirming the American belief that HIV/AIDS is a disease of substance abuse rather than sex between female and male or two females. In fact, during 1992 ("Update," 1993) more women contracted HIV through sex than through injection drug use. Researchers ("Women and HIV," 1993) have found that prevention programs in the San Francisco area targeting women who inject drugs have inadequately addressed issues of sexual practices. Although there has been a decrease in needle sharing and numbers of partners, many drug-injecting women continue to have unprotected sex. The researchers also conclude that messages that stress the risk of multiple partners but not the dangers of unprotected sex per se are confusing and ineffective.

A recent study (Mickler, 1993) has verified what many HIV/AIDS educators quickly recognized: The risk-group vocabulary offered a false sense of security and was counterproductive to their efforts. Among college students, increased knowledge about AIDS was associated with decreased perceptions of vulnerability, suggesting that education focusing on facts and high-risk categories may leave young people feeling reassured of their distance from the disease rather than with a sense of its relevance to their lives. Others are left more confused than reassured because they are unable to coordinate the medical facts, social meanings, and public health messages or to relate this information to their own lives (Bowen, 1993).

The epistemological structure that makes AIDS unknowable to college students also affects other target populations, such as men who have sex with men. Although estimates of homosexual contacts vary widely (from 37% of all men to 17% of adolescent males), to announce that AIDS is a disease of gay men can render prevention messages ineffective, since only a minority may identify themselves as gay (Kinsey, Pomeroy, & Martin, 1948; Sorenson, 1973). Similarly, although some students share needles when injecting steroids or street drugs, most do not think of themselves as drug users. On the other hand, young women who identify as lesbians but have sexual intercourse with males cannot afford to discount the risk of HIV despite popular messages suggesting that lesbians as a group are not vulnerable to infection.

Educators must avoid social labels and emphasize the specific practices that can potentially transmit the virus. We need to take full account of the discrepancy between how people see themselves and how others would classify them in order to do effective HIV prevention.

As Margaret Heckler's 1985 announcement made clear, membership in risk groups is most often contrasted with belonging to the general public. This distinction implies that risk-group members are somehow not part of "society," not entitled to the same rights and privileges as others. But media coverage of the epidemic has consistently positioned readers and viewers alike in contradictory ways, suggesting they both *are* and *are not* at risk (Watney, 1992). Even a concern for the heterosexual spread of HIV reemphasized the boundaries across which it must pass to reach the "general public." Allison Gertz, a college student from a white, middle-class family who became infected through a single sexual encounter, personified this new awareness. Her story did not so much change the basic discourse as modify the categories that signal potential danger, while the attention she received tended to mask the more obvious epidemiological evidence. Over half the adolescents aged 13 to 21 with AIDS are gay or bisexual males, a severely underserved population in which rates of new HIV infection are increasing at alarming rates (Cranston, 1992; Gardner & Wilcox, 1993).

Historians of the epidemic (King, 1993) point out that by the late 1980s HIV/AIDS had been "de-gayed." With the help of campaigns such as New York State's "AIDS Does Not Discriminate," public health officials set out to change the widespread belief that AIDS was a gay disease. But not everyone is at equal risk, not all groups have suffered to the same degree. While it is true that the early risk-group emphasis masked discrepancies between behavior and social identities, the de-gaying of AIDS functioned to direct resources away from one of the hardest hit populations and to obscure the pioneering role played by lesbians and gay men in responding to the epidemic. Some HIV/AIDS activists emphasize the "re-gaying" of a disease that continues to have such an overwhelming impact on the gay and lesbian community (Callen, 1989).

HIV/AIDS is best understood as a series of distinct but overlapping epidemics. Concern with "re-gaying" HIV/AIDS should be seen in the context of debates over how best to use limited HIV prevention and care resources (Des Jarlais, Padian, & Winkelstein, 1994; Schmidt, 1993). The National Research Council (Jonson & Stryker, 1993) argues that HIV/AIDS is an epidemic of socially and spatially isolated groups that leaves many geographic areas and strata of society untouched. For example, in this country 25% of people with HIV/AIDS are African-American and 15% are Hispanic, yet these groups make up 12% and 7% of the population, respectively. Three-quarters of women with HIV/AIDS are women of color, and 80% of HIV-infected newborns are of color. Increasingly sophisticated epidemiological evidence suggests the benefits of focusing on 23 to 30 urban neighborhoods across America, and even specific zip codes within those neighborhoods; reports from Australia, Scotland, and Sweden tell of the success of targeted prevention plans in other countries. Yet such an approach runs the risk of further stigmatizing specific racial and ethnic minorities and belies the complexity of individual lives.

HIV/AIDS POLICY AND OUR REPUBLICAN PAST

Traditionally, U.S. health policy involving risk assessment is based on judgments of the extent to which potential negative consequences should be determinative of policy (Rothman, 1987). Policy can be generated on a best-case scenario, stressing tolerance for risk, or on a worst-case scenario, heightening the requirements of risk avoidance. Public health officials have usually acted on the basis of the worst-case situation, counting all unknowns as negatives and implementing policy to maximize risk avoidance. This worst-case approach was exemplified by the response to the swine flu scare during the 1970s, when a massive vaccine campaign was undertaken because it could not be proven that a flu epidemic would *not* take place. A similar stand was taken in arguments over the placement of formerly institutionalized children with high incidence of hepatitis B into regular classrooms. Public health officials maintained that the risks outweighed the benefits, that individual rights to education in the least restrictive environment were secondary to public health concerns. In contrast, civil libertarian lawyers for the children held that it is wrong to penalize individuals in advance of proof of contagion simply because they belong to a group with a statistically higher incidence of disease. New York State courts ruled against the public health position, arguing that suspicion is not sufficient cause for exclusion.

The simplified bifurcation of reality into individual rights versus the public good limits options for community response while locating blame among specific persons. As with HIV/AIDS, when health issues are couched in military metaphors, actions based on confused notions of the enemy proliferate, since the goal in battle is victory at any cost. Critical standards of judgment and ethical evaluations of behavior are often suspended in a crisis. The Greek root of the word *crisis* means "to sever" or "to cut," and some would use the notion of an AIDS crisis to sever ties with those who are sick and so to cut off reflective thought. For most, however, AIDS is not yet a crisis, a critical turning point, a moment in time when clear danger exists about which nothing can be done. Rather, HIV/AIDS confronts us with an emergency, a set of circumstances that will exist over a period of time, demanding that we emerge with immediate, considered forms of action. As a professional group educators are facing such an emergency, requiring a reasoned response. Unfortunately, a reasoned response was not always forthcoming when communities first faced the emotionally charged issue of HIV-infected children in schools.

Communities in Crisis

From the beginning, my own experience working with suburban Long Island school districts indicated that the quality of community response was largely a function of existing HIV/AIDS education efforts. At the moment a school is confronted with a decision about a particular child or staff member, whether or not there is an approved policy, it is often too late. In two districts where I consulted, there was neither a policy nor curriculum in place when a crisis erupted, and it became impossible to communicate even the most basic facts. In a third district, an existing policy proved ineffective—in part, I believe, because it had never been supplemented by an educational program. Thus, while an advisory panel of medical and social service experts gave their unanimous approval to admitting a child with AIDS-related complex, the school board refused to accept this opinion or to meet with the panel directly. Placing the student on homebound instruction, the assistant principal herself had to visit the child twice a week since no special education teachers would accept the assignment.

The treatment people with HIV infection received, and the ability of the school to resolve apparently conflicting interests, also reflected the environment of trust or suspicion existing among parents, teachers, and administrators. In another district, one with an established policy and curriculum, parents threatened a boycott upon learning that an HIV-positive second grader had sought admittance to a local elementary school. Here strong administrative leadership, willing to bite the bullet and accept the disquieting consequences of its own policy, was able to build on existing goodwill to prevent an immediate confrontation and achieve a more positive community consensus.

Given the presumably fatal consequences of HIV infection and the history of public health responses, it might be seen as exceptional that in the mid-1980s school systems as diverse as those in New York City, Swansea, Massachusetts, and Arcadia, Illinois, would admit children with HIV/AIDS. Alternatively, knowing that the possibility of transmission of HIV in the school context is minuscule, it can also be said that excluding any or all people with the virus is morally and pragmatically contraindicated. The tendency toward apocalyptic thinking exemplified by communities (such as Kokomo, Indiana; Arcadia, Florida; and Oscilla, Georgia) that rejected HIV-infected children or children with HIV-positive parents must be evaluated against the claims of common sense. Why were such different conclusions reached? How did the theoretical possibility of transmission come to outweigh the real probability of such an event taking place?

David Kirp (1989) argues that those who entered the school debates were either well-intentioned professionals, or wise and caring parents, who struggled with the same impulses toward self-preservation and communion. Decisions like those made by the citizens of Arcadia, Indiana, to embrace Ryan White, a young hemophiliac with AIDS, and the citizens of Arcadia, Florida, to reject the Ray family's three HIV-positive children, are ascribed to differing cost-benefit analyses ("Family in AIDS Case . . . ," 1987; White & Cunningham, 1991). To the former, the values of community and inclusion were simply more compelling than any potential risk of infection. That Kirp does not offer a more systematic explanation of these differing perspectives has been attributed to his failure to situate the decision-making process in the broader social and political context (Raymond, 1990). As much as we may want to believe that the democratic traditions of town meetings and open, public debate will lead to the ultimate triumph of an ethic of care, we find ourselves reading a story in which a burning house in Florida, the Ray family home, has become an essential part of HIV in America. It is emblematic of the fierce passions ignited by the bringing together of HIV/AIDS and childhood.

Children with HIV/AIDS challenge our belief in childhood innocence, raise questions about our ability to preserve the uninfected from any hint of mortality and the infected children from death itself. Despite the harsh realities of many contemporary childhoods, perhaps even because of these realities, we adhere more tenaciously than ever to the ideology of childhood purity. To talk of HIV/AIDS and children in this society is to talk of innocence and blame, victims and crimes. Especially in small towns where the disease appears less frequently, more unexpectedly, as if out of context, the child with HIV/AIDS may be viewed as an unanticipated source of pollution. At a safe distance, in the hospital, a child with HIV/AIDS elicits pity, but in school or in the neighboring yard the same child evokes fear. Children with HIV/AIDS are perceived as a danger to our children and the body of ideas through which we seek to protect them.

Although the exclusion of HIV-infected children most directly affects their own futures, it clearly has implications for the uninfected as well. Not all communities want to understand that the exclusion of someone who is currently or potentially disabled sends a devastating message to everyone about those who are different or in need of care. The communication is straightforward: Difference is not to be tolerated; care is only to be provided by professionals in special settings. In contrast, we might choose to communicate to students an acceptance of difference, whether physical, emotional, or intellectual, and a commitment to care by and for everyone.

Policy statements serve an educative as well as a judicial function. Legislated decisions help to define the nature of the social and ethical climate in which we live, providing critical precedents and ideals toward which we can aspire as a society. But individual change also occurs more slowly, less dramatically, through face-to-face exchange in which those speaking the language of belonging attempt to communicate with those steeped in the language of isolation.

Welcoming the Stranger

In recent decades, schools have been institutions where critical issues of equity involving race, gender, and handicapping conditions have been hotly debated. Because of our belief in childhood innocence and investment in protective strategies, schools have also become the most charged arenas in which to work through our response to HIV/AIDS. Often these debates have been characterized by a tension between two coexisting communities in which we may hold joint membership: the community of compassion, celebrating connection and mutual engagement, and the community of fear, erecting barriers for protection against the unknown. It is the former that speaks the language of belonging, promoting an ethic of care and sense of affiliation, and the latter that offers the language of isolation, with its vocabulary of risk groups, mandatory HIV-antibody testing and reporting, and quarantine. Neither community is new: Both go to the core of our character as a nation.

The nineteenth-century traveler and social critic Alexis de Tocqueville (1838/1945) observed long ago that Americans vacillate between the attractions of individualism, with its glorification of rights, freedoms, liberties, and suspicion of group loyalties, and the commitment to a common good, with its reverence for the responsibilities of citizenship and popular sovereignty. In debates about public health policy, when the Republican tradition triumphs (Beauchamp, 1985), the harm principle, or a narrow paternalism based on self-interest, recedes. In its place a concern for the well-being of the community, our shared commitments and the promises in which they are grounded, emerges. This tradition reminds us that the public, as well as the community itself, has a reality apart from the individual citizens who compose it. As we shall see in succeeding chapters, this same tension between the individual and the group permeates many curricular debates as well as differing perspectives on human development and learning.

Some educators (Beyer, 1986) fear the loss of our Republican tradition to the growing technization of society and the disappearance of historical consciousness. Democratic communities are communities that recognize a common past and promote moral discourse and full participation of citizens in a variety of settings. Bellah, Madsen, Sullivan, Swidler, and Tipton (1985) refer to these as "communities of memory":

> Communities . . . have a history—in an important sense they are constituted by their past—and for this reason we can speak of a real community as a "community of memory," one that does not forget its past.
>
> The communities of memory that tie us to the past also turn us toward the future as communities of hope. They carry a context of meaning that can allow us to connect our aspirations for ourselves and those closest to us with the aspirations of a larger whole and see our own efforts as being, in part, contributions to a common good. (p. 153)

In such communities there are public arenas for the discussion of issues, with the implicit expectation that everyone is capable of discursive communication and the possibility of action based on consensus. Schools can play a central role in reconstituting communities. They can become places in which to prepare students for active participation in the world and in which to practice forms of authentic dialogue. If schools continue to promote the privatization of learning evident in the technocratic curriculum, they will deny students the communicative competencies needed to negotiate a democracy.

HIV/AIDS invites us to create public spaces out of which shared understandings of the social good, public virtue, and civic responsibility can emerge. This would be a world in which overt or covert acts of violence against the Other—racial, religious, economic, sexual—would be replaced by new forms of hospitality. The stranger in our presence asks for respect, for the openness to dialogue through which his or her uniqueness may be acknowledged and understood. This is the essence of caring relationships between teacher and student, parent and child, doctor and patient.

The manner in which we approach the stranger tells more about us than about them. Just as the fear of plague has become a metaphor for the spread of moral corruption in Western literature, so the approach of the stranger has become an occasion to understand the nature of community (Shabatay, 1991). In the Judeo-Christian tradition, denying hospitality to the stranger is a transgression of the community code that bonds host and guest in mutual respect. It is the stranger who calls us to account, offers the possibility of redemption through an acceptance of otherness, and reminds us of Arendt's injunction that educators take responsibility for the world as it is given. To claim this pedagogical authority would bring to the fore the political and ethical concerns that ground our practice.

As educators, we seek to do the right thing at the right time, basing our actions as much, if not more, in ethics as in technique. We hope that our students will be better off for having been in our classrooms, and will have learned not only to think wisely but to choose wisely what they will think about. While it is important for students to have the practical knowledge that will prevent them from *getting* and *giving* AIDS, it is equally important for them to grapple with the social implications of the disease. If we succeed, HIV/AIDS will not become another phenomenon to succumb to the technocratic thinking that threatens so much of our life worlds. These are the considerations I would ask you to keep in mind as we turn from policy issues to discussions of HIV/AIDS education in the succeeding chapters.

CHAPTER 2

Responding to Children in Time

The clock shows us the now, but no clock ever shows the future or has ever shown the past.

Martin Heidegger, *The Concept of Time*

This chapter is about responsibility, about the human obligation to respond to self, others, and the world in which we find ourselves. It begins with the story of how I cared about and learned to care for someone with AIDS. Such encounters with death, especially a death that occurs out of turn, inevitably remind us of the finite nature of life, of our need to nurture existence itself. This need links my immediate experiences with AIDS to a broader set of interests in the welfare of the young. The presence of HIV in our world has brought to the forefront of my thinking as an educator a concern for human temporality that might otherwise have remained buried among a myriad of seemingly more immediate issues pressing on the lives of children today. It has caused me to look more closely at the meaning of time we convey in school, how this meaning is embedded in particular curricular choices, and the sense of social responsibility that flows from a given understanding of human historicity.

As an academician of a certain age, I learned to write in an objective style designed to mask the presence of an authorial voice. As a person living his private and professional life in the midst of a health crisis, I have fought to reclaim my own voice, impelled to adopt a more narrative style. In part this is a response to the postmodern critique of positivism and to the feminist insistence on the significance of the situated speaker. However, I also believe it to be a way of resisting submergence in the overwhelming number of deaths that the last years have brought. And there is Isak Dinesen's reassurance, "All sorrows can be borne if you put them into a story or tell a story about them" (quoted in Arendt, 1958, p. 175).

Narratives chronicle the passing of time. They are built on the tensions between stasis and change, sameness and difference, tensions that we learn in our bodies long before language becomes a primary way of know-ing. Narrative is the final transformation of rhythms that have their origin in body time. It is a writing out of the body, a writing into life. I want to be assured that those whom I have loved and cared for are inscribed in the book of life.

From the beginning, I acknowledge the limitations of personal narra-tive and anecdotal records for producing cause-and-effect explanations or generalizable conclusions. First-person strategies, however, have the great-est power for drawing us into the difficult issues I want to address. They are inherently relational strategies (Noddings, 1991) requiring attention and flex-ibility, receptivity and discernment, hallmarks of a caring attitude. Narra-tive is a method of care, a method that allows me to move between the pro-fessional and personal as I find a single voice with which to speak of my experience. For it is undoubtedly true that I have become engaged by the only certain points in time: our natality, represented by the world of young children, and our mortality, as embodied in those who are living with HIV infection. For me, seeking to integrate these moments is the only way to live time authentically. Not to attempt this task would be to deny the facticity that defines my daily life.

CARING FOR MICHAEL/CARING FOR THE CURRICULUM

The hospital is located near the top of one of the many hills that define the San Francisco landscape. Two streets away are spectacular views of the Golden Gate Bridge and San Francisco Bay. Immediately below are the steeply pitched streets lined with private houses that appear on classic postcards of the city. Like other hospitals, this one goes on for blocks, but the buildings are low, made of brick and concrete, and do not overwhelm the quiet, resi-dential neighborhood in which it is situated. Inside the main entrance, a few people sit in the waiting room by the visitors' entrance, but there is no evi-dence of the suppressed tension and drama of other large urban institutions. Everything about this lofty setting is calm, reassuring, and respectable. This is the best that can be had.

Michael has been "unresponsive" since the second incident of grand mal seizures several days prior to my visit. I have lost track of how many times he has been in the hospital during the last nine months. I do not go every time. But although informed by his mother that there is no reason for me to make the cross-country trip, I know I will go. Not so much for Michael, who might not even be aware I am there, nor for his parents, whose courage and directness I have come to admire tremendously, but for myself. I did not want to have any regrets.

As it turns out, when I finally stand at the foot of his bed, his opened but unfocused eyes do find me. With an intensity that startles the others in the room, our eyes lock and his face breaks into the familiar smile of recognition, the welcoming smile that had greeted me so often before upon my arrival in San Francisco. He cannot speak, nor can I. My eyes fill with tears that I do not allow to escape down my cheeks. I begin to mutter some words of reassurance that he probably cannot hear. It does not matter. He knows me. As the others withdraw from around the bedside in the tiny, cramped room, I move closer and take his hand. We continue to look at each other for several minutes, but like an infant who can only manage so much stimulation, he begins to turn away with increasing frequency. The moments of focused concentration are too exhausting to prolong.

Over the next five days there are other moments like this, though none quite so striking, and there are many more when contact of any sort is impossible. I become involved in Michael's care. I help a nurse to change the IV needle. Luckily there is no need for oxygen masks or feeding tubes that might further medicalize the room and interfere with our ability to communicate. For Michael has only brain lymphoma that leaves his body strong and unscarred, surprisingly powerful.

He is in restraints, a vest of a metallic material that is secured underneath the bed. Watching him, I am overwhelmed by sadness and frightened by the unbridgeable gap that now exists between us. The restraints signal that all the words, arguments, even appeals to emotion we once used to influence each other are of no avail. It has come to this, the use of force. How can he be so strong and yet so helpless at the same time? It is the very incongruity of the situation that is most painful. He has been tied down in his own best interests so that he will not hurt himself. But by depriving him of free movement these same restraints also deprive him of any knowledge of himself in space and time, of his very being itself.

Michael sleeps clasping the protective rail of the bed as if he were holding on to life itself, even as the virus proliferates within his brain. His waking hours are spent in a detached, semiconscious state that mimics death. Is this some form of preparation, a practice period as his Zen friends might refer to it? At moments he is restlessly thrashing about, the usual silence broken by a few garbled words that send us all scampering after meaning as if to insist that verbal communication is still possible. We strain to keep life in view even as the modes of interaction are diminished and death moves closer. It is a space between hope and despair, denial and acceptance in which we are living out these last days.

At other times Michael fights to remove the restraining vest, symbol of incapacity. These are the worst moments of the day. When a nurse insists on calling two additional orderlies to change his bedding, I do it with her instead, holding Michael's attention with my eyes, calming him with my touch, as he resists the temporary discomforts of this procedure. The nurse admonishes him, "I'm not responsible for your being here. You only have yourself to blame for that." I cannot respond—me, the AIDS educator, gay rights activist—I am silenced by her vindictiveness. I only want the bed changed and Michael comfortable. But I fear for the night when she tells me she will give him a tranquilizer if he is "restless." Does she think I am reassured?

I am reassured only by the nurse who, as I am leaning over Michael trying to feed him some Jell-O, turns to me and asks what kind of person he was. I am stunned by this simple question. I am moved by her interest, appalled less by the task of talking about Michael's life than by having to do this in the past tense, knowing that the present tense is largely over and can now be summarized by a few words—*comfortable/uncomfortable, angry/relaxed, tired/awake*. I hide behind some stock phrases but try to make it come out right. I want to honor her request.

But there is no hiding, no time for clichés, between myself and Michael. Communication is rhythmic and physical and at the same time electric, metaphysical. He is responsive to the sensuous comfort of being kneaded, massaged, kept in close contact. Words and rational structures have been rendered useless by the disease. Our bodies and our sympathetic imaginations have become everything.

On the last morning of my visit, I bring my overnight bag, a Christmas present from the AIDS agency for which I work, and stow it in a corner of the tiny room. He is asleep and I step outside only to see two doctors enter. When I return from the coffee shop, Michael is groggily awake and a nurse is again trying to feed him. He is clearly out of sorts, probably tired of being poked and prodded. The nurse gives up and leaves. I move close, sit on the side of the bed, and take hold of his hand. He does not seem to notice me and is frowning. Is he uncomfortable, angry because I am leaving, or just off in some unreachable place? I tighten my grip and talk anyway. I say foolish things. I say good-bye. We have had our moments. It does not really matter.

The Narrator Reads His Own Story

As a teacher I have always given as much attention to how I think about the world as to what I think about it. I have wanted students to understand that my ideas do not take shape magically in full form but rather that they are dynamic constructions reflecting my struggle to make sense of experience. This requires that I read my own stories in a way that suggests their multiple layers of meaning. Some of these meanings are not surprising. For example, I read my last days with Michael as a friend, a member of a network who, despite geographic distance, participates in the caregiving and decision making that escalate with each new hospitalization. Such networks have become increasingly prevalent in the gay community when individuals have become alienated from their families of origin, settling in far away cities, and forced to create *de novo* the supportive structures necessary to human survival. Although it cannot be said that Michael was alienated from his parents, he had long ago moved away from the family home in order to participate in the burgeoning gay culture of San Francisco. Now his parents, with their limited financial resources, are forced to make terrifying choices about when to visit him based on assessments of which crises will be truly life-threatening and which merely indicators of others to follow.

At his bedside, Michael's parents express surprise and admiration for the ongoing stream of visitors, mostly gay men, who attend to his needs. They wonder aloud about who would care for them should they require it. I, in turn, more familiar with the way in which loosely associated groups of friends have transformed themselves into well-articulated families, am conscious of my own sense of insufficiency when judged against Michael's performance as caregiver. He had a gift for being with people as they died, for knowing how to manage the unmanageable, for organizing the living to sustain the dying. With his unusual powers of empathy, he was able to spend long hours in silence with others or join with them in reflecting on their lives. Grounded in these moments of intuitive understanding, he was also able to respond to the practical needs of the dying. He could draw up a will, translate medical jargon into commonsense meanings, and mediate among competing family interests. But now the caregiver has become the cared-for.

As the effects of illness are intensified, I find myself renegotiating my relationship with the one who is sick. So I also read this story in the role of the former lover whose desire has been unexpectedly peaked. In the midst of death, Michael's touch arouses a pleasure that is clearly experienced as erotic. This is both an echo of the past, a reminder of how we once knew each other, and a connection of the present. It is proof that we are still alive to the possibility of solace rooted in our physicality and to resisting the proprieties that have always impinged on our existence. I am in awe of the feelings that we call forth in each other and our determination not to be defined solely by the categories of patient and caregiver. So much of Michael's time is spent as passive recipient of the ministrations of health providers or claimed by the virus that has wreaked havoc with his brain. But then there are the moments when we seem able to recover the fullness of our humanity by being with each other as desiring, intending individuals.

But I am embarrassed by my own feelings. It is like the sensual pleasure that results from holding an infant or small child in one's arms. As adults, we want to offer security, comfort, and a sense of well-being without acknowledging the sensations that speak of the sexuality embedded in these attachments. These final moments with Michael offer an illicit pleasure, a pleasure stolen from the ever-increasing darkness that envelops Michael and places him out of touch. It is above all pleasure taken by two men, unsanctioned yet benignly accepted in this health care setting; men who have not only learned to meet each other's needs but who have responded to the needs of a community under attack. They bring to the immediate bedside their own histories as well as the histories of their friends and lovers who have struggled with the same disease. They are men who sought to build a world in which their desire would not be marginalized, their search to understand the erotic not trivialized as a matter of hedonistic self-indulgence. Their individual bond, their ability to express and share pleasure, must be viewed in the context of the community of which they are a part.

The Educator Reads the Same Story

I recognize, too, that even as I read my story as the story of friend and lover, I also read it as an educator—and with these words I feel as though I have crossed an invisible line. For if it is awkward to talk of death and desire in the same sentence, it seems far more threatening to bring young children into the text. Yet I reject the artificial barriers that are so frequently used to separate the private from the public, the personal from the professional, and the individual from the social. As I try to assimilate Michael's dying, it stretches and transforms my educational commitment. I do not want to set this experience aside and get on with the business of teaching children. The deaths I have witnessed are not only local events to be understood within the confines of family, friends, or special support groups. They are also political events, a fact clearly underlined by the nurse's accusation of Michael's culpability and my own reluctance to respond to it.

Agreeing with those who would define teaching as a political practice (Aronowitz & Giroux, 1991; Grumet, 1988), I want to explore how this unexpectedly political event of dying might affect that work. Is there a pedagogy for life hidden in the politics of dying? For me this has become a moment to assess the relationship between what happens in schools and the events that give shape to our lives; to assert that the hospital vigils, times of reassuring connection and painful separation, are not shameful adult secrets that occur in a different world from the one we share with children. Nor are we different people as we move between sickroom and classroom. I keep asking myself what this all means for the lives of children and teachers in classrooms. Are there experiences that children can have in school that would better prepare them to encounter death?

Perhaps it is not that the curriculum can prepare children for death, but that we might choose to live differently with them when keeping this knowledge consciously in front of us. For when we attempt to exclude death, we also exclude the life-affirming understanding of human temporality. The introduction of a discrete death curriculum allows us momentarily to hold mortality at bay, finally dismissing it to the edges of classroom life. Unlike some, I do not want to protect children from pain during a romanticized period of innocence, nor do I see children as a way to purchase immortality. Rather I want to argue that too much of the contemporary curriculum brings a deathly silence to the being of childhood and not enough of it speaks to the things that really matter in children's lives or in the lives of those who care for them. I want to argue that the curriculum has too often become an injunction to desist rather than an invitation to explore our life worlds. The curriculum remains lifeless as long as it is cut off from the roots and connections that feed it. If teachers cannot find themselves or the things that are important to them in the curriculum, it is little wonder that students have difficulty responding to it. A commitment to the curriculum must entail a commitment to the world, and none of us inhabits a world without death.

Mrs. Greene's Story: Not Enough Time

Shortly after Michael's death, under the weight of his death, I left full-time AIDS work and began an educational consulting practice. For the first time in several years I was able to observe classrooms and staff development sessions in schools. Although working on a project to infuse substance-abuse education and prevention into the early childhood curriculum, I had not moved very far afield in either a literal or figurative sense. Discussions with young children about substance abuse, like discussions about HIV, can easily implicate family members in behaviors considered to be marginal or illegal. Neither subject fits easily into the highly rationalized, technocratic curriculum, no matter how they are sanitized and packaged in a socially acceptable way. Substance abuse, like HIV, will lead to death if unchecked. An experienced teacher with whom I worked personified the determination to keep death outside of life and the subtle failure of responsibility that is reinforced by the standard curriculum.

I meet Mrs. Greene a few minutes before she is to conduct a workshop for new first-grade teachers. She is part of a mentoring program designed to provide ongoing support to inexperienced teachers. Expressing concern that these teachers would need ideas for activities to conduct with their students, she is busily assembling examples of curriculum materials, charts, and children's artwork. Tense, but controlled, she opens the session by welcoming the teachers and unexpectedly announcing that she has not had time to prepare adequately because of the death of her mother several days earlier. After apologizing for the introduction of this personal note into the work setting, she launches into an extended presentation of an array of projects that can be thematically linked to the changing seasons and holiday celebrations. Emphasis is placed on how to create eye-catching products that may be attractively displayed. Neatness, order, and conformity are given high priority, with many of the art activities requiring students to follow a teacher-made pattern. Room for individual expression is often left only to the choice of colors employed by the student.

At first glance this is the story of a master teacher who is reluctantly accepting that a personal crisis has interfered with the performance of her professional duties. Although the participants respond with sympathetic gestures during and after the workshop, it is clear that the announcement had placed a wall between them and Mrs. Greene. Delivered in a quiet but emotional tone, the communication has drawn the teachers into her suffering while at the same time signaling them to maintain their distance because of her evident vulnerability. This complex manipulation of feeling may have left the teachers wondering about the significance of their own concerns at a time specifically designed to help them cope with the stresses of being new teachers.

Let me be clear. I do not mean to pass judgment on whether or not Mrs. Greene should have told the group about the death of her mother. The decision to reveal such information remains solely with Mrs. Greene, and there is no easy answer to this difficult question. However, I was present to witness the manner in which she conveyed her information and its effect on the other participants. More importantly, this incident highlighted for me the way in which the structure and content of the workshop itself were geared to deny the realities that teachers and students face every day—an observation confirmed by subsequent workshops as well. With no opportunities for teachers to discuss the issues they were confronting, these sessions were more about how to keep children busy than how to create a responsive curriculum.

As presented, the managed curriculum is filled with an endless round of activities that are linked by reference to the seasons or holidays but have little to do with the socioeconomic contexts in which the school is embedded, the conflicted emotional lives of young children, or the existential dilemmas of adulthood. This turning away from affective and material realities alienates teachers from their work and students from the curriculum. A vision of schools as places where people search after meaning, and enrich that search through increasing access to the wisdom of the past as encoded in the disciplines, has become buried under mountains of photocopies, prepackaged materials, and curriculum guides. The curriculum is pregiven and standardized rather than emergent and negotiated.

A Death-Defying Curriculum

The paradox of Mrs. Greene's workshop is that, despite her acknowledged grief, she tries to offer the teachers a death-defying curriculum. It is
death-defying in the same way as the unexamined life described by Camus
in *The Plague*: In the midst of impending doom, the good citizens of Oran
cling to the rituals and routines of daily life that permit them to deny the
contingency of existence and the absence of meaning lying just below the
surface of normality. They will fight the encroaching plague by pretending
it does not exist. The futility of this denial, measured in attempts to ward off
death by collecting worldly goods, experience, and hoarding time, is also
described in Leo Tolstoy's *The Death of Ivan Illich*.

Existentialists refer to those who deny human temporality as living in
"bad faith." Phenomenologists (Schrader, 1972) suggest that we can live
irresponsibly, in bad faith, but not nonresponsibly. From this perspective,
responsibility is an ontological fact flowing from human reflexivity, from
the consciousness that is part of the human condition. We cannot escape being
liable, always answerable to ourselves for what we do and who we become.
This imperative to care informs more systematic ethical considerations. So I
ask myself about the connections between lives lived irresponsibly or in bad
faith and a school curriculum of senseless busywork.

Mrs. Greene expresses disappointment that she did not give the workshop participants "more." I suspect that she refers to more ideas to be stored
up against the endless days of winter, when they can be parceled out to mark
the passage of time. Research (Ben-Peretz & Bromme, 1990) confirms that
this approach to structuring curriculum, in terms of traditional time cycles
and their instantiation in the rhythms of everyday institutional life, is not
uncommon. This very approach to time appears to defy death as well. Time
treated as a succession of moments in the present, moments to be filled with
activity—in an effort to manage time as if it were an objective entity outside
of human experience. Phenomenologists (Troutner, 1974) refer to this as
machine time or clock time, in contradistinction to lived time, which contains both the past and the future in the present as it is experienced against
the horizon of our finite existence. Heidegger (1962) maintains that authentic time is experienced with the awareness that we are always living toward
the future, toward our death. By positing the life of the classroom as a series
of discrete moments without reference to past and future, Mrs. Greene excludes death from the curriculum. It becomes a painful intrusion, external,
rather than central, to the pedagogical project.

Although contemporary educators often recognize the need to respond
to children's queries about death, the fragmented and disjointed nature of
the curriculum itself ultimately undercuts a meaningful temporality. When

time is treated as a succession of present moments, the curriculum does not afford children the opportunity to make choices by reflecting on the past and hypothesizing about the future. The individual is thus imprisoned in routines and reduced to the mechanical. There is no acknowledgment of temporal development with all the uncertainty, indeterminacy, and contingency that allow for the new and unrehearsed to appear. Denied choices, unable to make an impact on the environment, children do not learn who they are and what they can do. A sense of authentic time, of the role of death in life, is essential to our becoming active, intending participants in the world rather than passive victims of circumstances in a one-dimensional present.

Huebner (1975b) inscribes this complete circle of temporality within contemporary curriculum discourse. He suggests that when educational environments reflect an understanding of lived time, the past will be in the present so as to become the student's basis for projecting a future. As do others who write about time and education, Huebner draws heavily on Heidegger's *Being and Time*. But in seeking clarifications of its many complex ideas, he turns to Kummel (1965), who speaks most eloquently for himself:

> No act of man is possible with reference solely to the past or solely to the future, but is always dependent on their interaction. Thus, for example the future may be considered as the horizon against which plans are made, the past provided the means for their realization, while the present mediates and actualizes both. Generally, the future represents the possibility, and the past the basis of a free life in the present. Both are always found intertwined with the present: in the open circle of the future and past there exists no possibility which is not made concrete by real conditions, nor any realization which does not bring with it new possibilities. (p. 50)

Huebner teaches us that the job of the curriculum maker is to select aspects of the past for re-presentation so that they call forth a response from the student in the present. In turn, the environment must be reactive to the student through objects, speech patterns, social interactions, and the structure of the disciplines. It must also allow for moments of vision so that the young may grasp the nature of temporality in general as well as their own possibilities in particular. When children are unable to project such a vision, they are deprived of a future. For Huebner, time is a political as well as existential reality.

From the perspective of the young child an existential concern for the future can be all too real. Continuously surrounded by admired older siblings, accomplished friends just two grades ahead, and myriad adults, all of whom appear to have achieved the impossible, children are quickly aware of what they have not yet become. In a world peopled by those who can, it is the lure of the future, when they too will be able to read, cross the street, or ride a two-wheeler, that propels the child forward. Children strive to make their own mark, to be someone in a world that would prefer to characterize them in terms of potential, unfulfilled promise. In *The Words* Sartre (1964) recalls this sense of futurity, about living toward a time yet to come: "I was often told that the past drives us forward, but I was convinced that I was being drawn by the future. I would have hated to feel quiet forces at work within me, the slow development of my natural attitude" (p. 237).

Thinking about Mrs. Greene, I understood more clearly why I read my experience with Michael as an educator. For I came to Michael's bedside with a commitment to learning environments that foster choice-making for both students and teachers. Being with Michael reinforced the multidimensional nature of time upon which such environments are based. I lived our past relationship in the present, aware that it would be absent from the future. Michael was simultaneously the vibrant friend and lover of the past as well as the semiconscious patient of the present. Slowly learning to draw on preverbal modes of knowing, the child within, to create the memories that I would need in the future, I had become the apprentice caregiver and Michael the patient teacher.

EXPERIENCING THE TIME OF CHILDHOOD

An incident occurring several weeks after observing Mrs. Greene helps me delve more deeply into the narratives of my own heart as well as into the heart of the curriculum. This experience raises further questions about the relationship between education and time in childhood.

I have been asked to accompany a staff developer, from the drug education project for which I am a consultant, to a school in another part of the city. Approaching the building, Adrienne informs me that two weeks previously a young teenager had stabbed and killed another in the schoolyard. As a 6-year-old carefully explains it to me 20 minutes later, "They were fighting over a woman and one of them had a weapon." Many of the children knew the participants as friends of older siblings, some as relatives. Relating news of the killing appears to be the only meaningful way to greet unfamiliar visitors, perhaps the only way to make an all-too-familiar event meaningful. These discussions continue as the children are engaged in drawing or writing exercises, through asides that are tolerated by the teachers unless they become overly animated, proving too great a distraction from the work at hand.

In the kindergarten Adrienne initiates a group discussion at story time about good and bad drugs, a topic that predictably turns to the schoolyard murder. Everyone wants to participate; everyone has something to contribute. An accurate and detailed recounting of the stabbing emerges, although it is increasingly punctuated by references to violence depicted on various television shows. Of special interest is the police drama "Rescue 911," for its very title raises the question of other telephone numbers to be used in case of emergency: fire, crime, or natural disaster. What can you do if you forget the number or do not know it? Where can you find it? Who can be of help? Almost imperceptibly the ground shifts from the real violence of the schoolyard, to the imagined or real crimes of television docudramas, to potential crises in the children's own lives.

The emotional turning point of the discussion occurs when a slight, dark-haired girl who has been patiently waiting a turn begins to talk. Julie's voice is halting, barely audible, but insistent and emotionally evocative. She describes being awakened in the middle of the night by the sounds of her parents fighting. She can hear them arguing through the wall that separates their rooms. She tells the rapt group of 20 5-year-olds that she was frightened, upset, and did not know what to do. She wanted to awaken her younger sister. Many sympathetic suggestions are spontaneously offered as to the appropriateness of such an action. I wonder if she is motivated by a desire to shelter her sister or by a drive to find reassurance in becoming one who can comfort another. Eventually Julie reports that the sounds died down but that she could not return to sleep for a long time afterwards.

This very personal and painful revelation inspires yet another round of narratives about family disagreements, most often between the narrator and a younger sibling. There is a great deal of disagreement about how much "my baby," defined as a brother or sister unable to speak, can understand. However, there is a general consensus that it is impossible to win disputes with these siblings, since they are perceived as having a moral upper hand due to their age. Strikingly, the entire meeting ends with attempts by the kindergartners to remember their own infancy, harking back to an apparently simpler time when greater vulnerability assured greater protection.

I know there are some who will read this discussion as exemplifying the untenable violence that permeates many urban neighborhoods. It highlights the difficulty of teaching children who must contend with constant threats to their safety and integrity. Others, such as Sylvia Ashton-Warner (1963) or Vivian Gussin Paley (1990), might read moments during which the real or imagined dangers of childhood are disclosed as the beginning of a caring pedagogy. From this perspective, these most emotionally powerful themes become the material for self-expression and the basis of a socially relevant curriculum. As educators we cannot control danger on the streets or in the private lives of our students. However, we can try to establish a safe zone in which the young come to recognize their own voices and know that they will be heard. And beyond our listening, we can fulfill our pedagogical response-abilities by placing their questions and concerns at the center of the curriculum. Learning how writers, artists, historians, sociologists, community, and family have responded to the existential themes they raise begins the process of connecting our immediate life worlds and the experience of others as codified in the disciplines and represented in the arts.

Having a Story to Tell

But how do I understand this kindergarten conversation? I read it as a text about time, about the opportunities and risks involved in caring for children, and about the changing time of childhood itself. Let me explain.

When children come to school they bring unique histories, comprised of all their prior interactions with the environment. Because every interaction involves potentialities and opportunities, there is always contingency and indeterminacy in their telling, the very qualities that the highly rationalized curriculum seeks to suppress. While educators may not be able to change the economic and political structures that promote violence and social injustice, they can play a transformative role in the lives of individual children by helping them to formulate strong, coherent identities. During simpler times a sense of continuity and identity could be assumed through participation in community life, but at moments of social disjuncture or individual upheaval, the construction of personal history takes on a special significance. It must be nurtured by institutions like schools where children learn about self in the presence of others, individuals define themselves in and through group membership, and pluralism is respected as the basis of democratic governance.

Such self-knowledge is a matter of re-collection. In this sense, being a self entails having a story. As educators we must foster the narrative knowing through which students can turn the fragmented and contradictory elements of the past into the wholeness and coherence that is our present identity. The process is both generative and restorative, giving us back the past in an understandable form and allowing new insight into its meaning (Crites, 1986).

According to Kierkegaard, we understand backwards but we live forwards. As we retrieve a self out of the past, we are also moving toward the future. It is our interest in the not-yet that frames our re-searches into the past. Narrative strategies for appropriating the past engage us with specificity and detail not possible when projecting the future. Here we work in the realm of uncertainty and the unknown; images are likely to be vague and sketchy, more improvisational in character. Yet it is this very indeterminacy that holds the promise of the future, that signals hope. Of course we can try to ignore or resist the future and remain lost in the past, just as we can attempt to forget or suppress the past, reducing it to a thin chronicle of events.

But by encouraging our students to become storytellers, we can help them to maintain the necessary tension between their work in the present as archaeologists of the past and architects of the future. I would argue that if the self is an aesthetic construct, albeit a psychologically necessary one, then schools should be workshops offering the tools, space, and support for students to become craftspeople of their own time.

To talk of the temporal rhythm of narrative is to talk of the way I as an author am both inside and outside my life story. When "I" in the present narrate stories about "me" in the past, I establish links among discrete events that make possible future projects. Time marks not only our passage into and out of this world but also the relationship between the objective and subjective, external and internal conditions that define our daily experiences. Temporality is a question of simultaneity as well as progression. Recognizing these traditional dichotomies now in narrative form sends me back to my own pedagogical roots. Grounded in an appreciation of rapid socioeconomic changes and committed to the belief that philosophical inquiry rather than instructional efficiency should guide our educational researches, Dewey (1938) framed his descriptions of the educational process in a dialectical manner that attempts to resolve apparent contradictions. He reminds us that effective teaching involves coordination between the psychological and logical, the conditions for learning that children bring to school and the demands that society would impose on them.

Adults can help children work outward from their more narrowly based, subjectively ordered concerns toward the world of abstract ideas, the objectively sequenced subject matter of the disciplines. These are not moments to be seen in opposition to one another, for the impetus to make sense of the larger world is always contained within the particular experience. Nor is the intellectual matter of the disciplines sought as an end in itself. Rather, it is seen as a means to reflect on and organize human experience. The curriculum itself is negotiated, moving in a measured way between the interests of the child and the interests of the community.

Although the schoolyard drama, with its intimations of adult sexuality, peer competition, and uncontrollable passion, was uppermost in the minds of these children, given time and space it proved to be only the starting point for an exploration of ongoing themes in their lives: the importance of family and siblings, moments of vulnerability and safety, techniques of communication, strategies for conflict management, and the separation of fact from fiction. Most educators would acknowledge that these themes ought to be part of a developmentally based curriculum. Undoubtedly, there is a cathartic value in their open presentation, but expression should not be an end in itself. Rather, the moment is best seen as the beginning of the curriculum maker's work, offering rich opportunities for dramatic play, block-building, language arts, and social studies. How, after all, do individuals and communities respond to danger? How do our communications systems work? How do we take care of the immature or disabled members of society? What does the community look like from various points of view—child, adult, man, woman, African-American, Latino, Caucasian?

As an intruder into this classroom, I could not help but notice the uneasy way in which the teachers had busied themselves with housekeeping chores throughout the discussion. How had *their* sense of responsibility led them to read the events of the past week? What had been the nature of their pedagogical response?

Later, in the vice principal's office, we talked with a small group of teachers. They spoke of the stabbing as only the latest example of the violence that saturates their students' lives. Given the primacy of this concern, they saw their role as one of providing a haven for the children, a space in which they could learns skills to insure their survival in the future. The teachers believed it was important to confirm what had occurred and not to censor the children's talk. But they also believed it equally important not to allow the incident to dominate the curriculum. They struggled to offer their students a refuge, moments in which they could leave behind distressing realities and glimpse other possibilities.

As I listened, I thought of the early childhood teachers I had interviewed 10 years earlier while pursuing research on pedagogical authority, who described their roles in terms of offering protective control to vulnerable young children (Silin, 1982). While I did not talk as extensively with the teachers this day, I sensed that their desire to cordon off a safe space in a threatening world was not so very different. Yet there was a new urgency with which they spoke about the time of childhood, about time in childhood; an urgency having less to do with a commitment to a developmentally appropriate curriculum, the overly determined standard of practice in the field, than with a desire to turn away from the world outside the classroom.

Responding in Time

I want to suggest that the way in which we define the nature of childhood is central to determining what forms our individual involvement with children will take and toward what ends our efforts will be directed. In Chapter 3 I discuss the value of incorporating the literature on the changing nature of childhood into teacher education (Woodhead, Light, & Carr, 1991). James and Prout (1990c) also offer a temporal dimension to the growing critique of scientist research on children. They point out that in many studies children are simply not *present* in their own right; they are effectively deprived of a presence in the present, in favor of a time past or future.

The systematic exclusion of children's voices in the scientific domain, which concerns James and Prout, is a reflection of our taken-for-granted assumptions about childhood. These cultural assumptions are embedded in the thinking of the teachers with whom I talked about the schoolyard death. They, like other adults, often locate childhood in time passing. Childhood is always in the past, a time that passes all too quickly, a social status to be remembered nostalgically: We constitute childhood as memorabilia. Each time we tell our story we enhance the authenticity of the past. The intensity of feelings we bring to these nostalgic reconstructions can lead us to deny the present. Blurred by sentiment and the nonspecific tonality of the remembered scene, we want to experience a feeling of time lost. It is not that we actually desire to be the lost child, although we may fruitlessly try to hold or capture the past as if it were a thing. Mostly we enjoy the process of contemplation itself, the longing from a distance that can never be fulfilled, of a space without social change or individual development.

At the same time as we freeze childhood in a personal past and in a less threatening historical time, we also understand it as a period of change—slow transformations and more dramatic disruptions. We imbue each stage of childhood with a distinct set of rights and responsibilities and eagerly celebrate the moments of transition. We construct it as continually directed toward a future time: Age is significant because it indicates a move forward. The present is important only as it foretells difficulties in future psychological adjustment or accommodation to the workplace (N. King, 1983). In a secular world, children are the future, holding our fate in their hands.

With the intensified surveillance of children and the professionalization of care, negotiating the challenges of "normal" development becomes more problematic, the need to watch for signs of deviance becomes heightened, and the future becomes more tenuous. It requires the help of more experts, longer periods of institutional life, and stronger family support. Waksler (1991b) asks about the political interests served by these adults, hovering over the child, who deny the present as an end in itself. Attending closely to the existing competencies of children may be threatening to adults, the knowledge they display having the potential for disrupting the present, for becoming a competing world view. Having made adulthood a tenuous and difficult achievement, we are reluctant to accept the challenges posed by other perspectives. In the guise of protecting children in the present, we judge differences as inadequacies or weaknesses rather than alternative but equally valuable ways of knowing. We also protect ourselves from looking at existing power arrangements across generations. When researchers do assume childhood competence, become anthropologists of another world, Waksler maintains they may be accused of incompetence or cognitive immaturity themselves. So we concern ourselves with what children are not, rather than what they are, assuring that the present will always be viewed in the service of the future.

The Child out of Time

Most pervasive, however, is the image of the child outside of time, living in a universal timelessness that is thought to insure both purity and innocence. The theme of childhood innocence and its loss is a familiar one in the Western literary canon and in popular media characterizations (Kincaid, 1992; Pattison, 1978). Jean-Jacques Rousseau, a prime exponent of cultural primitivism, tells us that the first principle of education is to "lose time." He claims that children live best when they live in harmony with nature and without the constraints of time and the limitations of the social world. Against this essentializing of childhood, progressive social scientists argue that childhood is a sociohistorical construction that cannot be understood outside of its spatial and temporal contexts. While I explore the epistemological meanings of innocence in Chapter 5 and its erotic underpinnings in Chapter 8, of more immediate concern here are the ways that teachers and administrators think about the children they teach. How do they manage the tension between the real and hoped-for childhoods of their students?

With this thought in mind, I listened to an auditorium filled with New York City educators convened to discuss their role in addressing contemporary social issues. While those present expressed both determination and frustration, one particularly angry principal railed against critics who blame schools for the ills of society. In his passionate defense of the schools, he asked that politicians, parents, and social service providers also be held accountable for the rising rates of crime, drug use, and child abuse. While a few teachers clearly welcomed these remarks, for most they caused a great deal of discomfort. The former group supported the focus on conditions outside of the school, while the latter suggested that such a focus for change was both beyond their professional mandate and impractical, given the constraints of their work. These teachers recognized their responsibility to address the immediate needs of their students, which included drug and HIV/AIDS education. However, they did not want to address the larger social problems underlying these needs. They defined themselves as instructional leaders in the classroom but not as child advocates within the broader community. This resistance to looking at the child and society together, the child-in-the-society, seemed to be part of a conscious strategy to manage their own lives in an unmanageable and unimaginable world.

To think of children out of their immediate contexts is to take them out of time, to leave them without possibility. The social and material context is the medium through which we define ourselves. By refusing to view the child-in-the-society, teachers are refusing individual biography, the right of every child to tell his or her own story; for our stories cannot be told without reference to the worlds in which they occur and to the interactions that give them shape and substance. We are all historical beings; time is at the heart of every biography. When we seek relief for ourselves and our students by excluding the world, of which it is so easy to despair, we conspire in denying those whom we claim to help. Hope resides in time and time can only be lived in the world, a world of many unsettling realities, a world that includes HIV/AIDS.

THE GARB OF UNIVERSAL TRUTH

Buber (1966) reminds us that life is only fulfilling when lived in dialogue. My experience with Michael taught me that even though his life had become little more than the narrative of his body, articulated by biological rhythms that had lost their natural synchronicity, I could still respond to his presence. Through his death, I am learning to tell my own story. But the teachers in Mrs. Greene's workshop and the students in the classroom I visited can also give direct voice to their lives, and they deserve to be heard and answered, to be part of a dialogue. Buber (1966) admonishes us:

> This fragile life between birth and death can nevertheless be fulfillment—if it is a dialogue. In our life and experience we are addressed; by thought and speech and action, by producing and by influencing we are able to answer. For the most part we do not listen to the address, or we break into it with chatter. But if the word comes to us and the answer proceeds from us then human life exists, though brokenly, in the world. The kindling of the response in that "spark" of the soul, the blazing up of the response, which occurs time and again, to the unexpectedly approaching speech, we term responsibility. (p. 19)

The Lived Realities of Children

The fullness of response to the children in our care reflects an understanding of the multiple realities in which they live. Collins (1974) describes the everyday life world of the student in terms of three perspectives. The first-person, stream-of-consciousness voice is constructed through the ongoing internal dialogue of the child. It may be characterized as phenomenological. The second-person, partner-in-dialogue perspective reflects the dialectical process through which we establish intersubjective communication. The third-person position, of the neutral observer, most adequately describes the political processes that inform the life of the classroom, where primacy is given to objectivity and compliance with rule-governed behavior. These perspectives do not represent a hierarchy but rather possible positions from which to view and respond to the world.

At home young children live in dialogic relationships with others. The primary caregiver is *a prioi* a significant other to the infant, who learns as necessity that which is in fact contingency. This is the world *tout court,* not merely one of many possible worlds. It is the world that is massively and indubitably real, the only kind of world that can lend credence to the caregiver's most frequent refrain, "Yes, everything will be all right." In early childhood most children succeed in building a complex set of typifications and role expectations that enable them to function effectively in a known world. At school, confronted with a problematic situation, children are not only forced to abandon these familiar typifications, this recipe knowledge, but also the comfort of dialogic interactions.

When children move from primary to secondary socialization, they move from intersubjectively negotiated relationships to objectively structured political processes. The words of the teacher do not carry the same affective charge as those of the first caregiver, learning no longer a matter of personal identification but of rational control. It is now possible for the child to play a variety of roles, detaching that part of the self that is necessary to the performance of a specific function.

> Subjective biography is not fully social. The individual apprehends himself as both inside and outside of society. This implies that the symmetry between objective and subjective reality is never [a] static, once-for-all state of affairs. ... In other words, the relationship between individual and the objective social world is an ongoing balancing act. (Berger & Luckmann, 1967, p. 134)

The emergence of this ongoing balancing act, of a self distinct from the world and the growing distance between self and role, permits the child to hide from the other, providing an essential strategy to survive the demands of institutional life.

In schools, teachers must establish their authority in a world of alternatives as children begin to live in several realities simultaneously—home, school, peer group. Mediating a reality lacking primary significance to children, teachers often resort to forms of mystification, intimidation, and objectification in order to make their world appear more desirable, if unachievable. These practices can keep students outsiders, marginal to the system. Collins would promote a pedagogy aimed at interrupting this definition of students as strangers, helping them to make objective assessments of the social context, and creating moments of one-to-one interaction that re-create the dialogic learning mode of home.

The Influential Teacher

But teachers cannot implement a liberatory pedagogy from a position of objectivity in which they themselves are deprived of their own being, their own life histories. In order for teachers to reclaim the curriculum, they must reject the myth of the neutral professional. Ultimately, education is about influence; we expect that children will be different for having been in our classrooms. Regardless of how uncomfortable it makes us, or what the technocratic planners suggest, there is no pedagogy without choice. Choice always involves selection, and when teachers choose not to engage in discussions of difficult subjects, the criteria of selection need to be examined carefully. This is not to deny the very real constraints under which teachers work but to insist that there is always room to negotiate, a thousand small daily choices that speak to the teacher as decision maker—and this is nowhere more evident than in classrooms with younger children, where the content of the curriculum has been most difficult to define (Cuffaro, 1991).

The curriculum that honors human historicity prepares students to be active participants in a democratic world. Even before the child enters a classroom, such a curriculum respects the whole person, purposes, and intentions of the teacher. Teachers do not simply implement curriculum but actively bring their own knowledge to bear on its construction. Mrs. Greene did not provide openings for new teachers to share their immediate concerns. The teachers I observed were uncomfortable talking about certain topics and found it difficult to read classroom discussions for their larger curricular implications. But have they been given a chance to make sense of the difficult issues they confront? Only a few staff development guides (Derman-Sparks and the A.B.C. Task Force, 1989; Sanders & Farquhar, 1991) structure sufficient time and experiences for teachers to educate themselves by exploring their own attitudes, values, and knowledge of social issues.

The curriculum teaches children the meaning of time by allowing them opportunities to make an impact on the environment. Teachers play a critical part by encouraging students to reflect on their past experiences before moving to new ones: Ideas then become hypotheses to be tested, consequences to be predicted, and results to be examined. This ability to exercise reflective control over impulsive behavior is cited by Dewey (1938) as at the heart of freedom and democratic process. Finally, through helping students to gain a perspective on the present moment, we can enable them to imagine its transformation into something different. Phenomena such as the "AIDS crisis," "homelessness," and "substance abuse" might best be studied as they are constructed over time, expressions of the structural inequities that plague our society rather than the willful result of individual behavior. The amelioration of social problems arises from an understanding of their history and timely, considered debate. Maxine Greene (1984) calls for creation of public spaces where such dialogue can occur and for education that respects the pluralism out of which real community is born:

> We need spaces . . . for expression, for freedom . . . a public space . . . where living persons can come together in speech and action, each one free to articulate a distinctive perspective, all of them granted equal worth. It must be a space of dialogue, a space where a web of relationship can be woven, and where a common world can be brought into being and continually renewed. . . . There must be a teachable capacity to bring into being . . . a public composed of persons with many voices and many perspectives, out of whose multiple intelligences may still emerge a durable and worthwhile common world. (p. 296)

Unfortunately, a void has been created by the absence of an ethical discourse that would bring social issues to the foreground—a discourse that was advocated by progressive educators long ago. Today we seem to feel more comfortable with questions of *how* and *when* than with questions of *what* and *why*. George Counts (1932), like Dewey writing in a time of economic stress, argued that education is of necessity about imposition and that teachers should accept this reality as part of their professional obligation. To deny this "involves the clothing of one's deepest prejudices in the garb of universal truth and the introduction into the theory and practice of education of an element of obscurantism" (p. 9). Counts's criticism was reserved for those teachers who did not seize the opportunity to create a pedagogical agenda informed by an articulated social vision. Acknowledging the successes of progressive educators in calling attention to the ways in which children learn, he pointed out that these methodological considerations are uselss if not employed to achieve a larger social purpose.

Counts's language now seems antiquated to my ears. It is very much of another era. Yet his impassioned plea for the engagement of progressive educators in the process of social reconstruction is very much to the point. Without such engagement teachers retain a narrow focus on individual children and refuse to accept responsibilities that would implicate them in larger issues of equity and justice. Too many classrooms remain isolated from the lived realities of the children who inhabit them. Engagement involves framing purposes, looking forward, projecting a vision. This insistence on the need for a vision and the assumption of responsibility joins social progressives like Counts, educational philosophers like Dewey, and temporal phenomenologists like Huebner. This insistence takes on special relevance in these times, when for so many a sense of the future has never been more tenuous or enticing.

I BEGAN THIS CHAPTER with a story of personal loss and remembrance, a narrative generated by one who, deprived of speech and action, could no longer tell his own story. I end it with reflections on teachers and students, politics and the curriculum. In between I have suggested how caring for Michael led me to care about an essential theme in educational theory and practice: human historicity. Concepts of time thread their way through every curriculum, from our appreciation of how children learn to the social purposes of education. They tell us about the distances we have created between adults and children and about the possibilities for narrowing them. If we are to respond to our children in time, then we must acknowledge the common world in which we live and the moments of our shared temporality that make it meaningful.

CHAPTER 3

HIV/AIDS Education: Toward a Collaborative Curriculum

AIDS radically calls into question the pleasures and dangers of teaching.

Cindy Patton, *Inventing AIDS*

AIDS makes no sense. However, the continuing proliferation of HIV/AIDS curricula speaks to our very real desire to claim epistemological rationality and epidemiological certainty in a world plagued by a new and as yet incurable disease. In defining HIV/AIDS as a biomedical event that can be addressed only by those trained in science and health education, we attempt to make it safe, contained within a specific discipline, so that it will not contaminate other areas of study. When the topic of HIV/AIDS is sanitized, teachers and students are protected from the truly unhealthy aspects of society that might otherwise be revealed; the status quo is ensured.

But diseases are constituted through dynamic interactions of biomedical, economic, psychosocial, and political factors. The existential realities of otherness, the politics of distancing, and our search for certainty suggest key elements in the social construction of HIV/AIDS. Understanding the meanings of a given illness involves far more then simply identifying a causal agent and a medical remedy. Just as efforts at prevention cannot be limited to the presentation of risk-reduction strategies, in the hope that exposure to a few facts and rehearsal of skills will lead to lasting changes in behavior, so coming to terms with the social ramifications of HIV/AIDS cannot be achieved through a limited focus on scientific knowledge. Effective prevention involves individual struggles with the meaning of sex and drugs, and a successful societal response calls for recognition of the multiple factors shaping the disease process.

56

HIV/AIDS presents a complex set of challenges for the curriculum maker. At first, school administrators perceived HIV/AIDS primarily as a policy problem requiring the attention of legal and public health experts to assess the feasibility of excluding students and staff with HIV. But as the crisis over the presence of people with HIV/AIDS in the schools abated, and awareness that HIV/AIDS was not confined to marginal risk groups grew, educators turned toward their pedagogical function. The process was hastened as more and more states mandated K–12 AIDS education.

Early curricular materials reflected simplified interpretations of the disease; they focused on prevention for adolescents and claimed to offer only "facts." But the assertion of objectivity is in itself a form of bias, carrying the implication that it is possible to separate fact from value, object from subject, the word from the world. It is this mindset that was exemplified by a New York City public school official who, in response to a film made to be shown in the city high schools, remarked, "There was a segment that was too long, simply to the effect that you should be nice to homosexuals. The attitude was not a problem, but this is not an attitude film. This is supposed to be an *educational* film" (CDC AIDS *Weekly,* 1986, p. 9). In the scene referred to, a heterosexual man recounts his first reactions to learning that his brother is gay and has AIDS.

If we acknowledge that attitudes and values play a role in shaping individual behaviors and the allocation of material resources in society, it is hard to understand how exclusion of these very factors can lead to a serious discussion of the problem at hand. The denial of subjectivity within the curriculum only falsifies experience and alienates students from their own possibilities. This is not to say that subjectively held opinions must be accepted uncritically but rather that they can become the text for examining the social determination of "private" ideas. Students can learn to question the sources of their knowledge and its reliability and to identify alternative reference points. HIV/AIDS provides an opportunity to practice the critical thinking skills valued so highly by educators today. It is an issue that most graphically illustrates the paradoxes and contradictions of our society.

In this chapter I seek to understand the fundamental inadequacies of our past efforts to talk with children about HIV/AIDS and to create new possibilities for such dialogues. Beginning with younger children and moving on to adolescents, I draw on my work with teachers, administrators, children, and parents in many public and private schools across New York State. These schools were located in a diverse cross-section of racial, ethnic, religious, and economic communities and reflected very different commitments to HIV/AIDS education.

LISTENING TO YOUNG CHILDREN

As an early childhood educator, I was trained to listen to and observe young children. Raised and educated in a Deweyan tradition, I understand curriculum as a negotiated process, an outgrowth of the interests of the child and the community. While teachers come to the classroom with an agenda based on knowledge of the community, their art rests in helping children move outward from more narrowly based concerns toward the world of larger ideas. At its best, education enables children to see the way that the concepts and skills offered by their teachers, and eventually encoded in the formal disciplines, amplify their powers of understanding and control. The role of teachers is to help their students make sense of the world. Imposing predetermined, formal curriculum on children without reference to their lived experience can leave them alienated from the possibilities of school-based learning.

When I was a doctoral student, encounters with Marxist and critical theorists made me conscious of the manner in which schooling functions to maintain and reproduce unequal distributions of economic and cultural capital (Apple, 1979; Bowles & Gintis, 1976). Recognizing that the most mundane classroom activities, such as recess, might be described as moments of ideological hegemony, I also began to think about the internal contradictions within any system that allow for reflection and transformation. But it is the phenomenologically oriented educationists (Barritt, Beekman, Bleeker, & Mulderij, 1985; van Manen, 1990) who are most mindful of the limitations of scientistically imposed frames of reference and of the need to ground our work in the world of childhood. They urge us to return to the children themselves to uncover what it is that seems to matter, to grasp how they make sense of experience. To accept such a challenge is to abandon the safety of science that allows us to know children from the privileged position of distanced adults. It is to risk the uncertainty of an engagement that threatens the boundaries between knower and known.

When called on to assist schools with curriculum formulation, I began by asking teachers what the children were saying about AIDS. This obviously reflected my commitment as a progressive educator as well as my experiences learning from people with HIV infection. The teachers' responses clearly indicated that HIV/AIDS had entered their classrooms through the voices of their students, regardless of age or formal instruction. Ironically, many of these opportunities occurred in elementary classrooms—that is, precisely those classrooms in which the prospect of HIV/AIDS education seemed most daunting. Sometimes these voices had been heard at unexpected moments, sometimes on more predictable occasions. Almost always, teachers had felt unprepared to take advantage of the moment to begin a dialogue that could lead to more structured learning.

Interestingly, teachers often had to work hard even to remember these incidents. Emblematic of this forgetfulness were the responses of teachers in a seminar I conducted in a semirural community on eastern Long Island. My inquiry as to what they had observed about their students' knowledge of HIV/AIDS was greeted with a painfully long silence. I began to wonder if I had arrived in the only area in New York State that had not been touched by the disease. Then a first-grade teacher tentatively raised her hand. She described the pandemonium that had broken out in her classroom that very morning when the principal announced, over the school intercom, that AIDS would be the subject of the afternoon staff meeting. Children started accusing each other of having AIDS and warning the teacher not to attend the meeting for fear she might contract HIV from the guest speaker. Given permission by the principal's announcement, the children had released their suppressed concerns. And then a third-grade teacher confirmed that for the past several months AIDS had been the reigning epithet on the playground during recess. It was the label of choice when a group of children wanted to ostracize someone. Games of tag were predicated on avoiding a child who was supposedly HIV-infected.

To these children the mere mention of AIDS provoked excited responses. Whether motivated by specific fears and anxieties, or simply the emotional resonance of the word in our culture, their behaviors accurately mimicked the responses of the majority of adults. To know in more detail what AIDS means to children would require the kind of probing by teachers that leads to a negotiated curriculum, a curriculum in which dialogue is respected and teachers learn with and from their students. For the moment, however, it should be noted that isolation and fear of contagion are being played out without interruption. Educators must recognize their complicity in discrimination by permitting children to use HIV/AIDS, if only in their games, as a means to exclude someone from the social arena. Like gender, race, ethnicity, and disability, HIV/AIDS is an issue of equity.

But children also reveal their awareness of HIV/AIDS in moments that are less incendiary and more focused. In an urban setting, for example, a teacher reported her consternation on a recent class trip upon hearing one child anxiously admonish a friend not to sit down in the subway for fear of contracting AIDS from the seat. The teacher admitted that it was only her concern for the children's safety in the moving train that prompted her to contradict this advice, which had been delivered in the most serious tone. A colleague at the same meeting described overhearing one little boy warning another not to pick up a stick in the park. The warning was based on the child's knowledge that people who use drugs frequented the area at night and his belief that they are the source of HIV infection.

There are few formal studies of young children's knowledge. Farquhar

(1990b) documents the practical difficulties in conducting research when we would prefer to protect children than provoke their curiosity. Although Schvaneveldt, Lindauer, and Young (1990) indicate that preschool children know very little about HIV/AIDS, this should not be taken as an indication that they know nothing at all or that AIDS education is irrelevant to their lives. As the anecdotes reported here suggest, HIV/AIDS can be a specter that haunts their movement in the world. For young children, and for many adults as well, fear needs to be replaced by understanding, misinformation by facts. HIV is part of daily life and should be treated as such in schools. To be meaningful, HIV/AIDS information should not be delayed till fourth-grade science curriculum or sixth-grade health class, where it may seem too abstract, removed from students' lived experience. Containing HIV/AIDS within the confines of the highly rational curriculum may offer adults a sense of protection but only at the price of placing their students at increased risk. If we avoid engaging with children about HIV/AIDS, even to counter false information about transmission, we foster the belief that HIV/AIDS is a mystery, a taboo subject that teachers cannot or will not address.

What teachers think about childhood also influences how or even if they will approach HIV/AIDS with their students. For some, children inhabit a very different world from adults. Despite what they may be exposed to at home, on the street, or in the media, they require educational settings where the flow of information is carefully controlled. In contrast, others suggest that what happens to children outside of school should become the object of classroom study. The school is a safe place to make sense of complex and confusing realities. Teachers who believe in this approach are more likely to provide opportunities for critical social issues to become part of the curriculum. For example, I observed a teacher of 6- and 7-year-olds open a class meeting with the simple question, "What do people use drugs for?" Information and misinformation poured forth from the children. They debated the ethical implications of the use of steroids by Olympic athletes (a subject very much in the news at the time), tried to understand how people actually snort cocaine (believing that it is placed on the outside of the nose), and struggled with why people do things to themselves that they know are harmful. The children saw drugs, rather than infected blood, as the source of HIV infection, and they clearly equated AIDS with death. They proved themselves to be curious, knowledgeable, and capable of thoughtful reflection. Their mistakes were surprisingly rational, the questions they raised worthy of any adult's attention.

In other classrooms the subject of HIV/AIDS may come up in a more oblique manner. A second-grade teacher reported, for example, that her AIDS curriculum began with the failure of two baby rabbits to thrive. Sitting near the cage with a small group of concerned children, one girl began to wonder out loud if perhaps they might have AIDS. The teacher told the children that, while she did not know very much about HIV/AIDS, she did not think it was a disease of animals. Picking up on their concern, the teacher sought more information from the health teacher, whom she also recruited to talk directly with the children. In the kindergarten classroom down the hall, the children had built a block city with a large hospital at its center. In questioning them one day about the ambulance speeding toward its entrance, the teacher was informed that it was carrying a person with AIDS who was very, very sick and going to die. For her, this was the moment to explore what the children really knew about AIDS, part of a larger commitment to understand her students and to bring greater definition to their worlds.

Farquhar (1990b), observing 8- and 10-year-olds, confirms that children's HIV/AIDS knowledge is variable in the extreme. Researchers using developmental frameworks suggest that knowledge is primarily age-dependent. However, Farquhar offers two insights that broaden our appreciation of children's social learning. First, students' emergent understanding of HIV/AIDS is closely associated with knowledge of related topics like sexual behavior or drug use. For example, an 8-year-old's belief that you could "catch AIDS . . . when you go to bed in the same bed" is not surprising given that the child describes "sex" as going to bed with somebody. Similarly, the statement by another child that "smoking causes AIDS" should be understood in the context of her knowledge that cigarettes contain nicotine, nicotine is a drug, and drugs are somehow implicated in HIV transmission. Second, Farquhar notes that many beliefs reflect the myths and stereotypes held by adults and promoted by the media. As they struggle to construct their own meaning, children's knowledge often mirrors that of the adults who surround them.

Even while those committed to conserving the past try to limit the role of the school, the majority are asking it to address an increasingly broad social agenda. Under pressure to do more and to do it better, in a world that offers fewer and fewer support systems for children, there is always the danger of reductionism. Schools reduce complicated social problems to simplified fragments of information, adopt pedagogic strategies that focus on measurable, behavioral outcomes, and define the child as a "learner," as the sum of his or her cognitive competencies. Many teachers see the curriculum in place as the biggest obstacle to effective education, for they recognize that issues such as HIV/AIDS cannot be segmented into discrete, 40-minute units.

THE CURRICULUM IN PLACE

Attending to children suggests the informal ways that HIV/AIDS enters the school and the daily openings teachers have for beginning a dialogue that can lead to a more formal learning plan. Unfortunately, most teachers learn about HIV/AIDS through the demands of a highly rationalized curriculum and without time for reflection. It is not surprising that they react with anger and frustration. Teachers need to be supported as curriculum makers who can respond to their students' immediate concerns while cognizant of the larger bodies of knowledge with which they may be connected. This approach is not compatible with the top-down imposition of lesson plans that are far removed from the children's lived experiences.

The New York State *AIDS Instructional Guide* (New York State Education Department, 1987) is one example of the technocratic mindset that undermines the role of teachers as decision makers. Although designed to be a "guide" and carefully labeled as such, it is worth considering in detail, since many districts adopted it *in toto* as the curriculum in order to save time and avoid controversy. This is an interesting political document, with its community review panels to assure decency, its denial of the sexual realties of teenagers' lives, and its careful attention to parents' right to withdraw their children from lessons dealing with HIV prevention. To educators, however, this guide may appear as a far more curious pedagogical document because of the way that it parcels out information across the grades.

The *AIDS Instructional Guide* presents a total of 37 lesson plans clustered by grade levels. The K–3 lessons deal with health in general. They barely mention HIV/AIDS at all, though teachers are told that some children may fear contracting the disease and that their questions should be addressed "honestly and simply." Somewhat less than half of the grade 4–6 lessons deal with HIV/AIDS. They describe communicable diseases, the immune system, how HIV is not transmitted, and how to prevent AIDS by abstaining from drug use. Only in the grade 7–8 lessons, a majority of which directly address HIV/AIDS, is there discussion of the sexual transmission of HIV and the possibility of prevention through sexual abstinence. Then, in a country where the median age of first intercourse is 16, and where a third of males and 20% of females have intercourse by 15—and of those currently sexually active, less than half report using condoms—teachers are instructed to emphasize the 13 ways that abstinence makes us free (*Chronic Disease and Health* . . . , 1990).

On the grade 9–12 level, the social and economic consequences of HIV/AIDS are confined to a single lesson featuring a debate on mandatory HIV-antibody testing. Although certain lessons are geared to elicit sympathy for people with HIV/AIDS and thus attempt to curb potential discrimination, never does the guide address the homophobia, racism, and addictophobia underlying much of the HIV/AIDS hysteria that the curriculum is ostensibly trying to dispel. This superficial approach to "humanizing" the disease belies the extensive introductory comments about the importance of pluralism and democratic values. It also denies the fundamental reality of HIV infection in our country—that it has disproportionately affected groups of people who have been marginalized and subjected to various forms of physical and psychological violence (Fraser, 1989). Convincing students to listen to any messages about HIV/AIDS and to understand personal vulnerability cannot be accomplished without interrupting the "us-versus-them" mentality that pervades our social thinking.

There are two assumptions underlying this curriculum guide that bear careful scrutiny. The first is that children's minds are compartmentalized, able to deal with HIV/AIDS information in a logical, sequential order. It assumes, for example, that children can discuss how HIV is *not* transmitted while holding in abeyance for several lessons and/or years how it *is* transmitted— and how to prevent its spread. No attempt is made to assess what knowledge children come to school with or the kinds of questions their personal experiences may have generated. The child is read as a *tabula rasa* with respect to HIV/AIDS. The New York State planners appear to have been attending more to the logical order in which they wanted to present a specific body of information than to the psychological order that may reflect children's questions and interests. It seems only fair to ask for the voices of the children in the curriculum—the voices heard on the playground, on the subway, and in the block area. But who is listening? Who has the time?

The second assumption is that HIV/AIDS is a medical phenomenon to be located within the confines of the health curriculum. If we accept that there are economic, political, and social as well as biomedical strands in the Gordian knot that is HIV/AIDS, then an effective educational response does not reside in the province of the health teacher alone. A successful response is a collaborative one involving teachers from all the disciplines, administrators, and parents. In order for students to understand the disease, they must understand the cultural context in which it is occurring. For it is this context that defines how individuals and society at large respond to people with HIV and assign resources to prevention, research, and care.

From this perspective it is easy to see how HIV/AIDS lends itself as a subject for current events and social studies classes. HIV/AIDS raises many questions about access to health care and its costs, the ethics of confidentiality, diseases of poverty, availability of new drugs, and conduct of scientific research. Sloane and Sloane (1990) report on the integration of HIV/AIDS in a class on the history of the United States since 1877, which already includes discussion of the living conditions of North American cities in the late nineteenth century and the incredible toll of epidemic diseases, such as yellow fever, scarlet fever, influenza, and consumption. Here the modern-day epidemic can help students understand the fears and responses of earlier generations and offer the opportunity to clarify the differences between airborne diseases and HIV/AIDS.

There is also a growing body of novels, plays, and poetry emerging in response to this disease, and they provide further opportunities to introduce HIV/AIDS into language arts and English classes (Klein, 1989; Murphy & Poirier, 1993; Nelson, 1992; Pastore, 1992; Preston, 1989). More and more artists and musicians are also turning their attention to the issue, as well might our students in their own work (Klusacek & Morrison, 1992; J. Miller, 1992). The curriculum should reflect the richness of all these imaginative reconstructions, as they offer alternative routes to understanding the impact of HIV/AIDS (Brunner, 1992; Engler, 1988).

In effect, I want to argue that students would be best served if the assumptions underlying the curriculum in place were inverted. First, rather than creating elaborate instructional guides based on a formal ordering of facts, it would be far more helpful to ground the curriculum in the issues that children themselves find challenging, a principle upheld by progressive educators from Dewey to Friere. Second, our very definition of the disease needs to be reexamined in such a way as to permit its multiple ramifications to emerge across the disciplines. This is not to deny the importance of messages about prevention but to underscore the less visible interconnectedness of our social institutions. Successful prevention efforts at all age levels do not seek to abstract and control specific behaviors but rather to help people examine sexual and drug-using practices in the context of their total lives.

THE TEACHER'S PERSPECTIVE

My own research on pedagogical authority in early childhood (Silin, 1982) revealed that teachers think of themselves as objective professionals acting in the best interests of children. By legitimating this self-definition in their knowledge of child development, teachers could speak authoritatively about other people's children while suggesting a space for family prerogatives with respect to the inculcation of values. Interviews with primary school teachers illustrate the commitment to keeping personal attitudes and beliefs out of the classroom (Farquhar, 1990a). One teacher commented:

> It would be very wrong of me to put my personal interpretation, the standards I use for living my life, to tell them "this is how you should live." . . . It is not the place of the school to criticize in that way, or the teacher to criticize or to imply that one way is right and another way is wrong. (p. 12)

Teachers want to believe that the primary school is simply a purveyor of objective knowledge, that "we present a neutral sort of attitude to facts" (p. 12).

My work on HIV/AIDS curricula with teachers, however, suggests that personal values, prejudices, and preconceptions play a critical role in determining what information they do and do not provide. When people first began to take the facts about HIV transmission seriously, they had to explore previously unrecognized moments of vulnerability in their own lives. The middle-aged woman whose husband had just been through major surgery needed to calculate the odds that he might have received a unit of infected blood; the young male teacher needed to assess his resistance to carrying a condom on his weekend date; and the mother of a grown daughter who shared an apartment with two gay men needed to come to terms with her anxieties about casual contact as a source of HIV infection. Although everyone is better informed today than in 1985, when I began working with teachers on HIV/AIDS curricula, immersion in this issue inevitably leads to rethinking potential risk. When this does not happen, the lack of personal relevance can in some cases lead to a lack of interest. As one of Farquhar's (1990a) interviewees commented:

> This is a big turn-off. It's a big bore for me, because I know I've got nothing to worry about. I've led a monogamous life, I know I'm clear, and I'll always be clear, and I'm not going to come into touch with it. I'm not going to get caught up in drugs, I'm not going to go injecting myself. The blood contamination is the only one that could get me. (p. 12)

In a sense HIV/AIDS happens all at once. Coming to learn about HIV/AIDS in the context of their professional lives, most teachers recognize that this disease has meanings that extend far beyond the clinic office or hospital room, meanings that will seep into conversations with their own children, affect attitudes toward friends and family, and change lifelong behaviors. It has meanings that even challenge their sense of safety in the workplace. This is the all-at-onceness of HIV/AIDS, a disease that not only destroys an individual's immune system but also breaks down the artificial barriers that we construct between professional and personal lives.

Successful preservice and inservice education depends on the provision of adequate time for teachers to express their feelings about HIV/AIDS and their reactions to talking with children about HIV-related issues (Basch, 1989; Sanders & Farquhar, 1991). For only after these feelings have been acknowledged and discussed can teachers attend to the task at hand. In describing the introduction of an anti-bias curriculum, for example, Derman-Sparks and the A.B.C. Task Force (1989) provide a model for staff development about HIV/AIDS. They emphasize group consciousness-raising for teachers as the first step in creating new curricula on social issues. This process is one that respects the teacher as an adult learner, providing an opportunity to understand the subject matter in more than a superficial manner. A reading of the anti-bias curriculum also suggests that teachers who have placed equity issues high on their own agendas will have less difficulty integrating HIV/AIDS into the ongoing curriculum; these teachers have already created environments in which human differences are discussed and valued. HIV/AIDS education must proceed out of a meaningful context, so students can recognize the familiar and understandable as well as the new and unexpected in this issue.

Institutional Constraints

Talk of staff development, consciousness-raising groups, and adults as learners is not to deny the real constraints under which teachers work. Ironically, the press for school reform initiated by the publication of *A Nation at Risk* in 1984 has resulted in increased demands for required courses, quantitative measurement, and universal standards. The introduction of HIV/AIDS education has meant that teachers must squeeze an additional topic into their already overcrowded, overorganized days. It becomes another requirement that impinges on what little discretionary time remains to them. Even as leaders of industry and labor are calling for greater teacher autonomy to increase school effectiveness, and experiments in teacher-based school governance proliferate, state mandates for HIV/AIDS education allocate few resources for staff development (Kenney, Guardado, & Brown, 1989). If teachers are to engage in the decision-making activities that would define them as professionals, then they must be given the opportunity to develop the knowledge appropriate to such responsibilities (Wirth, 1989).

Thus for teachers, the introduction of HIV/AIDS into the curriculum has also meant preoccupation with negotiating school bureaucracies and calculating the risks of fomenting change. In most school districts where I have worked, teachers are in agreement about institutionally imposed limitations on what may be said. However, they are often in disagreement as to what their individual responses should be. Three solutions to this dilemma are common.

The first solution accepts the limits but recognizes that there are ways to work around them. The second solution, more cynical and despairing, resists any participation in what are perceived to be duplicitous practices. For teachers advocating the first solution, compromise is essential in order to get critical information to their students. For teachers adopting the second solution, however, the main compromise—that they may respond to questions as raised by students but not initiate certain "hot" topics—is unacceptable. Placing teachers in a position where they rely on student questions, and then refer students back to their parents or to after-school counseling sessions, can undermine the teacher's authority. Unfortunately, the legitimate anger expressed over the moral bind in which they are placed is too often projected onto the subject of HIV/AIDS itself rather than directed at creating a changed educational context.

A third solution to institutionally imposed limits is premised on the teacher's sense of privacy and control when the classroom door is closed; these teachers feel that they are free to say what they want when they are alone with students. Grumet (1988), exploring the experiences of women teachers as well as the histories of women writers and artists, suggests the self-defeating nature of this strategy. Describing the importance of private spaces for the development of ideas, she also points to the incipient dangers of isolation and privatization that can result when the doors to these rooms are never opened. The potential for community change can be fostered or thwarted by our willingness to make public that which has been nurtured in private.

But the institutions in which we live and work are often far more permeable than we imagine (Sarason, 1982). If teachers are to be successful change agents—and HIV/AIDS always involves change—then professional education programs must prepare them for their extra-classroom roles. Knowledge of institutional power structures, budget making, and community relations is as appropriate for the classroom teacher as for the administrator. All school personnel need to understand that institutions are often less monolithic and more heterogeneous when looked at closely with specific ends in view. Internal contradictions provide openings for change. Frequently it is our own perception of hegemony that is the biggest block to creating effective local strategies.

Primary Ideology

Finally, while for some adults the reluctance to talk with children about HIV/AIDS reflects their own lack of knowledge, for others it is part of a consciously held belief system about the nature of childhood. For example, Robin Alexander (1984), in a study of British primary and junior schools, found teachers committed to the idea of childhood as a time of innocence. Although the "primary ideology" recognizes that children are capable of unacceptable behavior, it also deems them free of any malicious intent. Ideas about original sin once promoted by religious reformers have been abandoned, replaced by images of moral purity. In an observational study of three schools, R. King (1978) confirms teachers' determination to protect young children from harsh and corrupting realities of the adult world. In America, California kindergarten teachers have opposed any discussion of HIV/AIDS in their classrooms because they want to protect children from any unpleasant and, in their view, irrelevant subjects.

When *Young Children*, the Journal of the National Association for the Education of Young Children (NAEYC), published its first HIV/AIDS article, entitled "What We Should and Should Not Tell Our Children About AIDS," it

emphasized that the role of the teacher was to soothe the potentially frightened child and avoid presenting unnecessary information (Skeen & Hudson,
1987). Two years later an article on substance abuse prevention in the same
journal reinforced a similar philosophy. Misleadingly titled "Drug Abuse Prevention Begins in Early Childhood (And is much more than a matter of in-
structing young children about drugs!)," it deals solely with the need for
parent education and calls for an analysis of parenting styles that promote
positive self-images among young children (Oyemade & Washington, 1989).
There is little recognition in either article that children may be all too aware
of the social problems that exist in their communities. While teachers are
constantly reminded to structure environments that are psychologically supportive of personal growth, never is it suggested that they take the lead in
providing information about HIV/AIDS or drugs. Nor are they encouraged to
help students sort through the multiple meanings they may have already
assigned to them. The message is that as long as we follow developmentally
appropriate practices, little must change in the way we think about children's
lives.

PREPARING CLASSROOM TEACHERS TO TALK ABOUT *HIV/AIDS*

To accept that children live in a world where they come to learn about
HIV/AIDS, drugs, poverty, and homelessness at a far earlier age than most of
us would prefer does not mean we are participating in the denial of childhood. But it does mean we need to create classrooms in which children feel
comfortable exploring these issues. Teacher educators can foster this process in two critical ways. First, they can highlight for their students the tension between what we have learned about the social construction of childhood, the embeddedness of our ideas in specific historical contexts, and what
we may believe to be optimal conditions for children's growth (James &
Prout, 1990a). Wanting the newcomer to feel at home in the world, we each
struggle with the degree to which we see childhood as a separate life period
requiring specialized protections and professionalized care, and the degree
to which we see it as a time for full participation in the ongoing life of the
community. The work of those who look at how the social environment is
changing the experience of childhood—from the growth of electronic information sources, parental pressure for achievement, and the increasing isolation of children in age-segregated institutions, to the pervasive violence in
young people's lives—would be especially helpful with this project (Elkind,
1981b; Garbarino, 1992; Polakow, 1982; Postman, 1982).

Second, given the stressful lives of contemporary children, it is important for teacher educators to emphasize their competencies as well as their

developmental deficiencies, a theme I pursue at greater length in Chapter 4. Here I would mention the use of the anthropological or sociological lens (Felsman, 1989; Glauser, 1990) to focus on the strengths and healthy adaptation rather than weaknesses or pathology of children living in difficult circumstances. I also refer to our increasing knowledge of young children's narrative skills, their use of and understanding of abstract concepts, binary oppositions, metaphor, and humor (Egan, 1988; Sutton-Smith, 1988). Like Robert Coles (1989), we need to listen to the moral energy coursing through the stories of older children living in poverty, as they question and reflect upon their experiences. These stories can tell us how children resist despair, claim dignity in dehumanizing situations, and create redemptive moments out of sorrow.

A Question of Authority

Preparing classroom teachers to integrate HIV/AIDS into the curriculum is a complex process not just because it raises personal concerns for individuals or because it may force them to address new subjects such as sex and death. It is complex because it provokes inquiry into basic philosophical issues about the nature of pedagogy, the meaning of childhood, and the role of the teacher as change agent. An incident in the spring of 1986 crystallized for me the underlying theme of this inquiry and much of the teacher discourse on HIV/AIDS. At that time I was asked to talk to a group of angry parents and teachers who were attempting to exclude a 5-year-old girl with AIDS from their school. Within a few minutes of my opening remarks about the severity of the HIV/AIDS problem in the community, I was interrupted by an angry, bearded man in his mid-30s who announced himself to be a teacher, a historian of science, and a parent in the school. Citing the newness of the disease and the constant flow of information from the medical world, he began to question the credentials of the panelists—a physician, a public health official, a school administrator, a parent leader, and myself—one by one. At that moment of attack, rather than becoming defensive as many of the others did, I began to relax. As a former teacher, I recognized a familiar issue emerging, the issue of authority. This irate father was challenging not only the specific information we offered but, more significantly, our fundamental right to influence his children. The shadow of the school–family struggle for the child was lengthening to include HIV/AIDS.

Although this scene took place at the height of HIV/AIDS hysteria, it exemplifies a critical and ongoing theme in the HIV/AIDS discourse: the challenge that the disease poses to traditional concepts of authority. For many, authority implies certainty, the right to guide others based on full knowledge of the outcomes of the recommended actions. But HIV/AIDS is not about absolutes.

It is defined by a series of changing practices, bodies of knowledge, and contexts. AIDS educators and policy makers are skilled at juxtaposing theoretical possibilities against actual probabilities, an unsatisfying dialectic for those who feel personally threatened and seek safety through guarantees. Yet physicians and other officials who assert certainty lose credibility as well. For in their attempt to reassure, they fail to acknowledge the reality of indeterminacy, an acknowledgment that would allow them to form a sympathetic alliance with an anxious audience. The ethical and practical implications of HIV/AIDS test our tolerance for uncertainty as well as our commitment to live the democratic principles that speak to inclusive rather than exclusive modes of behavior.

While the father described in this incident was particularly direct in his attempt to discredit our authority, or perhaps more accurately, even the possibility of the existence of authoritative knowledge about HIV/AIDS, he was raising the same question that emerged in countless sessions with teachers at that time. Teachers were faced with a dual quandary. They saw themselves as possibly in danger, not only because they were acceding to policies based on calculated risks, but also because they were being asked to initiate HIV/AIDS instruction without feeling confident about the information they would be transmitting. Obviously, HIV/AIDS also meant talking about sex, drugs, and death, often taboo subjects that are not easily packaged into highly rationalized lessons. Without certainty, lacking definitive research or a legitimated history to support current assertions, teachers wondered what stance to adopt with regard to the subject. They wondered how not to place their own authority in jeopardy with students. When teachers believe their ability to influence students rests in the control of information, the lack of that control can lead to a lethal silence.

Teachers now recognize that their failure to respond to many teachable moments reflects a lack of confidence in their own HIV/AIDS knowledge. A subtle but more positive shift in attitudes has occurred when professionals refer to their ignorance rather than to lack of scientific proof. The reservations are less about the validity of scientific knowledge than about their familiarity with it. Yet there is something fundamentally askew when teachers are unwilling to admit to students that they do not know the answers to their questions and use this as a rationale for pretending that the subject does not exist. While the obvious remedy to this situation is to provide all teachers with a good basic education about HIV/AIDS so that they feel competent, a long-range response must also be pursued by encouraging teachers and those who work with them to examine the sources of their authority. For HIV/AIDS is not the only difficult issue teachers face in the classroom where the willingness to model the role of learner takes precedence over the traditional role of knower.

Collaboration in Health and Education

The high degree of control and standardization in American public schools that undermines the initiative of teachers has been amply documented by historians and sociologists of education (Apple, 1982; Tyack, 1974). Frequently denied the choices that would express their pedagogic expertise, teachers are reluctant to take on subjects like sex, illness, and death that leave them in undefined territory where previous understandings of authority may seem less relevant. In such territory, student–teacher distinctions based on the ownership of knowledge may break down in the face of the greater commonalities that we all share regardless of age.

The breakdown of hierarchical authority that may ensue when certainty becomes doubtful has been actively sought by people with HIV/AIDS and their advocates and is a development educators might watch carefully. As individuals confront radical care and treatment decisions, the authority of institutions and private practitioners has come under increasing scrutiny. People with HIV/AIDS often have more information about new drugs or treatments than their health care provider; at other times, the provider may have to acknowledge that little is known about how a drug works or even if it is effective. A collaborative model of health care in which the patient is a full participant seems only appropriate given these circumstances. Such a collaborative model has implications for all professionals who may have once defined their right to practice by the exclusive control of a particular body of knowledge and skills.

As more and more people with HIV/AIDS strive to become involved in the decisions affecting their care, they set an agenda for themselves that does not sound so very different from one that good teachers may set for their students—or indeed that teachers as a group may have for their own development. This is an agenda of increasing independence, autonomy, and self-reliance. Illich (1976), in a book written just prior to the emergence of HIV/AIDS, makes an illuminating distinction between medical and health care, associating the former with the highly rationalized scientific management of illness offered by experts in institutional settings, and the latter with the sociopolitical process that enables people to make life-affirming choices on a daily basis. To Illich, medical care is only a part of a larger set of contextual issues that facilitate or inhibit health. This is not to deny the critical role of technology and professional care but to question how reliance on them affects our sense of dignity and agency.

It would seem that teachers express a similar set of concerns, not only when they question the ultimate meanings of the technocratic curriculum but also when they assess the administrative structures that frustrate their ability to decide how and what they will teach. For the belief in expert control undermines teachers who are asked only to implement curricula designed by others, undermines students forced to learn in classrooms in which they are not active participants, and undermines sick people made passive observers of the healing process (Rosenberg, 1987). Collaboration, in education as in health care, may appear risky because it means that experts relinquish some of their control. But it is also a recognition that not all knowledge is about control. While there needs to be space for mastery, there also needs to be a role for understanding and acceptance, for emancipation and liberation.

IS THERE SAFETY IN SAFER SEX?

The interests of early childhood and elementary classroom teachers in becoming knowledgeable and establishing a rationale for HIV/AIDS education with younger children are different from those of teachers working with adolescents. In junior and senior high schools, health teachers are trained to talk about sex and sexuality, though permitted to do so with varying degrees of freedom. It is now assumed that HIV/AIDS education is relevant to all students who are potentially sexually active. This has not always been the case.

It is understandable that adults were at first reluctant to admit the presence of a complex, wily virus such as HIV in a chameleon-like population that itself often appears to have no other goal than to test the limits of human possibility. During the earliest years of the epidemic, this reluctance to view teenagers as vulnerable to HIV infection was reinforced by the dominant risk-group vocabulary, which suggested that the virus would be contained within specific populations. The social and political marginalization of gay men and injection drug users allowed many to discount their experiences. Today, although there continues to be widespread denial of the existence of gay-identified youth in our classrooms (Rofes, 1989), there is a greater acceptance of the fact that any teenager may experiment with behaviors or accede to peer pressure in such a way as to place him- or herself at risk for contracting HIV. Indeed, it is these very attributes that are most frequently cited as the reasons for making HIV education so daunting.

Whether motivated by irrational fear or realistic assessment of the problem, a strong national consensus exists in favor of HIV/AIDS education for young people (Center for Population Options, 1989). Although compliance may be inconsistent and resistance from the religious right fierce (Gallagher, 1993), over half of the states have mandated HIV/AIDS education in their schools and most others strongly recommend it. Only 13 states have established complete programs including published curricula, training or certification requirements, and inservice education for staff (Kenney et al., 1989). The absence of resources for staff development is especially notable given recent calls for greater teacher autonomy to increase school effectiveness and the proliferation of experiments in teacher-based school governance. In many of the nation's largest school districts, education about HIV has begun to take precedence over education about sexuality. While the majority of schools address both topics, the transitional and often confusing nature of the moment is evidenced by the number of sites that offer HIV/AIDS education but not sexuality education, and others where the situation is reversed.

HIV-related curricula tend to have a strong prevention focus. Not surprisingly, the prevention method of choice is clearly abstinence. Of the 27 state-approved curricula, only 8 address abstinence and strategies appropriate for sexually active students in a balanced manner and provide comprehensive information about the epidemic. Indeed, the subject of safer sex is one of the least likely to be discussed with students. While teachers blame their own discomfort with this topic on parental and administrative constraints, lack of appropriate materials, and the embarrassment with which students approach discussions of sexuality, they report little difficulty teaching abstinence and sexual decision making (Kerr, Allensworth, & Gayle, 1989). This suggests that the latter topic is not so much about learning to make choices from a world of possibilities as about deciding to say "no" to sex, based on a predetermined set of behavioral rules. That decision making has become a code phrase for a "just say no" message is underlined by teachers' responses to survey questions. There is almost universal commitment to programs that enable students to examine and develop their own values; yet three-quarters of the same teachers believe that students should be explicitly taught not to have sex (Forrest & Silverman, 1989). The values clarification discussion becomes the critical vehicle for persuading students to own the adult perspective.

Despite media and school-based efforts, teenagers remain woefully ignorant about HIV and ill disposed toward people with AIDS (Brooks-Gunn, Boyer, & Hein, 1988; Hingson & Strunin, 1989). This is of increased concern for African-American and Latino communities whose youth represent 34% and 18% respectively of adolescents with AIDS but who, in comparison with their white peers, are less knowledgeable about HIV and the effectiveness of condoms for prevention (DiClemente, Boyer, & Morales, 1988). Overall, AIDS is the sixth leading cause of death among those aged 15 to 24 (*Chronic Disease and Health . . . ,* 1990). While adolescents are only 2% of total AIDS cases, for the past six years the number of cases among 13- to 19-year-olds has doubled every 14 months, the same rate of expansion seen among gay males in the first years of the epidemic. Other studies indicate that 7% of homeless and runaway youth and 1% of all teenagers in high-incidence cities like New York and Miami may have already contracted HIV (Society for Adolescent Medicine, 1994). Most disturbingly, over one-fifth of people with AIDS are in their 20s. Because the average latency period between initial infection with HIV and the onset of CDC-defined AIDS is 10 years or more, it can be inferred that many of these people contracted the virus as teenagers.

State-approved HIV/AIDS curricula usually give priority to information about healthful lifestyles, communicable diseases, and HIV transmission and prevention. But many pose constraints to the discussion of subjects that might be interpreted as facilitating sexual activity—contraception, safer sex, and sexuality—even though studies indicate that sex education leads not to more sex but to more responsible sex, including the postponement of first intercourse, safer practices, and fewer unwanted pregnancies (Altman, 1993a).

Unfortunately, evidence also suggests a lack of practical efficacy in our efforts; only 8% of males and 2% of females reported condom use after exposure to AIDS education. Among homosexual/bisexual males, those who reported using condoms increased from 2% to 19% after AIDS education (Bell, 1991). Studies (New York City Board of Education, 1990) conducted two years after implementation of specific curricula point to little or no change in actual knowledge. When asked, students report that they learn about HIV/AIDS primarily from the media and interpersonal sources—for example, friends and parents ("What High School Students Want . . . ," 1990). Schools are listed third, and teachers are described as ill informed, reluctant to talk about disease and sexual activity, and uninterested in HIV/AIDS education. Students themselves request more extensive and intensive education, beginning earlier, and including presentations by people with HIV/AIDS, targeted information about prevention, condom availability, and discussion of the psychosocial impact of the disease.

The Life-Skills Approach

In order to create more effective programs, some curriculum makers (Basch, 1989; Keeling, 1989) have focused on what they perceive as a critical gap between information and/or self-perception and behavioral change. Mickler (1993), studying AIDS-preventive behavior among college adolescents, found that knowledge of AIDS was not predictive or strongly related to safer sex practices. Others (Koopman, Rotheram-Borus, Henderson, Bradley, & Hunter, 1990), working with adolescent runaways and self-identified gay males, reported that both groups had moderately positive beliefs about their self-efficacy and self-control in sexual situations. Yet in focus groups they were unable to role-play safer behaviors, such as asking about their partners' sexual history or asking their partners to use a condom. More significantly, although three-quarters had engaged in sexual activity in the previous three months, with a mean of 2.7 partners, all reported infrequent condom use.

Increasingly, HIV/sexuality education curricula emphasize an ill-defined cluster of behaviors variously labeled as coping, problem solving, or life skills. Depending on the commitment of the particular curriculum, it is claimed that these skills will enable teenagers to remain abstinent until marriage, delay intercourse until an unspecified time in the future, or negotiate safer sex practices as necessary. Through active participation in role-playing, brainstorming sessions, and games, students are taught resistance or refusal skills so that they will not succumb to pressures from peers. These skills are often reduced to a set of sharp retorts that permit students to say "no" to sexual activity without losing face among their friends. In some instances a few lessons are added to more traditional, direct-instruction curricula, while in others, information is interwoven into a consistently interactive format (Brick, 1989).

But as progressive educators have asserted since the last century (Dewey, 1900/1956), students learn most effectively when in the midst of meaningful activities. Programs that abstract social skills provide neither the motivation nor intentionality required for substantive learning. A curriculum that attempts, in a few brief lessons, to teach students how to make critical decisions cannot make up for years of education that have denied them the right to become autonomous, self-determining learners. Friday afternoon "magic circles" to build self-esteem or Monday morning rehearsals of refusal skills divert our attention from the realities of contemporary children, who too seldom have the opportunity to make meaningful choices, follow through on them, and reflect on their consequences.

Skill-based approaches are built on the understanding that the lack of a positive self-image is the biggest factor preventing teenagers from making healthy decisions. Nationally distributed curricula such as "Project Charlie" (Charest, Gwinn, Reinisch, Terrien, & Strawbridge, 1987) and "Growing Healthy" (National Center for Health Education, 1985) are being described as panaceas to a wide variety of problems, including high school dropout rates, lowered academic performance, widespread alcohol and substance abuse, and teenage pregnancy. As in similar programs designed to improve adult productivity in the workplace, the focus on changes in self-perception and interpersonal skills masks material barriers to real equity and autonomy (Steinberg, 1990; L. Williams, 1990). Self-esteem has become a popular buzzword for efforts to promote better psychological adjustment to the political status quo.

The seemingly humanistic techniques of self-empowerment models often become a means to reproduce a hegemonic ideology, instantiating subtle but powerful forms of social control (Young, 1990). This occurs, for example, when the press to insure safer sex, whether condom use for gay men or abstinence for teenagers, impels facilitators to assume responsibility *for* group members rather than *toward* them. The most sympathetic educators may fail to exercise pedagogical tact when confronting HIV/AIDS. Programs are coercive to the degree that they compromise the participants' abilities to draw their own conclusions from experiences that take place within a context that specifically proclaims the importance of individual choice. Experiential learning becomes a means to an end rather than an open exploration of possibility, including the potential rejection of safer sex practices.

Both individual behavior change and self-empowerment models are based on the instrumentalist assumption that behavior can be isolated, analyzed, and understood apart from the socioeconomic context in which it occurs—an assumption that negates the necessity of addressing issues of the differential distribution of economic and cultural capital. Brandt (1987) comments:

> These assumptions with which we still live regarding health-related behavior rest upon an essentially naive, simplistic view of human nature. If anything has become clear in the course of the twentieth century it is that behavior is subject to complex forces, internal psychologies, and external pressures all not subject to immediate modifications, or, arguably, to modifications at all. (p. 202)

The historical record not only documents the past failure of narrow approaches to the control of sexually transmitted diseases but also the degree to which they are constructed upon a set of moralistic judgments about the nature of sexual activity (Fee & Fox, 1988).

In a democratic society that is respectful of pluralism and accepting of different rates and ways of learning, the public health goal of zero transmission, 100% risk reduction, is not only counterproductive but politically unacceptable (Bell, 1991). Compromise is inevitable in societies where absolute control over citizens' (mis)behaviors is given up in the interests of the responsible exercise of individual freedom. It is as inappropriate to employ coercive measures as it is to gauge the success of HIV/AIDS education by gross measures of behavioral change.

The Collective-Action Approach

While much is to be learned from the cognitive social learning theory (e.g., active engagement of students, multiple levels of learning, and variable strategies) underlying skill-based programs (Flora & Thoresen, 1988), its limitations are highlighted by a tri-phasic map of health education including individual behavioral change, self-empowerment, and collective action models (French & Adams, 1986; Homans & Aggleton, 1988). The underlying assumption of the first two approaches, also referred to as direct-instruction or experientially based programs, is that increased information about HIV transmission, or the practice of specific skills, will result in a decrease of high-risk behaviors. This in turn will translate into a reduced number of new HIV infections (Eckland, 1989). The linear reasoning embedded in these approaches, along with questions of long-term effectiveness and ethics, is exposed when they are juxtaposed against a collective-action model of health education. In addition to addressing the need for information and communicative skills, the collective-action approach encourages organizing to transform the social and political forces that shape and give meaning to individual behavior.

When the connection between health status and poverty, employment, income, and social class is fully recognized, then socioeconomic factors appear to have greater significance for health than do individual behaviors ("Demand side," 1993; Hubbard, 1993). These factors are best addressed through collective action in the political process. While this position is consistent with radical definitions of health and illness (Illich, 1976), it threatens the official governmental position on disease causation, as summarized by the presidential commission on the Human Immunodeficiency Virus Epidemic (1988), which is that "the heaviest burden of illness in the technically advanced countries today is related to individual behavior, especially the long-term patterns of behavior often referred to as 'life-style'" (p. 89). Paradoxically, it is this attempt to define critical social issues as private and personal rather than as public and political that heightens the very bigotry that the Presidential Commission seeks to dispel.

In fact, safer sex organizing began as a grass roots political movement within the gay community (Patton, 1990). Its greatest successes occurred in the first years of the epidemic prior to the professionalization and bureaucratization of HIV prevention. Some continue to understand that health education, community building, and political resistance are inextricably linked. Cranston (1992), for example, proposes HIV/AIDS education among gay and lesbian youth based on Paulo Freire's concept of the community of conscience. Consistent with a collective action model, this is HIV prevention that leads to political engagement because it values and fosters respect for gay histories, identities, and futures. Others (Gasch, Poulson, Fullilove, & Fullilove, 1991) understand the disproportional impact of HIV/AIDS on African-American populations as part of a more generalized pattern of excessive risk and mortality. They stress the role of the social and material environment in conditioning health-related behaviors. Poor African-American communities are best served by developing an analysis that will enable their members to work toward reversing the pervasive social decay. Educating for contextual self-efficacy means connecting individual behavior to larger social changes.

Assessing the impact of a curriculum requires an exploration of the knowledge assumptions on which it is based. This assessment is critical to dispelling the myths about sexual identity and behavior that prevent effective HIV/AIDS education. Limiting the terrain of HIV/AIDS education to that of a "solvable" social question involving risk-reduction strategies has led to correspondingly limited answers focusing on either behavioral or attitudinal changes (Diorio, 1985). Valued knowledge is construed in the former case as the sum of facts and skills and in the latter as the ability to understand the intentions of others through improved communication abilities. However, HIV/AIDS is not only a question of individual behaviors and social norms. It is also a question of material conditions and resources, and structural inequities based on race, class, gender and sexual identities.

SEX, *HIV*, AND THE PERMEABLE CURRICULUM

AIDS is a disease of contradictions. It is a disease that is not a disease, a biological reality that has had a greater impact on sociopolitical practices than on medical care, an illness of hiddeness that has led to irreversible changes in public discourse. Unfortunately, HIV infection has also become a disease of adolescence, a period characterized in our society by its own unique logic—moments of sudden growth and regression, of open search and certain definition, of personal power and extreme susceptibility to the influence of others. An additional conundrum now presents itself: Safer sex alone will not make us safe from the effects of HIV.

The complexity of HIV/AIDS mandates a multifaceted approach. Reconceptualizing HIV/AIDS education means abandoning the instrumentalist assumptions of information- and skill-based programs that have led many to theorize the problem of HIV/AIDS education as one of bridging a gap between knowledge and behavior. Preventing the transmission of HIV involves not only learning about condoms, spermicides, and negotiating sex; it also means developing tools of political analysis, a commitment to social change, and an ethic of caring and responsibility. In short, we must shift our attention from HIV prevention narrowly defined as a means of behavioral control to a broader focus that would more accurately reflect our students' life worlds. HIV/AIDS education should further the goal of preparing students to become active participants in a democratic society. But what are the elements of such an approach?

First, HIV/AIDS education needs to begin with the youngest children and permeate the curriculum in order to break down the taboos with which it is associated and to make the subject a more comfortable one for discussion (Quackenbush & Villarreal, 1988). Our efforts should be informed by an appreciation of the developmental levels and experiential bases of different groups of students. We must ask whether the curriculum ensures equal access to HIV/AIDS information for all students. Access means that students not only have the opportunity to hear information but that it is presented in a language and style easily understood by specific target groups (Nettles & Scott-Jones, 1989). At the same time, as with other subject areas, we must be concerned with unwarranted differences in curriculum predicated on the race, class, gender, or sexual orientation of our students (Apple & Weiss, 1983; Willis, 1977).

Effective sexuality education itself, education that empowers students by building their sense of entitlement and decreasing their vulnerability, is based on our willingness to listen to and work with the experiences students bring with them. This requires giving up presuppositions about the nature of sexuality and the outcomes of our efforts in favor of a sociohistorical appreciation of the ways in which sexual meanings are constructed and changed (D'Emilio & Freedman, 1988; Rubin, 1984). Safer sex can be less about the limitations imposed by HIV and the inculcation of specific behaviors and more about exploring multiple zones of bodily pleasures and the transformation of culturally determined constraints (Patton, 1985). In a time of HIV/AIDS, a discursive analysis becomes essential to re-imagining sexual practices in life-affirming, sex-positive ways.

Our goal should be to replace isolated lessons calculated to build self-esteem and social skills with an ongoing discourse of desire that problematizes violence and victimization (Fine, 1988). If the experiences of our students are valorized, they will be better able to understand the sources of pleasure and danger in their own lives. This process begins when students find a safe place in which to tell their stories. To accept these narratives is not only to foster respect for individual differences but also to reveal their distance from officially given versions of human sexuality, a distance that is clearly identified by recent studies of the high school curriculum (Trudell, 1992; Ward & Taylor, 1992). At the same time it is impossible to ignore externally imposed constraints to liberation, for even the best-intended pedagogic efforts may have little impact without increased life options for poorer students and easy access to birth control materials, health clinics, and substance-abuse treatment for everyone.

The permeable curriculum requires balancing our concerns about individual responsibility for transmitting HIV with an analysis of the changing social context in which it thrives. At a personal level, the curriculum causes students to reflect on their own behaviors as they affect the transmission of HIV and the lives of those who already carry the virus. At a social level, the curriculum provokes critical consciousness, fostering responsive and responsible citizens. Students should be asking questions about the societal responses to HIV/AIDS and learning to see themselves as citizens who can make decisions that will give direction to that response in the future. They need access to all kinds of citizens, especially those living with HIV, who model active responses to the disease (Navarre, 1987).

And what does the permeable curriculum say about people with HIV infection—gays, injection drug users, and others? Fear-based appeals have never been successful in preventing the spread of sexually transmitted diseases (Mickler, 1993). Greater familiarity with HIV, not less, is needed in order to break down the distancing mechanisms that allow us to feel that we can remain untouched. Images of diversity remind us that people with HIV/AIDS are a part of all our lives. Although some have real anxiety about what they perceive as a disintegration of culture and an erosion of values in the modern world, HIV/AIDS is not an appropriate metaphor for these concerns. The permeable curriculum is about caring for others and inclusion, not about isolation and exclusion.

Just as effective sexuality education is based on an entire school experience that encourages decision making, problem solving, and self-worth, successful HIV/AIDS education is built on a continuing appreciation of equity and pluralism in society. It cannot be assumed that an absence of negative comment signifies a lack of bias or commitment to social justice (Croteau & Morgan, 1989; Vance, 1984). Educators must take an active role in bringing the full spectrum of human difference to the classroom, acknowledging the ways that these have become sources of conflict and domination as well as the ways that they enrich and form the basis of participatory democracy. A curriculum that is permeable to the impact of students, one through which they can learn the skills of responsible citizenship, lays the groundwork for all AIDS education. For the history of HIV constantly reminds us not only of individual suffering and pain but also of the power and creativity that reside in a collective response.

Although HIV/AIDS may challenge our prior ideas about pedagogical authority, it also offers us an opportunity to examine new models that more accurately reflect who we understand ourselves to be and what we would like our students to become. From HIV/AIDS we learn about the limits of science and the importance of human vision, the frailty of the body and the strength of the spirit, the need to nurture the imagination even as we direct our attention to rational cognitive structures. In the end, the HIV/AIDS curriculum can be more about life than about death, more about health than about illness, more about the body politic than the body physical.

CHAPTER 4

Developmentalism and the Aims of Education

... the real political task in a society such as ours is to criticize
the working of institutions which appear to be both neutral and
independent; violence which has always exercised itself obscurely
through them will be unmasked, so that we can fight fear.
Michel Foucault, *The Archaeology of Knowledge*

There is a well-documented body of literature demonstrating how psychology can function as a subtle but pervasive form of social control, encouraging our dependence on increasing numbers of professionals and our adaptation to the political status quo (Berger & Luckmann, 1967; Foucault, 1965;
N. Rose, 1990). There are also more private moments that cause us to reflect on the role of psychology in our lives. Such a moment occurred for me
upon receipt of the communication reproduced below. It was written by
Michael Merrill two years prior to the scene described in Chapter 2. At the
time, he was a resident at the Mitre AIDS Hospice, run by the Hartford Street
Zen Center in San Francisco, and an incisive critic of its practices.

March 3, 1987

Dear Jonathan,
  Our friend at Hartford Street, J.D., is doing pretty well. He came
in November after being discharged from the hospital to die. They
gave him two weeks at that time. Last week he walked with a walker
for the first time, and he has progressively recovered his physical coordination and has gained in every impaired area. Yet when I arrived
at Hartford Street, there was a nurse-type person in J.D.'s room.
These people come every day, sometimes a couple of times a day, to
monitor his "paranoia" and to conduct tense and anxiety-producing

discussions about the blips in his moods. Anyway, I heard her voice saying something in tones of great moral urgency. Presently she leaves. Issan comes downstairs and reports that she has said to J.D., "Your body is trying to die but your mind won't let it." What do you think of that? The clear message was that the body in its wisdom knew what was best and that the intellectual or conscious will to live was a form of false consciousness standing in the path of a spiritual understanding of the situation.

I fear that there are many people who are making their living paying visits to bedsides and suggesting consciously and directly, as well as unconsciously and indirectly, that people hurry up and die. I think this is a dangerous form of moral insolence, and a by-product and pitfall of the death and dying fad.

I think the incident Michael describes is emblematic of a larger cultural tendency to modulate the distance between people, to keep us safe from the more chaotic emotions that lie beneath the surface of our daily encounters. After all, is the impulse to guide the sick in their dying so very different from the impulse to manage the young in their growing up or to encourage the homosexual in turning to the opposite sex? In each instance it is the presumption of normative stages that allows the professional to proffer an interpretation of the client's experience. I know what you need because I am not you. I am not dying, am no longer young, do not exist on the sexual margins. Yet who does not live toward his or her own death, does not know the child that lingers below the affectations of adulthood, has not channeled erotic energies to exclude once powerful possibilities?

Michael's communiqué asks us to examine our reliance on the expert to coach us through difficult transitions and how this reliance reinforces the belief that we cannot manage on our own. Perhaps we might not go through the proper phases, perhaps we might even hang on too long. Is this moral insolence or mortal fear? Unfortunately, we do not hear J.D.'s response to the "nurse-type person" at his bedside, although Michael's own resistance to her formulaic offering is loud and clear. How can I explain his instinctual resistance to the balm of psychology? Michael, a founder of the Zen Center, was a gay liberationist steeped in radical political traditions that brought him to San Francisco in the 1970s. He was also a person with AIDS. Is he responding out of the endless hours of silent meditation, out of the years of engagement in social analysis, or out of the months of illness through which he had recently suffered?

Finally, Michael's position cannot be adequately explained. Indeed, I suspect that even the notion of adequate explanation would not be consonant with his world view. For we occupy contradictory subject positions that permit us multiple perspectives and defy certainty. But resistance must be marked, for it signals the conflictual spaces in which we become self-aware subjects fighting for our lives.

Experiences caring for people with HIV/AIDS, experiences of loss, have led me to ask new questions about popular uses of psychology. However, it is the experience of educating teachers about HIV/AIDS that has drawn me back to earlier assessments of the developmental knowledge base in early education (Silin, 1988). For in my work with teachers I hear the reluctance to initiate discussion of subjects such as AIDS, substance abuse, and homelessness couched in the language of the developmentally appropriate curriculum (Bredekamp, 1987; NAEYC, 1990). Echoing my own teaching vocabulary, they tell me that their children have more pressing needs—the need to play and to make sense of their immediate family lives. They imply that these needs are somehow separate from rather than enmeshed in the realities of the contemporary social world. I am repeatedly told that it is the children who are not ready for these difficult topics. What can they understand of such complex and disturbing phenomena? I am left to reflect on whose readiness is really in question. For in the end, we are probably most disturbed by the questions for which there are no answers and the ethical dilemmas raised by a society that shuns people in need.

But teachers do not work in a professional vacuum, as I was reminded when perusing a recent book based on the developmentally appropriate guidelines, *Engaging Children's Minds: The Project Approach* (L. Katz, 1989). Drawn to a discussion of teacher planning, I found a curriculum based on the hospital, illustrated with a wonderful diagram including spokes and topic headings like "people," "materials," "operations," etc. My interest sparked, I notice that AIDS is listed under "illnesses" and then, upon closer inspection, see an asterisk leading me to the bottom of the page where, if the book were in color, I would have seen a little red flag instead of the words: "only if raised by the children." Apparently we are allowed to initiate discussion about transplants, diabetes, jaundice, even having a baby, but not about AIDS. It seems to me that this project web teaches the teacher that, among other things, there are acceptable and unacceptable or less acceptable reasons for going to the hospital. Of what is the author afraid? On what knowledge did she rely to make decisions about where and when to place the asterisks?

This chapter explores the predominant knowledge base of early childhood education that leads to the kind of asterisks encountered above. I want to place the commitment to developmentally appropriate practice in historical context, articulate the connections between this paradigm and our reluctance to address difficult issues in the classroom, and suggest how both a reconsideration of the role of psychology in education as well as postmodern approaches to subjectivity might support new thinking about the curriculum.

THE EARLY CHILDHOOD KNOWLEDGE BASE

Within the broad domains of educational praxis, people committed to young children have always displayed a unique sense of mission. In 1984 Bernard Spodek invited early childhood educators to renew this sense of mission, this common identity, by examining the history of the field and the issues that have consistently informed its discourse. Shortly thereafter I responded to this invitation (Silin, 1987b) by exploring one aspect of our past, the knowledge base upon which we have relied for making curricular decisions. This exploration suggested that despite the distinct sense of mission possessed by most in the field—perhaps even because of a certain forgetfulness about the history that has shaped the profession—early educators have borrowed heavily from some academic disciplines while totally ignoring others in order to rationalize existing practices and to project new ones.

During the twentieth century, the field of early childhood education was most permeable to the influence of psychologists, and psychology was its primary "supply" discipline. Thus theoretical discussions about curricular goals were predicated upon distinctions within psychological rather than educational paradigms (Kohlberg & Mayer, 1972). Educational programs for new teachers were designed to reflect different approaches to development (Seaver & Cartwright, 1977), teacher education was analyzed in terms of the psychological theory employed by the practitioner (Porter, 1981), and programmatic innovations were evaluated in terms of developmental appropriateness (Elkind, 1981a). This "psychologistic" orientation was most pronounced in the 1960s, with the proliferation of Head Start models. Whether one was a behaviorist advocating a narrowly academic agenda, a Piagetian subscribing to a broader conception of intellectual growth, or a developmental-interactionist concerned with socioemotional as well as cognitive growth, psychological criteria became the basis for educational decision making.

Today there is some evidence of change in the field—a new understanding of the complexity of learning, including a merging of once discrete developmental constructs; an openness to qualitative research methods; and sensitivity to cultural differences (Bowman, 1993). Yet the discourse of early childhood continues to give precedence to psychological considerations and to suffer from the conservatism of the 1980s (Spodek, 1991).

A Historical Perspective

Early educators not only have a strong sense of mission; they also have a history documenting how the sense of mission has been realized. This saga and the origins of modern childhood can be traced to the sixteenth-century recognition that young children were not simply immature adults (Aries,

1962). While the Reformation focused attention on the need for appropriate forms of religious education and moral suasion, the publication of important pedagogical treatises by Comenius, Locke, and Rousseau indicated a growing awareness of the early years regardless of religious commitment. However, it was Froebel's work that most surely catalyzed the early education movement in America. A man of deep religious convictions, Froebel claimed his program was based on revealed truths—the unity of life, whole/part relations, the interconnection of all things, and the law of opposites. He designed a group of pedagogical apparatuses and exercises, the gifts and occupations, to symbolize these truths and to make them evident to children. As a rationalist, Froebel was less concerned with teaching specific content than with helping children to recognize universal values. He conceived of education as a process of "unfoldment" through which children were given the opportunity to make the inner outer and outer inner.

A challenge to the Froebelian kindergarten was mounted during the last decade of the nineteenth century by those for whom scientific method and direct observation took precedence over religious conviction and intuited forms of knowledge. Based in a philosophy of pragmatism rather than idealism, the progressives believed that the early childhood curriculum should be built on psychological rather than logical principles. They were convinced that real experiences expressing the immediate interests of children, not symbolic materials revealing eternal verities, should form the core of curriculum. The teacher acts as democratic guide, not authoritarian director of activities. The school helps children learn appropriate behavior through social interaction and the reconstruction of experience, not through the imitation of moral models. The progressive reformers wanted not only to change the very look and feel of the early childhood classroom but also to modify the knowledge base on which it was constructed.

The shift from a religious/philosophical knowledge base to a secular/psychological one was consistent with the nineteenth-century demand for scientific legitimation in all fields of endeavor. Darwin's *The Origin of Species* (1859), published three years after the opening of the first German-language kindergarten in America, was emblematic of this nineteenth-century scientific mindset. The popularity of evolutionary theory itself also created a new interest in the mental life of children. The concept of change over time as a progressive evolution from primitive to sophisticated structural forms was extended from biology, to anthropology, to child study. Borrowing from embryologists, educators asserted that, just as individual members of the species repeat the stages of evolution experienced by their phyla in prenatal development—ontogeny recapitulates phylogeny—so humans after birth repeat the stages of cultural change undergone by humankind as a whole. This assertion also made for an equation of the primitive with the childlike that had political implications for non-European people and pedagogical ramifications for children (Cleverley & Phillips, 1986; Gould, 1981). To be meaningful and efficient, education had to be child-centered, based on the developmentally determined interests of the child.

In the United States, it was G. Stanley Hall's child study movement, with its emphasis on the direct observation of children and questionnaire inquiries, that was to contribute the knowledge of children necessary for structuring educational environments. Although signaling the acceptance of what later was to be called the child development point of view, child study itself soon lost ground to the new science of child development that required a more rigorous approach to data collection, including objective, quantitative measures; standardized testing techniques; and experimental laboratory procedures. The university-based researchers sought acceptance from other scientists through the use of these positivist methods and through disassociating themselves from the more practical concerns of educators and parents. The professionalization of child study involved a growing distinction between those who produced knowledge about children and those who were to use the knowledge. The resulting lack of communication between practitioner and researcher has often been commented upon (Almy, 1982; Desforges, 1986; L. Katz, 1977). This expert/implementer dichotomy and the hierarchy of functions that goes along with it is not unique to the field of early childhood; rather, it appears to be an inescapable outcome of positivist science and the technical-mindedness that pervades education today.

The field of early childhood has always drawn heavily on a range of psychological theories but has been far less successful in establishing its own theories of practice. The 1920s, for example, saw the dominance of behaviorist approaches to learning and the measurement movement, as well as a concern for the formation of proper habits. Although this influence remained strong in the kindergarten, perhaps because it seemed well suited to programs designed to prepare children for the elementary grades, during the 1930s other early childhood institutions, such as the nursery school, were more affected by the dissemination of Freudian theory. Then, in the 1940s and 1950s, the role of normative studies of children like those conducted by Gesell at Yale firmly took hold. Their widespread use marks the success of the well-articulated child development point of view. As defined by Jersild (1946), this meant:

> an effort to apply to the education of children lessons learned from the study of children themselves. Research in child development has provided many findings which have implications for education. . . . But the child development approach does not represent merely a collection of fact. It represents a point of view. (p. 182)

Despite the pervasive shift during the 1960s and 1970s to more cognitively oriented curricula and the less prominent role given to socioemotional adjustment, early educators continued to rely on psychological rationales for program design. For example, Evans (1982), in his description of the components of early childhood programs, claimed that their theoretical foundations rest equally in psychological and philosophical thought. But when he categorized different models—behaviorist, dynamic, constructivist—he unwittingly revealed the dominance of the former over the latter. The substitution of Piaget for Gesell or Berlyne for Freud may have changed the specifics of our knowledge, but it did not alter the terrain in which it was located. Bettye Caldwell (1984), past president of NAEYC, confidently summarized this history: "Our field represents the applied side of the basic science of child development" (p. 53).

THE LIMITS OF PSYCHOLOGY: THE PIAGETIAN PARADIGM

Although the child development point of view has predominated, it did not go unchallenged, and it is the challenges that suggest openings for more socially relevant curricula. Reviewing the growth of early education during the post-*Sputnik* era, Spodek (1970) made an important distinction between curriculum sources and resources, noting that, while the former are a set of goals which are the aims of education, the latter are only a means to help achieve these ends. Among the resources are certainly developmental theory and learning theory. Egan (1983), in a more extensive analysis, asserted that the specific function of educational theory, as opposed to psychological theory, is to tell us how to design curricula to produce educated people. A deceptively simple definition, at its core is a concern for the kind of person who will result from the educational process. To talk about the result of education—the educated person—is to talk about the context in which this person can reach his or her full potential. A theory of education is not only a theory of individual growth but also a theory of political and social power. If the goal of education is to inculcate the knowledge and skills that will prepare persons to be successful political and social agents, then it must be informed by a vision of the *polis* the student will eventually enter.

In Egan's view, psychological theory is not only different from but secondary to educational theory. The former becomes meaningful only as it is part of the latter. In fact, the role of education is to shape the forces that produce psychological regularities, not to be bound by them. This is the case because psychological research is concerned with behaviors and thoughts that are the result of personal and historical experience. It is a descriptive rather than proscriptive discipline, reflecting what has been and what is, but not what ought to be (Kendler, 1993). Psychology can help us to understand the empirical consequences of social policy decisions but cannot guide us toward the ethical imperatives and political goals that should inform our curriculum work. Psychologists, whose goal is the pursuit of knowledge, can afford to isolate particular skills or characteristics for study and can at least claim to be objective in their practices. The work of educators, on the other hand, is more clearly culture-bound and value-saturated because it prepares children to live within specific communities and traditions. Education is concerned with erudition and learning as well as with cognitive and socioemotional development.

The limitations of the psychological perspective are best understood through the critique of Piaget's (Piaget, 1954) work that emerged during the 1970s. Becoming popular at a time of mounting concern over math/science education and growing interest in the open classroom, Piaget's theories are still pervasive in early childhood education. More than psychodynamic theory, with its limited implications for curriculum design, or behavior modification strategies, which were confined to specific program models, Piagetian constructs directly affected many different settings. And although Piaget's theory is clearly exceptional in its richness and complexity, its very popularity speaks as much to its uniqueness as to its representation of widely accepted assumptions about development. Criticisms of Piaget's work underline the difficulty of producing objective, definitive research about subjects who are by nature immature, unstable, and not given to the control of experimental procedures.

Decontextualized Knowledge

In the 1920s, when Piaget's work first was translated into English, mainstream American psychology was dominated by behaviorism and procedures relying on quantitative data for validation. Piaget's structuralist hypothesis and clinical method were inimical to these principles. His writings did not find a large audience.

Ironically, it was an English educator, Susan Isaacs (1930), working not from a behaviorist position but from a psychoanalytic one, who offered the most trenchant commentary on Piaget's method. Her concerns were not that his findings lacked the corroboration of large-scale studies but that the clinical interview itself did not promote the optimal use of the child's intelligence. Isaacs believed that many of the interview questions assessed the possession of specific information, not the ability to reason, as Piaget claimed. In the interview, questions were asked *of* children, not *by* them, and were thus suggestive of particular answers and related to limited, stereotyped situations. Children's intelligent thought was not revealed because children were neither naturally interested in nor motivated to seek answers to questions raised by others. Alternatively, Isaacs suggested that reason was best studied in real-life situations where it arose spontaneously in response to the child's desire to find out about the world and to solve meaningful problems.

More recently, Donaldson (1978) reviewed a series of experiments that replicated, with slight but significant modifications, those done by Piaget (1954) on decentering, class inclusion, deductive thought, and conservation. She concludes that children's success in these experiments was influenced by their knowledge of language, their assessment of what the experimenter intended, and the manner in which they would represent the situation to themselves whether or not the experimenter was actually present. Performance level was affected by minor changes in language, format, apparatus, and procedure. Failure to deal successfully with many tasks reflects the adult's inability to decenter, to understand the world from the child's viewpoint, not necessarily the child's inability to reason. Donaldson's findings, consistent with Isaac's earlier assertions, suggest that Piaget's conclusions are ill founded because children fail to grasp the nature of the problem presented to them, or the problem is irrelevant and they lack motivation to seek an adequate answer. Isaacs's and Donaldson's similar criticisms of Piaget led Isaacs to insist on the role of the school as supporting the child's learning in the context of his or her ongoing experiences. In contrast, they suggest to Donaldson that the school must articulate and provide more direct instruction in the abstract, disembedded forms of thought valued by Piaget and society at large.

Short (1991), too, has described how Piaget's sequential developmentalism leads to an underestimation of children's cognitive abilities and a reluctance on the part of teachers to stretch and test the limits of their students' intellectual competence through the introduction of controversial issues. Alexander (1984) stresses the link between Piagetian developmentalism and popular ideas of "readiness"—the idea that children's capacity to cope with specific types of learning is determined by their developmental stage. Piaget himself did not believe that children's passage through cognitive stages could be accelerated to any great degree, an idea he derided as the "American question." The teacher is caught in a paradox, for if a child is ready to change, this will occur naturally and without adult assistance. Any intervention is largely superfluous, even harmful.

Short notes how Piaget's assumption that the preadolescent is unable to appreciate a range of arguments or to evaluate conflicting evidence mediates against the introduction of political education into the primary school. He catalogues the stream of research that confirms and extends the Piagetian framework to new areas, from social perceptive taking and moral development (Damon, 1977; Kohlberg, 1981; Livesley & Bromley, 1973; Selman,

1980) to political literacy (Furth, 1979; Jahoda, 1963; Leahy, 1983; Hartley, Rosenbaum, & Schwartz, 1948). Short contrasts this work with a less widely read research tradition indicating that primary level children are more politically sophisticated (Stevens, 1982) and have greater awareness of issues regarding race and prejudice (Horowitz, 1936/1965; Jeffcoate, 1977; Short & Carrington, 1987), gender and sex-role stereotypes (P. A. Katz, 1983; Kuhn, Nash, & Brucken, 1978), than is generally assumed. The Piagetian lens may be helpful in understanding the child's logical reasoning skills, though even here it has been challenged (Matthews, 1980), but appears inadequate or irrelevant to the discussion of social issues in the classroom.

Reason and Values in Psychology

As a group, the authors discussed so far are representative of those who have questioned Piaget's method, resultant data, and the nature of his theory qua theory. They provoke us to examine how psychological research is conducted and to ask if its methods are consistent with the more contextualized, less fragmented ways early educators experience growing children. There are others, however, who attend less to methodological issues than to the emphasis on logicomathematical structures in Piaget's work (Merleau-Ponty, 1964). These critiques highlight how competing schools within psychology shape our interpretations of common childhood activities, focus on different aspects of human potential, and contain alternative world views.

It is not surprising that Piaget's work, with its attention to rational modes of thought, has achieved wide popularity in a culture obsessed with technological accomplishments and scientific approaches to the management of human problems. What Piaget's theory excludes from consideration are nonrational, but not necessarily irrational, modes of thought: intuitive, mythical, religious, aesthetic, imaginative. This omission is not a neutral exclusion; a definite value system is operative in the Piagetian framework. For example, Piaget (1962) understands symbolic play as a function of underdeveloped thinking processes. Play is significant when young children's needs to assimilate information, to distort reality to conform to their existing picture of the world, is greatest. As cognitive structures become more adequate, as they accommodate to reality, children enter the period of concrete operations, giving up symbolic play in favor of rule-governed games. To Piaget, imaginative play is a compensatory activity rather than a source of new concepts or ideas and is clearly irrelevant to adult functioning. Always in the service of cognitive development, play is a necessary step on the road to formal operations.

Focusing on directed rather than on divergent, creative, or imaginative thought, Piaget interprets play as an epiphenomenon, although admittedly serving a cathartic purpose in the emotional lives of the young. In contrast, others (Herron & Sutton-Smith, 1971; Vandenberg, 1971) see play as a primary phenomenon, an essential mode of being in childhood, with its own structures, purposes, and sources for generating novel ideas. If play is considered an end in itself, it may represent an irreducible challenge to contemporary values. That is, because play is a nonproductive, pleasure-oriented, aesthetic activity, it may be seen to threaten a society built on material production, repression, and control. Play expresses the child's refusal to be organized by adult conceptions of reality (Alves, 1972).

To embrace Piaget as the basis for educational programming is to embrace a particular conception of what is essential to human development and to success in adult life. It is also to accept the belief that intelligent action is the human expression of the biological process of adaptation (Piaget, 1950). The implication is that education, in promoting intelligent behavior, promotes adaptation to the environment. In the end, every psychology is embedded in a politics as well as a world view, and the politics of adaptation is certainly not the politics of resistance or revolution. While educational decisions should be based on more than our knowledge of children, it is how and what we choose to know about them that is immediately in question.

The Developmental Metaphor

If Piaget's perspective is one that leads us to view children as incomplete beings, falling short of adult standards of functioning, part of the explanation lies in his belief in the superiority of reason over other forms of knowing. But part of the explanation also resides in the basic metaphor of development itself. This is a metaphor borrowed from the biological sciences; its use implies not only a continuity of physical and psychological growth but also an adult-centered perspective in relation to children. Research making this assumption begins with a set of adult characteristics, usually defined by middle-class Western standards of maturity, and examines growth as progress toward the achievement of these characteristics (Speier, 1976). The imposition of these standards is rationalized through the further assumption that, because developmental processes are biologically based and best exemplified in Piaget's assimilation/accommodation model of adaptation, they are also universal. Although environment or experience may affect the speed of development, the attainment of higher levels of thought, or even the way that specific tasks are accomplished, the sequence of stages and laws of development are assumed to be cross-culturally valid.

This is an assumption challenged by Egan (1983), who raises doubts as to whether Piaget described a natural, universal pattern of development, as claimed, or whether he described the results of particular methods of sociocultural initiation. Egan marshals cross-cultural evidence to suggest that Piaget's stages are not universal or invariant in sequence; this evidence casts doubt on Piaget's explanation of why children at certain stages can perform some tasks but not others—specifically on the ambiguous role attributed to experience and the meaning of *decalage*. If, as Egan maintains, Piaget's stages reflect a logical rather than psychological necessity, then they are not amenable to proofs from empirical data at all and their scientific validity is again thrown into question. Egan is skeptical about the educational commonplaces drawn from Piaget's work, such as the active nature of learning, the importance of readiness, and the assessment of individual differences. And indeed, growing numbers of early childhood educators have come to view stage theories of development more metaphorically than literally (Weber, 1984) and to recognize the impact of diversity in all its many forms on learning in schools (Banks, 1993; Zimiles, 1991).

PERENNIAL PROBLEMS IN EARLY CHILDHOOD EDUCATION

When educators rely on psychologists for their knowledge base, they may be avoiding difficult philosophical and social issues while believing themselves to be acting in a "professional" manner. They also may be succumbing to a subtle, but nonetheless potent, form of technical-mindedness because they are taking educational decision making out of the realm of moral and political consideration, where it more properly belongs. Early educators are particularly vulnerable to this form of instrumental rationality because they tend to regard themselves as objective, if well-intentioned, protectors of the young and because they are members of a low-status field seeking to improve its position in a society that places primacy on scientific knowledge. Age-related differences should not be obscured in developing educational environments; nonetheless, what age means needs to be explored from many perspectives, and knowledge about how people change over time should be part of an articulated social philosophy.

Curricular Content

The absence of social theory in many early childhood programs underlines the limits of our current knowledge base and contributes to two perennial problems—the nature of curricular content and the grounding of professional expertise. Appropriate knowledge for young children has been a subject of controversy among early educators and is ill defined in many programs (Evans, 1982). Diverse conceptions of the child's developmental abilities, concerns, and needs have led to differing approaches to curriculum design (Maccoby & Zellner, 1970). Historically, custodial programs have tried to provide a benign environment, acting *in loco parentis* to inculcate behaviors and attitudes not learned at home. The play curriculum in middle-class schools was geared to support socioemotional growth. Grace Owen (1920), an influential British educator, summarized this position:

> No mention has been made of instruction in the Nursery School because in any formal sense it has no place. No reading, no writing, no number lessons should on any account be required—no object lessons as commonly known should be allowed, for the time for these things has not yet come. Up to the age of six, the child is usually fully occupied in mind and body with learning from actual experience: he is busily taking in ideas from the world about him, he is gaining information by means of his own questionings of grown-up people—he is experimenting with his limbs, his senses, his hands, in a thousand ways. (p. 25)

Today many early childhood educators find themselves torn between their training in developmentally appropriate practice and the press for academically oriented programs that Owen fought off so long ago (Hatch & Freeman, 1988). Some (D. J. Walsh, 1991) suggest it is their resistance to this, rather than positive consensus, that unifies those believing in developmental education. But perhaps it is the preoccupation with developmental correctness itself that has left early educators without clear guidelines for content selection. The model of child-centered pedagogy that emerged in the 1970s was grounded in the Piagetian epistemology that not only gave precedence to the individual over the group and the cognitive over the socio-emotional, but also to the concept over the content.

> His [Piaget's] personal role in the movement towards naturalization of mathematical and scientific knowledges as individual capacities, developing in a quasi-spontaneous fashion given the correct environment, was a central part of that movement which permitted the curriculum to be understood as spontaneous and permitted the teaching of facts to disappear in favor of the monitoring of the learning of concepts. Recognizing such a movement is absolutely crucial to understanding how the present pedagogic common-sense "facts" themselves have become concepts, structures—stripped of their content and located in individuals. (Walkerdine, 1984, p. 178)

Kessler (1992) suggests that by attending to context variables—the culture of the family, school, and community—we can make curricular content less problematic and more reflective of local visions of the "good" life. If education is about initiating the young into an already existing world, if it is to teach them not only *how* to live but also *what* the world is like, then considerations of psychological process are insufficient to the task.

Nurturing Professionals

The second longstanding problem in the field is intertwined with the first and involves the basis for the educator's professional expertise. Is such expertise grounded in knowledge of child development, understanding of materials, possession of a nurturing personality, or ability to teach correct school behaviors? I want to suggest that professional status is also grounded in an ability to understand the sociopolitical context in which we live and work. We have a responsibility to propose an ethical vision of the world in which our students will one day participate. But the reliance on psychological research for validating program decisions and the resulting ambiguity about content and traditional conceptualizations of the teacher's role mediate against such considerations in our thinking.

I became aware of the absence of ethical and political considerations when I tried to understand the lack of response by many in the field to the serious critique of American education begun in the 1960s. This critical literature began with the work of revisionist historians (M. Katz, 1971; Tyack, 1974) who described the failure of the schools to promote social mobility, equality of opportunity, and democratic forms of interaction. It includes the radical critics (Illich, 1970; Kohl, 1967), who focused on issues of depersonalization, apathy, and alienation, as well as the educationists (Giroux, 1980; Macdonald, 1975), who analyzed the nature of curricula, overt and covert, and the way that they were structured to fulfill the needs of the postindustrial workplace.

In part, I saw the lack of response from the early childhood field as a weakness of the critiques themselves and their failure to address early education per se. But British critical sociologists (Bernstein, 1975; Sharp & Green, 1975) also offered important insights about early education. They argued that progressive methods encouraging children to display an ever-greater variety of behaviors at school also provided increased opportunities for professionals to inculcate values reinforcing the political and social status quo. Although the conclusion that open classrooms in British infant schools, which resembled many American early childhood settings, allowed for more subtle but extensive forms of social control was foreshadowed in Gramsci's (1971) writings, it was new to many American readers.

Bloch (1992) suggests that in part the resistance of early education to critically oriented perspectives can be explained in terms of its institutional history. Elementary and secondary teachers have been trained in schools of education; research, professional training, and laboratory schools for children aged 2 to 5 are frequently affiliated with university departments of psychology, psychiatry, home economics, or family/child study. Schools of education maintained a strong interest in the kindergarten and social welfare agencies in day care, but most research and study about young children was conducted in the confines of the developmental sciences. Ending the isolation of early childhood education within academic settings is essential to opening the field to new influences. I am less sanguine than some (Kessler, 1992), however, about the integration of early childhood programs into the public schools, where it is often difficult to resist the pressures for academically oriented programs.

The impact of our institutional history was evident during interviews I conducted with early childhood teachers working in a variety of schools during the early 1980s (Silin, 1982). As a group the teachers preferred to see themselves as objective and apolitical, concerned only with the best interests of the child. I found early educators to understand their work in terms of protective control; that is, they viewed children as open to the world, curious and eager to learn, yet vulnerable to the threats posed by either internal emotional turmoil or external sources of influence. Thus they saw their task as one of protecting children through controlling the educational environment.

An emphasis on developmentally adequate curricula allowed teachers to think they were noncoercive, unprejudiced practitioners. Because children were viewed as vulnerable and fragile, teachers did not want to see themselves as influencing them in any way that had ideological or political ramifications. Their job was to facilitate, to enable children to learn and grow. They did not seem to recognize the degree to which different developmental schemas speak to different aspects of growth and embody particular values and diverse conceptions of human possibility. Nor did they seem to possess a sense of choice about their work, which would indicate that they saw themselves as self-determining agents rather than as beneficent technicians responding to the demands of their charges.

This self-image of early childhood teachers reflects the progressive era's commitment to "keeping politics out of the school" and the traditional American belief that schools function in an equitable manner, allowing the talented to succeed on merit alone. Perhaps, too, it reflects the gender of the early educators and the social expectations of their role. From the first, this role was modeled on images of maternal nurture, and the educational rhetoric of the nineteenth century made it difficult to think of maternal nurture in terms of political practice or social empowerment. Women were encouraged to enter teaching, at least until their own child-bearing years, because it was argued that their instincts allowed them to know children better and to manage them with ease:

> That females are incomparably better teachers for young children than males, can not admit of doubt. Their manner is more mild and gentle, and hence more

in consonance with the tenderness of childhood. They are endowed by nature with the stronger parental impulses, and this makes the society of children delightful, and turns duty into pleasure. . . . They are also of purer morals. (Elsbree, 1939, p. 201)

While early childhood theoreticians such as Pestalozzi (1907) also idealized the mother as the first teacher, and others such as Montessori (1912) spoke of early education as "communizing a maternal function" (p. 66), it is clear that for most the common ground shared by child and adult was a devalued ground, ruled by emotionality and impulse. Women teachers were seen as able to develop the character and moral behaviors so valued by school reformers in America like Horace Mann and Henry Barnard, but later intellectual achievements were to be guided by men:

> In childhood the intellectual faculties are but partially developed—the affection much more fully. At that early age the affections are the key to the whole thing. The female teacher readily possesses herself of that key, and thus having access to the heart, the mind is soon reached and operated upon. (Elsbree, 1939, p. 203)

The low status and pay offered to women does not negate the significance that teaching had for them, nor does it suggest the pride, enthusiasm, and professionalism with which they approached their work (Hoffman, 1981). Oral histories (Munro, 1992) reveal complex processes of resistance to male stereotypes regarding careers, agency, and the meanings of "scientific motherhood." For working-class and lower-middle-class women who gravitated toward the early childhood movement, teaching was not only a means to an independent life but also a way to realize their interests in social reform (Snyder, 1972). The commitment was to the child's growth and development and to the context in which it occurred.

A concern for bettering the circumstances of the poor was one of the distinguishing characteristics of those who first created early education programs; this theme connects the work of such diverse individuals as Rachel and Margaret Macmillan, Maria Montessori, Robert Owen, and Johann Pestalozzi. The location of kindergartens in settlement houses and the structuring of teachers' days so that they might make home visits in the afternoon was part of this commitment. As was the case with later progressive reformers, educational strategies for young children were integrated into broad social visions (Almy, 1975; Takanishi, 1978).

It is true that, for a brief period during the War on Poverty, early educators tried to address the relationship of social class, curriculum, and schooling outcomes. This interest took the form of a debate over compensatory education. While some (Bereiter & Englemann, 1966) argued that children of the poor needed more academically oriented programs in order to catch up to their middle-class peers, others (Biber, Shapiro, & Wickens, 1971) maintained that all children, regardless of background, benefited from the same kind of developmentally oriented approach. From the beginning of this debate, a few (Lazerson, 1971) were skeptical of the ability of schools to effect the larger changes that were needed in the economic system outside the class-room.

The majority of educators, however, seemed to have been caught up in the belief that schools could in fact equalize opportunity and create a more just society. Programs like Head Start and Follow Through can be attrib-uted less to a recognition of systematic weaknesses in the schools than to the limited acknowledgment that problems existed in the society at large for which education could compensate. The demand for curricular revision need not be predicated on fundamental social critique but on a return to an early childhood tradition—the amelioration of poverty through education. The new research on the importance of the early years for later cognitive development (Bloom, 1964; Hunt, 1961) was used to rationalize change and to meet the scientific and industrial challenges posed by the Cold War. A more political indictment of our own system qua system was avoided: The revisionist cri-tique need not apply.

Although the cultural deprivation paradigm popular in the 1960s (Bloom, Davis, & Hess, 1965; Riessman, 1962) was challenged by cultural difference theorists of the 1970s (Baratz & Baratz, 1970; Ramirez & Castaneda, 1974), it reemerged in the 1980s under the label of "at-risk" populations (Cuban, 1989). And today, many discussions about bilingual and multicultural programs mask issues of class and structural oppression (Banks, 1993). What are the sources of a more politically sophisticated analysis of the early childhood endeavor for the next decade? How might we emerge from the shadow of the developmentally appropriate paradigm to create a more socially relevant curriculum?

RETHINKING DEVELOPMENT

In recent years a growing critique of developmentally appropriate prac-tice directs us to sources for renewing early childhood education—the multivocal subject, a better balance of source disciplines, alternative modes of knowing children, a collaborative research base. In an immediate way, it has been argued that we have been unsuccessful in bridging the gap between developmental theory and classroom practice (Fein & Schwartz, 1982), that the application of developmentally appropriate theory (Bredekamp, 1987; NAEYC, 1990) often leads to diametrically opposed practices (Jones, 1991), and that the concept itself is too inclusive, without internal consistency and unsupported by research (Weikart, 1988). Bowman (1993) raises further questions about the difficulty of defining developmentally appropriate practices in a multicultural society:

> Not only do various groups differ regarding the ages for achieving "appropriate" objectives, but the translation of developmental principles to specific practices confronts the differences in how various communities organize interpersonal and material relationships to achieve similar developmental results. (p. 117)

Research by Jipson (1991) and Delpit (1988) echoes earlier findings by Joffe (1977) that there is often a discrepancy between the values and programs of white, middle-class educators and African-American families. This discrepancy can lead to a devaluing of the culture many children bring to the classroom as well as to the educational goals and aspirations of their parents.

Kessler (1991), initiating an unusually acrimonious dialogue, suggests that developmentally appropriate practices should no longer be the endpoint of our work but must be subsumed under a broader set of social goals. She proposes that our ultimate educational purposes have to do with preparing active citizens for a democratic society, reflecting the social reconstructionist aspects of the progressive tradition. Bredekamp (1991) of NAEYC, responding to this challenge, argues that we must continue a singular focus on the developmental rationale as an effective strategy to gain legitimation as professionals with recognized standards of practice and to resist the imposition of inappropriate academic programming from those who do not understand or value young children. Both talk the language of politics and power, though the former is concerned with the relationship of schooling to society and the latter with the relationship among professional groups.

This interest in the social goals of schooling, combined with the concern for how to respect cultural pluralism, points to a central paradox of American life. For we are simultaneously recognizing the complexity of intergroup differences, with the polarities this may cause, and seeking to create communities with increased participation and common purpose (Greene, 1984). There is a dialectic to maintain between the recognition of difference, otherness, and marginality that has been the project of postmodern discourse, and the commitment to community, solidarity, and moral imperatives that leads to political engagement and transformative social practices. Beyer and Liston (1992) support the importance of pluralism while warning against the dangers of social disintegration:

> We agree that personal social conditions need to be continually created, recreated, and reinforced that will encourage, respect, and value expressions of dif-

ference. Yet if the valorization of otherness precludes the search for some common good that can engender solidarity even while it recognizes and respects that difference, we will be left with a cacophony of voices that disallow political and social action that is morally compelling. If a concern for otherness precludes community in any form, how can political action be undertaken, aimed at establishing a common good that disarms patriarchy, racism, and social class oppression? What difference can difference then make in the public space? (p. 380)

I want to suggest that, for early childhood educators, addressing this dialectic means examining how our highly psychologized understanding of childhood fosters a belief in individuals as autonomous, self-determining agents, separate and distinct from the social world they inhabit. How might our programs change if the self were seen as constituted in and through the social rather than in opposition to it? What if this individual, whose growth we so carefully monitor and whose autonomy we promote, is no more a permanent fixture of the social landscape than the U.S. Constitution is universal to the political world? These are not easily asked questions in a field that some psychologists have criticized for being dominated by a "nursery ideology of extra-ordinary dogmatism" (Bruner, 1980, p. 203) that even resists advances in developmental theory.

The Multivocal Subject

While educators (Sylva, 1986; Walkerdine, 1984) debate the full extent of Piaget's influence in England and America, it is clear that the individualism inherent in his genetic epistemology has long been countered by an alternative, if weaker, tradition emphasizing the social aspects of human growth. Educators working in this tradition attended to theorists like Mead and Vygotsky who—the former from a social interactionist, and the latter from a Marxist perspective—attempted to more fully account for the functioning of the social within the individual. Vygotsky (1956) understands intellectual potential as created in the process of the child's enculturation to a particular society, not as a biologically determined given. Learning is social, an experience mediated by the language, beliefs, and politics of the adults surrounding the child. Reversing our assumptions about learning and development, he proposes the former as preceding the latter. Learning makes development possible as the child internalizes adult meanings. Thus current development is assessed by what children can do without adult help, and their potential is recognized by what they can accomplish with it. Vygotsky refers to the gap between these levels as the zone of proximal development. In contrast to Piaget, Vygotsky encourages the teacher to take an active role in assisting development (Rogoff & Wertsch, 1984).

Dewey also makes an important contribution to understanding the movement between the individual and the social, the child and the group, heredity and environment. Initially describing their connection in terms of *interaction*, he later substituted *transaction* to emphasize the transformational relations of these elements rather than their fixity or discreteness. It is the social individual that emerges from Dewey's work. Cuffaro (1995) makes this clear:

> From a Dewyan perspective, *social* and *individual* are not a question of balancing elements but a spatiotemporal affair of a whole that has "phases and emphases marking its activity." As Dewey presents the evolving person, the social and the individual may be said to be "two names for the same reality." It is not either the social or the individual but the *social individual*, each element functioning within the whole, named as separate elements for the purpose of analysis but in actuality transactionally related. Such a view ensures continuity and connections. It attends to process, time, and context. (p. 23)

Within psychology itself, a multivocal concept of subjectivity has emerged in the last decade, one that posits the individual and the social not as binary opposites but as parts of a single reality and that asks us to rethink our ideas about age-appropriate curriculum (Henriquez, Hollway, Urwin, Venn, & Walkerdine, 1984; N. Rose, 1990). To accomplish this task we must set aside our belief in the fixed pregiven subject found in traditional psychology and European humanism. We can seek out the historical resistance to disembodied notions of the self that support the ideology of bourgeois individualism and Enlightenment rationalism (Hermans, Kempen, & van Loon, 1992). The earliest forerunner of this resistance, the seventeenth-century historian Giambattista Vico, rejected the ahistorical conception of the human mind embedded in Descartes' famous dictum, "I think, therefore I am" in favor of a view of mind and body as inseparable—"because I consist of body and mind, therefore I think." The human mind is in the body, therefore it is in history, makes its own history. History does not exist objectively outside of human experience but can be grasped within the structures of the mind. In the twentieth century others share in this absolute belief in the human capacity for imagination and the mind as an active, organizing structure. For example, the German philosopher Hans Vaihinger (1935) added to the constructivist position by explaining the conscious, practical, and fruitful role that fictions play in the development of thought, and the American psychologist George Kelly (1955) challenged the belief in objective reality by asserting the importance of alternative interpretations or hypotheses through which we make sense of experience, the personal construct.

This understanding of the self as moving through space and time and able to imaginatively occupy a number of positions that permit dialogical relations is one that leads to a narrative concept of the self (Hermans et al., 1992). Writers from James and Mead to Bruner and Bakhtin have posited distinctions between the *I*, or author, and the *me*, or actor (Sarbin, 1986). The dialogical self can be seen as a multiplicity of *I* positions or as possible selves (Markus & Nurius, 1986). The difference, however, is that possible selves (e.g., what one would like to be or may be afraid of becoming) are assumed to constitute part of a multifaceted self-concept with one centralized *I* position, whereas the dialogical self has the character of a decentralized, polyphonic narrative with a multiplicity of *I* positions. This scene of dialogical relations, moreover, is intended to oppose the sharp self–nonself boundaries drawn by Western rationalistic thinking about the self (Holdstock, 1990; Hsu, 1985). The self is essentially social, the other is not outside but inside the self-structure. It is not so much that we can take the role of the other who is outside of the self (Mead, 1934), but rather I construe the other as a position I can occupy, creating an alternative perspective on the world and myself that may or may not be congruent with the perspective of the actual other.

Educators like Dewey as well as social theorists like Mead and Vygotsky are firmly grounded in the material realities transforming life in the twentieth century. Alternatively, postmodern psychologists attempt to integrate the psychological and the social, the individual and society, in discourse theory. A discourse includes both the concepts and language through which the child is imagined, as well as the social practices and institutions embodying that imaginative construction. Thus the discourse of child-centered pedagogy employed in British infant schools encompasses the academic and popular ideas of Piaget as well as the classroom arrangements, materials, and student evaluations designed to implement Piaget's ideas. There is a reciprocal and inseparable relation between our modes of speaking, the language that codifies behaviors, and the behaviors that are constitutive of language. They form a single discourse.

Postmodernists reject structuralism for the way that it abolishes the subject by conceptualizing individuals as bearers of social roles, and they criticize recent attempts to view development in a social context for ultimately sustaining a subject–object split (James & Prout, 1990b). Thus Urwin (1984), looking at infant development, theorizes that subjectivity is produced as we assume different positions in a variety of discursive practices. In contradistinction to traditional psychologists, she does not presume a universal set of developmental processes or a "real" child that might be revealed by peeling back the layers of social meanings attached to childhood. We are no more nor less than the accumulated subject positions we learn to occupy as participants in various discourses.

The goal of the postmodernists is to abolish the individual/social dualism inherent in formulations that pose a pregiven subject, one that is discrete, coherent, and existing prior to social experience. In its place, they seek to define a more complex, decentered, at times contradictory subject embedded in the social world. The challenge is to maintain the tension between individual agency and the limits imposed by material constraints. In rejecting naive realism, reality as directly given and without mediation, postmodernists risk a solipsistic textualism with no referents outside of language itself. Again, Beyer and Liston (1992) comment from the perspective of social reconstructionists on the implications for pedagogic action:

> Questions of non-discursive veracity and accuracy presume, to some degree, that our knowledge of the social world refers to a reality that exists, in some fashion, apart from us and our operant system of discourse. Such questions presume, in other words, something very much like "the metaphysics of presence" that postmodernists reject. We agree that reality may be described in various ways, and may be more or less accurately rendered for particular purposes, and these purposes are not necessarily equally valuable. Yet postmodernism provides us with little moral guidance about how to choose from among those purposes and descriptions and thus about how to act in the world. (p. 386)

Urwin (1984) tries to avoid the pitfalls that occur when the child is read only as a social text, the biological body reduced to an effect of socially constructed interpretations, by drawing both on Lacan's semiotically driven description of development and on Foucault's analysis of power/knowledge. From the former, she understands that coming into subjectivity is disjunctive and discontinuous, the struggle for continuity and identity ongoing rather than a completed accomplishment of adulthood. With the assistance of the latter, she is able to conceptualize a historically situated subject and to account for the possibility of social change lacking in purely linguistic explanations. Focusing on the behavioral regularities that precede language, but that are part of larger discursive practices through which we learn to occupy subject positions, Urwin is able to link the psychic and the cultural, power and desire, continuity and change.

Pedagogical Subjects

Walkerdine (1990) adopts a similar postmodern perspective in her critique of child-centered pedagogy. She argues that the child who develops "naturally" under the ostensibly benign gaze of the nonintrusive teacher is only a product of the particular discourses that have created contemporary educational space. These spaces and the disembodied subjects we create to inhabit them are not without a history. Foucault (1980a) allows us to see that the conditions that gave rise to a nursery school practice focusing on the developing child are historically specific, part of the larger process through which the idea of mental health has achieved its hegemony in our society. It is not that he spoke of early education. Despite the omnipresence of pedagogical vocabulary in Foucault's work (for who but Foucault has brought to our attention the multiple meanings of the examination, discipline, and power–knowledge?), there is little direct attention given to the institution of schooling. What he does attend to, however, is the nineteenth-century penchant for quantitative measurement of human characteristics used in the service of establishing distributive statistical norms within a given population. It was this drive to normalize human growth and behavior that allowed specialists to pass judgment on the abnormal as well as the normal, to create exemplary case studies, and to define the subject as the object of developmental surveillance.

The subject postmodernists seek to deconstruct, the very sense of self we believe to be most private, is created in and through the social institutions—courts, schools, hospitals, and clinics—that proliferated during the nineteenth century. The new legal, pedagogical, and medical practices helped the individual to recognize needs, desires, and wishes consistent with expanded forms of governmental control. The "tutelary complex," as Danzelot (1977/1979) refers to the interlocking technologies produced in these discourses of the self, inscribes the citizen as an individual with rights and responsibilities. Social regulation is secured through the production of emotions and attitudes that will enable us to claim our rights and adhere to our responsibilities as members of the body politic rather than through overt coercion. Beyond establishing limits and laws, power functions through the proliferation of knowledges that allow us to "know" the individual with ever greater certainty. Through the observation and classification of psychological characteristics, we not only record the socialization of those in our charge, we also describe the very domains in which to seek expressions of individual differences. In this sense we participate in the production of subjectivity, that which is considered essential to the self.

DISTANCING THE CHILD

It is not my purpose to unpack all of the meanings new theories of subjectivity might bring to the work of early childhood education but more simply to bring these developments to our attention. I am only too aware of the gap between expert knowledge and pedagogical acts as they occur in specific, concrete situations. Yet the obvious limits of the developmentalist perspective currently in place impel me to look elsewhere for an understanding of how to think about children and childhood. When the individual and the social are seen as discrete domains, we construct two significant, often unbridgeable distances.

The first is the distance between adults and children created by stage theories of development. In the twentieth century normal development is increasingly problematic, a minefield of potential hazards posed by uneducated parents and societal ills that can only be navigated with professional assistance. The laying down of this minefield, begun in the nineteenth century with the new mental measurement technologies and child study movements, escalated in the early twentieth century with the popularity of behaviorist, Freudian, and normative research studies (Gesell, 1940). It is a minefield continually being reseeded with new points of danger—the importance of a single, maternal caregiver in the 1950s, the role of early intellectual stimulation in the 1960s and 1970s, the significance of mutually regulated communication patterns in the 1980s. Although we have learned to chart the path of individual growth with greater specificity, we have made it a far more tortuous one. With the accumulation of empirical and theoretical knowledge, the accomplishment of adulthood appears to be ever more complex and far from the haunts of early childhood.

The second space we have created expands the distance between children and the disquieting material realities in which they live. The children we have inscribed in our pedagogy are *a priori* individuals with capacities that mature over and against the world. To decrease these distances, I have suggested we substitute a notion of subjectivity as constituted in the domain of the social for the prevailing individual–social dualism. This would enable us to recognize the role of our own discursive practices in producing the subjectivity that heretofore appeared to prefigure our educational interventions. In short, I contend that we undermine our best intentions when we consider the child and the world as separate entities. The subject of our pedagogical attentions might better be construed as the child-in-the-world. And this is where we turn from early childhood as the applied side of child development to early childhood as a discrete field of theory and practice permeable to a wider variety of influences.

REVISIONING EARLY EDUCATION

Early education can only benefit by becoming permeable to disciplines other than psychology. While developmentalists themselves are moving toward a more contextualized understanding of human growth and learning (Rogoff, 1987; Scarr, 1992), a familiarity with history and sociology can make us aware of the social meanings of our work. For example, a Foucaultian perspective places early schooling in the context of other institutions that exert subtle forms of control through the imposition of normalizing standards of assessment (Ball, 1990). In a Marxist analysis of the economic implications of the expansion of early education, Chamboredon and Prevort (1975) suggest the need to study the lag between the functions delegated to the nursery school by different social classes and the functions it actually fulfills. This is not only to alleviate the social ills created by poverty, a recurring theme in the history of early education, but also to analyze how educational institutions reproduce and promote resistance to underlying socioeconomic structures.

Schooling, even nursery schooling, is one of the central ways that society organizes power and influence. Recognizing this means that early education should not be exempt from a more political analysis of its program. We need to delineate the social commitments that inevitably lie behind all our programs. Teaching needs to be viewed as more than the professionalization of a maternal function that occurs in a protective environment. It must be seen in the context of the larger societal processes that both shape and are shaped by it. Even the smallest pedagogical acts have meaning for students that extends beyond the classroom. If teachers are to be more fully in control of their professional lives, they must assess this meaning and incorporate it into their knowledge base.

Historical and political analyses alone are not enough, for they refer to the past and the present but not necessarily to the future. A grounding in philosophy encourages us to think about the kinds of people who will emerge from our programs and the nature of the society in which they will live. It would also provide a better basis for evaluating new programs and trends as they appear. With increasing numbers of prepackaged and prestructured materials on the market, we need to ask whether their use is consistent with our values and goals for children.

Alternative Modes of Knowing

While a better grasp of new developments in the academic disciplines may help educators to understand the social implications of their work, an expanded knowledge base also includes investigation of alternative modes of knowing. This will affect both how we view children and how curriculum is implemented. The use of universal, theoretical constructs can obfuscate the complex realities of lived experience. Some within the field have already adopted a phenomenological approach to children, emphasizing the uniqueness and integrity of each child. As defined by Weber (1984), this means that "the existential moment-by-moment environmental interaction of the learner supersedes an interest in—even a recognition of—developmental factors. The departure from stage theory is in part out of discomfiture with a designated end point for all children" (p. 206). As the phenomenological research agenda has been defined with increasing clarity (Barritt et al., 1985; Pinar & Reynolds, 1992; van Manen, 1990), more and more researchers are putting it into practice (Adan, 1991; Sinclaire, 1994; Smith, 1991).

Literature and the arts can also provide access to knowing children and childhood (Coe, 1984). As autobiographical methods have been advocated for use in teacher education, there is a renewed interest in how prospective teachers can turn their own early experiences into stories for children (Graham, 1991; Vascellaro & Genishi, 1994). Novels, plays, and films can frequently stimulate new insight into children's realities as well as our own. Imaginative constructions of fictional events can be as evocative and helpful as scientific descriptions of developmental processes. Paley (1991) places this search for our connection to children at the heart of the pedagogical project:

> In the matter of the self we are not connected to one another by accumulations of skills and facts, but, rather, by inner fears and fantasies, impulsive urges and pleasures. That which every child feels we all feel; that which every child fears we all fear. The challenge is to uncover what we seek and fear and fantasize and desire, so we may proceed toward the understanding of another person. And if that person happens to be a child in our classroom, we will need some strict rules to go by, for the roles we play in a classroom are too unequal. It is hard enough to find common cause in the faculty room, but in the classroom we automatically become judge and jury and there is seldom a witness for the defense. (p. 155)

At one time, emphasizing the uniqueness of young children as a group was a necessary strategy to draw attention to their special needs and interests. Now it is time to look at the continuities as well as the differences between children and adults. Such investigations of the commonalities between the generations, hidden in stage theories of development, find their roots in the writings of nineteenth-century romantics like Coleridge, who proudly proclaimed that "to carry on the feeling of childhood into the powers of manhood . . . is the character and privilege of genius" (quoted in W. Walsh, 1959, p. 18). To acknowledge that children possess a moral integrity, a power of vision that has become submerged in adults, is to acknowledge that education itself is a form of moral persuasion, embodying values, promoting ways of being, and teaching ethical behaviors that are less subject to the laws of empirical validation than to the rigors of democratic discourse and the problems of intersubjective communication.

As early educators use diverse knowledge sources in understanding children, they might give renewed emphasis in the curriculum itself to multiple modalities of experiencing the world. Teachers of young children have long valued artistic/aesthetic elements in the curriculum as a way of enhancing personal expression. But the arts also provoke self-reflection and understanding. They help children to break with the taken-for-granted world and open new possibilities, creating privileged moments when new visions can be achieved (Greene, 1978).

Similarly, while early educators have always paid attention to physical development and growth, we need to reaffirm the centrality of the body as a vehicle for teaching and learning in the contemporary world. Linking language, thought, and sensuous experience of the self in the world, Levin (1982) describes a grounding for teaching moral valuing, while Grumet (1985), drawing on diverse philosophical sources, asks us to rethink the meaning and learning of reading. These curricularists are writing in response to the growth of educational environments in which control, certainty, and quantification are given precedence over subjectivity, wonder, and intuition. They seek to foster a rich, multilayered education of the imagination in place of a narrow, unidimensional education of technical competence.

Creating a Research Base

Finally, early childhood specialists need to create their own research base. Some (Spodek & Saracho, 1982) decry this lack of a highly developed body of knowledge and a reduced emphasis on theoretical and conceptual work within the field, and others call for the creation and/or systematization of our unique fund of knowledge in order to assure professional status (Ade, 1982). No matter what the rationale, inadequate descriptions of the teaching role, imposition of inappropriate theoretical constructs, and impractical or incomplete curriculum recommendations have too often resulted from the distance between practitioners and researchers from outside the field. Takanishi (1981) argues that early childhood education is a unique cultural system with its own history, traditions, and values. In their socialization to the field, new teachers learn to see children and development differently. Because they work in classrooms rather than universities, they have another perspective on learning in educational settings.

Especially relevant to a revitalized knowledge base in early childhood is the incorporation of the new scholarship on women in education (Sadker, Sadker, & Klein, 1991). This scholarship underlines the need to reconceptualize our ideas about research and who conducts it. Historical research done by men tends to record women's experience, if at all, as incidental and nonessential (Tetreault & Schmuck, 1985). In most histories men are the subject and women are the other, differentiated only in terms of the male experience. Shakeshaft (1986) has explored the facts that shaped women's professional lives as researchers, noting their marginality and isolation from the mainstream, which largely ignored their work. Techniques for uncovering the history of early education must move beyond traditional methods to identify contributors who may not have been part of a university community or other male-dominated organization. Our definition of the nature of research—work that formed the basis of programs but did not receive academic acknowledgment—will need expansion, as will the sources we explore. Diaries, letters, and school reports will have to be added to formal treatises on educational practice and philosophy.

In the past it has been suggested that there is a basic conflict between researchers, who are theoretically oriented, and practitioners, who are more clinically focused (Sergiovanni, 1985). Teachers aim at action, not knowledge per se. They help to construct social worlds and to create meanings rather than to seek truth or the right solution to a given problem. Teachers tend to emphasize indeterminacy and uncertainty rather than regularity and scientific laws (Darling-Hammond, 1985). They rely heavily on their own experience and the experience of others in similar settings. Ultimately, too, teachers need to believe in what they are doing, because they often do not see immediate results from their work. They cannot afford the detachment of healthy skepticism demanded of pure scientists.

Early childhood education needs a research literature that looks directly to child-care workers to define questions for investigation, to corroborate findings, and to insure practical meaning (Richardson, 1990; Cochran-Smith & Lytle, 1990). This research would articulate the knowledge that already exists and make it accessible to others. It would give recognition to the unique perspectives of the early childhood educator. Researchers have emerged from the paradigm wars more open to qualitative techniques involving ethnographic standards, interpretive interviews, and participant observation (Gage, 1989; D. J. Walsh, 1991). They have increasingly come to understand the value of the teacher's personal practical knowledge and collaborative research strategies (Berliner, 1986; Elbaz, 1983). Unlike traditional hierarchically structured modes of inquiry, collaborative research assumes the teacher's ability to comprehend the complexity of schooling or to engage in reflective action. True collaboration requires equal responsibility and status for both teacher and researcher, which is often hard to achieve in a real-world context that stresses competition, individual autonomy, and well-defined lines of authority (Oakes, Hare, & Sirotnik, 1986). Research employing good qualitative methods respects the intricacies of the teaching–learning situation, sees the teacher as a whole person, and acknowledges his or her purposes and knowledge. It is consistent with the best traditions of the field.

Toward a More Socially Relevant Curriculum

I came of age as an educator within a liberal, progressive context, at a time when Piaget was just beginning his ascension into the pedagogical sphere and the most popular article summarizing contrasting approaches to early education was titled "Development as the Aim of Education" (Kohlberg & Mayer, 1972). My professional training was dominated by a broad array of psychologists who were employed to interpret children's behavior and to make decisions about curriculum. With a singular emphasis on individual development, there was little space for consideration of the political and ethical ramifications of our work.

The 1960s and early 1970s were also a period of increased attention to early childhood education. Despite President Nixon's 1971 veto of the Comprehensive Child Development Bill, many new early intervention programs flourished. Unfortunately, this interest in young children did not continue in the 1980s, nor did it result in improved salaries, better working conditions, or an increased role in decision making for child-care workers. To correct this situation, organizations like NAEYC focused on a professionalization agenda, including an emphasis on credentials, licensing, nomenclature, and public relations, geared toward standardizing practices and improving the status of the field. While supporting the goals of this program, I found the agenda of professionalization a problematic means to achieve them. First, it tends to mask issues of race, class, and gender, the structural barriers to improved lives for early childhood workers. Professionalism has as often been used to promote docility and occupational control by those in power as an occupational strategy to resist external regulation of the workplace and strengthen teachers' positions relative to their employers (Ozga & Lawn, 1981).

Second, professions have always sought to establish a monopoly over the provision of a particular service through the negotiation of cognitive exclusiveness. But it has been especially difficult for early educators to establish a claim to the possession of a unique body of information and skills. That is, the nurturing instincts assumed to be at the heart of the early educator's practice are also assumed to be inherently feminine characteristics. Women enter the field with the requisite ability to care. Therefore they do not merit compensation equivalent to those whose work demands prolonged periods of preparation. Joffe (1977) cuts to the heart of this issue:

> The problem for childcare workers is that the care of normal preschoolers is very "familiar to everyone," and especially to their parent-clients. Thus for a "weak" profession, like early childhood education, the main struggle with cli-

ents is not, as in the powerful professions, to withstand unacceptable demands; rather it is to be acknowledged as "professional" in the first place—to make the status leap from "babysitter" to "educator." (p. 22)

It is exactly this problem that early childhood leaders sought to address though the promulgation of Developmentally Appropriate Practice Guidelines. Now, in the 1990s, this concept has become institutionalized and reified. Intended to improve the quality of child care and the status of those who provide it, developmentally appropriate practice has become a conserving and conservative force in our teaching rather than a vehicle for change. It has led to an underestimation of children's intellectual abilities and the significance of race, class, gender, and ethnic differences as well as to a denial of a critical pedagogic function—helping children to make sense of difficult social realities. A revitalized knowledge base is essential to a more inclusive, socially relevant pedagogy, one that furthers our students' interests as well as our own.

CHAPTER 5

Contours of Ignorance

Ignorance is not just a blank space on a person's mental map. It
has contours and, for all I know, rules of operation as well.

Thomas Pynchon, *Slow Learner*

As a gay man, I have become preoccupied with the question of our ability to
touch one another, of the distances that make us feel safe or place us at risk.
How can I not be? HIV has made it impossible for me to touch and be touched
without the specter of death. I think about the strong, youthful, and not so
youthful bodies turned into living corpses that have become so hard to touch.
I think of the proliferating claims of some to a therapeutic/healing touch and
of my own modest efforts to stay in touch with those who are dying. I do
not read Michael Cunningham's novels, Paul Monette's poetry, or Andrew
Holleran's short stories that tell of our difficulties and successes in becoming caregivers, of what it means to be a man nurturing other men through
the mundane realities of a terminal illness. Nor do I watch the public television specials documenting the lives of those I do not know being cared for in
distant cities. Rather, I remember Ralph's words from the winter of 1985,
uttered shortly after he was admitted to intensive care, no longer able to hide
the debilitating symptoms of pneumonia that would kill him within 10 days:
"I have already endured enough indignities to last a lifetime." I believe that
Ralph's spectacular decline was precipitated by his desire to avoid further
intrusions by the gloved hands of the professional caregivers who surrounded
him. He did not want to endure the challenge they posed to his sense of dignity and to the integrity of his body.

When my friend and colleague Jo Anne Pagano asks me to participate
in a symposium on the difficult questions children ask, I think about these
scenes, about the matter of distances. I presume that Jo Anne is interested in
the questions about life and death, survival and annihilation, truth and dis-
simulation that inevitably catch us off guard as we are rushing to get to the

dentist, escorting a boisterous group of 4-year-olds to the park or on a crowded bus, all eyes focused on our response to the query of the ingenuous 6-year-old at our side. I know her invitation to be predicated on the set of papers I have written that attempt to articulate the concerns of children, adolescents, and adults about the rising toll of HIV/AIDS. Yet I am hesitant to accept this new opportunity to examine the anxieties fueling the contentious debate over an appropriate public response to the disease. At some moments these anxieties have mirrored my own, and this writing clearly served a cathartic function. At others the public debate seems far removed from the concerns that inform my daily life as a caregiver and gay man.

It has always been an intellectual challenge to bridge this gap between my own perspective and that of people not directly affected by HIV/AIDS. However, it has been an even more difficult personal struggle to manage the distances—physical, psychological, social—between myself and those for whom I have cared. And it is this struggle that has created my own most difficult questions, questions that have turned me into a sometimes impassioned, sometimes reluctant writer. Admittedly, the presence of HIV in my world has increased my sense of vulnerability, calling into play a vast armada of defensive strategies. Moreover, it has placed into question the distance that I once assumed separated health and illness, and from that point all the other binary oppositions upon which our educational institutions are constructed—teacher and student, adult and child, parent and educator.

THE GEOGRAPHY OF *AIDS*

In prior chapters I have described the silence surrounding HIV/AIDS in early childhood education as a function of the institutional constraints under which teachers work, the developmentally appropriate curriculum operative in many classrooms, and a reluctance to acknowledge the social realities framing all our lives. In this chapter I want to address a related issue—how we modulate the emotional distance between ourselves and our students. I have come to believe that the manner in which we take up our place in the classroom and signal to students the positions they best occupy has a significant impact on our willingness to engage in HIV/AIDS education. This is to suggest that at some moments we stand so far from children that we do not hear their queries and that at others we stand too close. In effect, I want to argue that our difficulties talking about HIV/AIDS with children, like our failure to mount an adequate public health response to this disease, might best be located in the distance we have produced between "their" bodies and ours, your life and mine. I understand this distance as a function of our definition of the child as innocent and ignorant, and the corollary assumption that the adult is indeed the one who knows. I also understand it as a reflection of broader cultural barriers we have created between those in need and those in control of material resources necessary for establishing caring environments.

The dictionary tells us that at one time *distance* was synonymous with *discord, dissension,* and *quarrel.* There is little doubt that these meanings have been a part of the pedagogical landscape as well as part of the terrain in which I have sought more equitable HIV/AIDS care and policies. But I have also learned that distances can connect and hold people together. Today the primary meaning of *distance* is the portion of time between two events or an event and the present: an interval, as in "the ~ between birth and death." As I read this definition I am fascinated by the tiny, spermlike mark that stands for *the* distance, apparently too sacred to spell out, between birth and death. If the mark appears an insignificant moment on the page, suspended in midair, not even anchored to the bottom of the line, the very next example confirms its tenuous existence. Here we are warned that the actual ability to sustain life is in question, for we are "not sure he could endure the ~ to the time of his release from captivity." Now I want to reassure our hero, captive of the dictionary page, that he will endure if he can make connections, locate himself in a supportive social web. It is a matter of finding the right distance, enduring the longer distance by structuring many smaller ones.

Only those, like Ralph, who are HIV-positive can speak to the specific ways this disease tests our ability to endure (Callen, 1991). But others of us can address the questions it raises about our educational purposes and the uncomfortable intervals it can leave between teacher and student. Hopefully we can locate a common ground on which people with HIV/AIDS can share the stories that constitute the disease with educators who have knowledge of and access to students who will shape its future. My own exploration of distance in caring relationships begins with a story.

The Distances Traveled

I am preparing to conduct a workshop on AIDS for teachers at the school in which I first taught. As with other requests like this one, months of anxious phone calls have preceded the selection of the speaking date. The director is cautious, wants to move carefully, has already been criticized for not moving fast enough. It is 1991 after all, 11 years into the epidemic. In our conversations, I learn that the school has already spent considerable time preparing itself to address HIV/AIDS in the classroom. There have been other speakers, expert advisors, curriculum review committees, and losses to the disease in the community itself.

I sense that the school cannot be more prepared; needs only to be encouraged to test the waters, has tested them; needs to take the plunge, has already plunged. The discussions are interminable, and my patience is worn thin by the desperate attempt to decipher whether I am the best person to lead the staff seminar. Like so many, they want to get it right, and they want me to tell them how to get it right. I fear I will only frustrate them by declaring that there is no sure way to get it right. There is only a process of listening to and observing children, of sharing amongst each other, of reflecting, of learning to do it better and better each time.

However, when the appointed day finally arrives, I am unable to summon the confidence that informed these earlier conversations. As I circle the block gathering courage to enter the familiar building, my mind is filled with thoughts of that first year of teaching. How can I forget my discomfort at being called by my last name, constantly looking over my shoulder for my father, the only person I knew as "Mr. Silin." I was 24 and it was 1968. I had just graduated from Columbia, just stood at the university gates demanding a greater role in institutional governance while secretly reveling in my imminent departure from academe. For in the last tumultuous months of college, I had rejected what had once appeared as the inevitable next step, graduate school, in favor of a job working with young children.

Initially, the idea of teaching appealed to me because I saw it as a vehicle for social change. Once in the classroom my interest was sustained because I realized that children, in their way, were asking the same questions about life that I was asking of myself as a young adult: Is it possible to make my way in the world, unaided by parent or family? Can I negotiate a social identity that is consistent with who I feel myself to be and what others deem acceptable? What is the connection between my inner life, which so easily runs amok with the most unimaginable emotions, and the orderly world of the school and the formal disciplines? As I grappled with these questions, I could not help but feel myself to be an outsider. I was an anomaly in those days—a male in an early childhood classroom, a gay person in the pre-Stonewall era, the product of a progressive education in a traditional setting.

Although circumstances had clearly changed, I wondered if I would feel any more at home today than I had 25 years ago. Can one ever be at home when the subject is HIV/AIDS? Specifically, how can I account for the distances traveled since 1981, when friends began to report the strange swellings and purplish lumps that were the first indications of infection? The task is formidable. I feel the need to ground myself, to remember why I do this work and how I have come to manage the critical distances in my own life. I comfort myself with memories of last summer, of the final lessons taught by my oldest friend.

Terminal Conversations

I am standing on a hillside in southern France. In the distance I can make out other small towns like the one in which we are living, really no more than a collection of stone dwellings built centuries ago to house the people who till the fields below. We have no telephone, and I must call Bill from the public booth located at one corner of the town square, which offers what the Michelin guide refers to as a "panorama." Bill sounds more breathless than I would want him to be. He has not been able to answer the phone himself. A stranger's voice greets my request to speak with him. I am not surprised. We have not been in communication for three weeks, too long a time in the life of someone with AIDS. So I am prepared, am never prepared, to hear Bill tell me that, in his own words, "The news is not good." He has had a biopsy: Kaposi's sarcoma throughout his lungs. There is no use in further invasive procedures. This is it. After so many years of so many drugs, treatment regimens, doctors, hospitals, decisions. The virus wins out.

Bill reports that there is someone from his family with him all the time now. He is well taken care of, feels loved, is not in pain. There is a new acceptance and finality in these words, along with a familiar directness, a matter-of-fact quality that has made it easy to be with Bill during his illness and for which I will be ever grateful. Living across the country, now in another country, I have never been part of Bill's daily world, of the routines of care, of the social network that structures itself to make the unbearable bearable. Always at a distance, he knows I worry about these things, need reassurance, can count on him to show concern for the other even now.

But how do you end a phone conversation when the distance is so great and the time left so short? I promise to call in a few days. I must sound uneasy, overly solicitous, projecting the end before he is ready. Steady and confident, he is quick to reply that he does not think his situation is "*that* terminal." He uses *terminal* as if it were relative rather than absolute, not an end, a terminus, but a hazy boundary that is not reached suddenly, all at once, but slowly, by degrees. I wonder if he is being honest with himself, with me. His breathing sounds so labored, the diagnosis so final.

I wonder, too, if Bill is trying to save us from further, more painful communications. He has managed so well up to this point, has been a model for me and for many others. He has always known when to fight and resist and when to conserve his energy, let the body do its own work. I have been in awe of this wisdom, never questioned its sources or meaning. So I wait a week before calculating the hours between Sebastopol, California, and Lacoste, France, careful to call in the morning, when he will be strongest. Anticipating who might answer the phone, I do not expect to hear his father's voice. I instantly realize that this was the one time I should not have trusted Bill's analysis. He was overly optimistic, I too cautious of his feelings. And if I had been more assertive, insistent on frequent contact? What could we have said in one last halting conversation, his voice barely audible, my own trembling with emotion?

I understand now that critical, summative conversations occur when you least expect them. Indeed, they only become the "final conversation" in retrospect. For example, there are the moments Bill and I shared several months prior to his death as we traveled through the tropical landscape of Hawaii. Bill is too weak to drive but not too weak to make the forests come alive as he names and describes the growth patterns of the strange vegetation. When I stop the car, he does not want to get out. In truth, I want not only to see the dramatic scenery unfolding below us but also to seek relief from the intensity of our conversation, to believe for a brief minute that we are only two gay men on holiday, nothing is wrong, no one is going to die, no one is going to be left behind to chronicle a friendship that began 23 years earlier on the beaches of eastern Long Island.

We have managed the geography that has separated us over these years with well-placed visits, phone calls, and occasional letters, Bill's usually filled with pictures of his ever-expanding house and garden. Especially in this last year, I have tried to be psychologically present as I listened to the most immediate medical developments and long-range plans. Bill needed little practical help, knew how to care for himself, had cared for his lover, Jim, who died 14 months before him. Can I ever forget the visit in 1988 when I found them sitting on the back porch tethered to the same oxygen tank, recovering from their first pneumonia? What was the distance then that separated Bill from Jim, them from me? Why did Bill survive for 14 months after Jim's death?

Even now as I sit at the computer recording the past, re-presenting these scenes to myself, to others, my solitude is disrupted by a call from Allen. Our close friend George has finally been assigned a hospital room after seven hours in the emergency room corridor, still no diagnosis, still no production of red blood. Again I must be ready to draw this new map before the ink on Bill's has had time to dry, before I have assimilated what road he actually followed. Yet another illness to be monitored and managed, another death in the making.

PROTECTING OURSELVES/SAVING THE CHILDREN

These are the experiences that fuel my passion for HIV/AIDS education. I want to communicate the ways in which my life has been irrevocably changed by this disease, most especially my increased awareness of the fragile arrangements educators create to fend off knowledge of mortality. Ralph's absolute dignity before death, Bill's resilient spirit, even George's hospital ordeal present universal themes for our consideration as adults, as educators of young children. HIV/AIDS raises existential questions about choice and contingency as well as practical concerns about sexual practices and the structure of contemporary courting rituals. How can we create opportunities for discussion of the compelling issues that bind us most closely to others, regardless of age, without collapsing the distance between ourselves and our students in such a way as to reduce all knowledge to matters of intersubjective communications?

My talk that day at the school in which I first taught was well received and confirmed my belief in the power of HIV/AIDS to provoke critical reflection about the curriculum among teachers. I am especially moved by the comments of a mustachioed young man, timelessly dressed in blue jeans and work shirt, who has been laboring over a reading experience chart throughout the afternoon. I imagine he is the same age as I that first year of teaching. He has listened silently to a discussion of possible parental opposition, school policies, and the impact of HIV/AIDS on the local community. Thoughtfully, self-critically, he looks up from his handiwork and reflects on his reluctance to talk about death, most especially to his first-grade class. He says he is unprepared to confront his own mortality. The tension in the room affirms that we have come to a turning point in the discussion. Although I am more familiar with death now than when I began teaching, I try to appreciate the distance, the resistance to embracing death as part of a life-sustaining curriculum. But it is the kindergarten teacher, a woman near retirement age, who is quickest to come to our aid, by describing how the loss of her husband made it possible for her to talk about illness and death in the classroom. Having been physically closer to death, more intimate with its meanings, it has become a less fearful subject, more familiar ground. The teachers have started a dialogue that neither they nor I will long forget.

Many educators tell me that this dialogue, and my personal experiences with HIV/AIDS, have no relevance to life in the classroom. David Elkind (1987) cautions that our belief in the malleability of young minds can lead us to burden them with inappropriate knowledge:

> To be sure, children are fresh learners to the extent that they are not handicapped by previous ideas and concepts. But this does not mean that they are ready to learn everything and anything—far from it. Their openness to learning is limited and we need to recognize these limitations. There is a time and a place for everything and early childhood education is not the time nor the place to teach children computer programming, the threat of nuclear war, or for that matter, the dangers of AIDS. (p. 6)

Classifying HIV/AIDS with knowledge of computer programming—an abstract, intellectual skill—and nuclear war—a distant and yet unrealized event— Elkind informs us that young children do not have the conception of biological death necessary for understanding the disease. But AIDS is here and now. Elkind's avoidance of death is based on two critical assumptions. First, that death is ultimately knowable by adults and second, that this knowledge is conceptual in nature. Others might argue that our knowledge of death is always fragmentary and partial, our important knowing not conceptual and cognitive but rather affective and social. In this instance, it is Piaget's investigations into young children's understanding of animate and inanimate objects, reversible and irreversible scientific processes, that reassure us of the superiority of adult knowledge. But what about death considered as an issue of loss and separation, our understanding a function of aspirations for immortality and fear of the unknown? What about the intelligent young teacher trying to respond to the needs of his students?

Too often the official curriculum focuses on children's cognitive limits and not on their lived realities, masking our own anxieties about contemporary events. In a paper on the restructuring of social studies, Minuchin (1990) highlights two obstacles to creating more relevant social studies curricula. The first is the traditional program, with its sequence of topics based on child development principles designed to reflect changes in cognitive capacity, meaningful content, and thinking styles. This familiar sequence begins with family, moves outward toward neighborhood and community, and eventually leads to cultures of other times and places. The second impediment is our desire to present a manageable world to children when we as adults feel increasingly powerless and ineffective to influence the direction of modern life. While Minuchin (1990) makes an important contribution to demystifying what appear to be radical shifts in the family and offers concrete suggestions for new curriculum, her most incisive comments have to do with differences in adult and child perceptions about social change:

> "Social change" is an interesting concept, implying that we all approach "then" and "now" with the same framework. But of course, our perceptions vary, and the differences are particularly important in the teaching–learning enterprise. What represents "change" for teachers, who are adults, is simply "now" for children. That's how it is; this is the world. One implication of this difference in perspective is that we may be more impressed or disturbed by changing elements of social reality than the children are. They may be readier than we think to make their reality a subject of study. (p. 4)

That's how it is; this is the world. But educators have always been selective in their re-presentation of the world. The desire to sanitize the curriculum is an enduring theme in our work. Here I want to suggest that this desire and our consequent ability/inability to recognize children's concerns are a function of the emotional distance that separates us from them. This idea is neither original to my work nor uncontested. It begins with the history of childhood itself. This is a history first written by Aries (1962), whose investigations into medieval and Renaissance art revealed that childhood was not always perceived as a discrete period of development requiring the attentions of specially trained caregivers. There was once a time when children mixed freely in society, were portrayed as miniature adults, and survived through a certain benign neglect.

This same history was later edited by DeMause (1974) and the psychohistorians, who believe that "the history of childhood is a nightmare from which we have just begun to awaken" (p. 1). By contemporary standards, children were frequently brutalized and abused. Boswell (1988), for example, vividly chronicles the practice of abandoning unwanted, out-of-wedlock, and deformed children, which was common from late antiquity to the Renaissance. Challenging Aries' interpretation that life has become increasingly constricted and limited for children, psychohistorians posit a complex schema for charting changed attitudes which indicates that over time adults have become more skilled at meeting the needs of the young child. The new adult competencies emerge through effective control of the anxieties inevitably generated by the unsocialized child. As we spend less time projecting our adult anxieties/concerns onto children or demanding role reversals, we become more empathetic listeners. The nearer we move toward our children, the closer the identification permitted by psychodynamic processes, the better able we are to care for them. Children have realized only benefits from these growing attentions.

The optimism inherent in the psychohistorians' account is itself placed in question by the postmodern critique of the mental health perspective (Foucault, 1984; N. Rose, 1990), suggesting that all the psychological knowing has become an omnipresent form of social control rather than a liberatory move toward freeing children of intrusive adult involvements. The history of testing and labeling, inappropriate institutionalization, and warehousing of students until the marketplace can assimilate them attests to this reading of the nineteenth-century reconstruction of childhood. Polakow (1989) describes how those who want only to nurture the young may unwittingly be implicated in a regulative project. She is insistent in her claim:

> To talk of child development is also to talk of motherhood and domestic ideology, of family and patriarchy, of power and control. In the case of childhood, it is also to link power and the site of control—the body—to a social history of surveillance, classification, and regulation: in short, to the "biopower" (Foucault, 1984) that we, as child developers, increasingly employ in

our discursive practices as we chart taxonomies of thinking skills, scale norms of psycho-social and cognitive development, and assess the staged progression of performance outcomes. (p. 75)

At the same time that our attempts to know children have uncovered increasing numbers and kinds of differences between their worlds and ours, the boundaries separating them may actually be less secure. While some critics decry the demise of childhood, Zelizer (1985) suggests that our history is one in which the child has become economically worthless but sentimentally priceless. Once viewed as economic assets of the individual family with obligations to repay parental expenses for their upbringing, children have become social resources to be nurtured and educated in public institutions. The goal has shifted to maximizing their potential contribution to future societal progress. Universal, state-mandated schooling, promoted as the best means to protect children from the physical hardships of the factory, also removed them from the "moral decay" of the working-class family and guaranteed middle-class dominance of the social order. Children were to be protected from "abusive" situations and society was to be kept safe from the potential civil chaos threatened by unregulated masses of the poor (Plumb, 1972). Everyone was to benefit from an increasingly skilled, educated, and docile work force.

The Innocent and Ignorant Child

Underlying this transformation was the image of the hapless, innocent child essential to the romantic imagination. Replacing Reformation notions of the child as innately sinful and given to moral corruption, in need of harsh physical punishment, the romantic ideal enshrined the child as qualitatively different from the adult. The vision cast children in a new light:

> as assets of the race, to be conserved at any cost—as the torch bearers to the civilization of the future, as the links in the chain of human endeavor. With this vision before mankind, the child has in our own day entered into his rights. For the first time in the history of the race, he has become an entity in himself: his physical needs, his mental requirements, his moral training as considerations to be studied entirely apart from the adult. His life has become an autonomous world set within that of maternity. (Plumb, 1972, p. 7)

The child who in earlier centuries was potentially redeemable only through unrelenting parental vigilance became the child redeemer (Wishy, 1968); child advocates popularized the slogan, "A little child shall lead them" (Breckinridge, 1912).

For nineteenth-century writers the child became a symbol of innocence juxtaposed against social experience, imaginative sensibility against bureaucratic conformity. Emblematic of the artist's dissatisfaction with society, the child—vulnerable, fearful, and alone—became a frequent subject of aesthetic interest. Unfortunately this identification with children led as easily to escapism and nostalgia as to productive self-exploration and social protest. Romanticism had the potential for both objective awareness and morbid introversion. The child offered an image of growth and involvement with life as well as retreat and disengagement. This was the tension successfully maintained in the poetry of Blake, Coleridge, and Wordsworth and ultimately lost in the Victorian novels of Dickens, when the image of the child became reified. Once the source of power and integrity, the child was now associated with morbidity and mortality. The sentimentalized children of Victorian novels either succumb to their own innocence, as in *Dombey and Son,* or become the foil against which an elderly adult is rejuvenated, as in *Silas Marner, Oliver Twist,* and *Our Mutual Friend* (Coveney, 1967; Pattison, 1978).

The popular images of childhood embedded in the literary masterpieces of the nineteenth century supported a political order as well as an aesthetic one. As Hendrick (1990) suggests, proliferating images of childhood—the factory child, delinquent child, school child, psychomedical child, welfare child—brought new opportunities for public interventions in children's lives. Ignoring differences in class, geography, and culture, children's advocates proclaimed a universal childhood with rights and special needs that demanded protection. The right to health and education, the right to play and to freedom from work, and, above all, the right to be treated with special consideration spawned a multitude of institutions from schools and juvenile justice systems, to mental health clinics and child welfare agencies, to playgrounds and open-air camps. A compulsory relationship among family, state, and social welfare agencies was legislated into practice.

The idea of a natural childhood, embedded in a bourgeois ideology of domesticity and care, established standards against which to judge the childhoods of working-class children. This ideology had very practical consequences. The new investment in children led to declining infant mortality rates through the improvement in basic care practices (Shorter, 1977). It also meant the removal of older children from socially significant activity as institutions were created to protect and educate them. Although additional resources were put at the disposal of the family, the effect was only to weaken its authority while strengthening the state's. The family was given responsibility for newly defined problems of psychological development, social adjustment, and language acquisition at the precise moment that it was deemed unable to provide adequate care. Family life became the focus of a new breed of helping professionals, the child savers.

The adults who designed and implemented programs for children saw themselves as part of the larger progressive movement for social reform (Takanishi, 1978). They set out to save the children, not to imprison them, to free them from adult tasks, not to make them more dependent. In the process childhood became a social issue and the belief in childhood innocence that rationalized their work became a belief in childhood ignorance. When innocence is defined by the absence of the experience presumed to characterize adulthood, the protection of childhood requires controlling access to the knowledge that would signal its loss. The school was one of numerous institutions in which the child was increasingly defined as ignorant and in need of adult supervision. The assumption of childhood ignorance became an essential element in constructing the new pedagogy and the sciences through which it was instantiated. Schools became sites that produced and applied knowledge about children. They consistently affirmed how much students did not know, encouraging their dependence on formal education.

Although a minority of educators have always sought to connect the student's life inside and outside of the school (Dewey, 1916; Freire, 1986), ethnographers and phenomenologists, in studies of contemporary education, document the way that schools continue to keep students at a safe distance (Delpit, 1988; Lightfoot, 1978). Removed from the familiar context of home and family, the child's prior knowledge of the world has little relevance. It is the teacher's knowledge and the school's text that take precedence. Valuing the abstract over the concrete, the distant over the near, difference over connection, schools insure that children are viewed in terms of what they do not know, rather than in terms of already-given competencies and commitments. Because students are kept ignorant of the objective analysis necessary to understanding the multiple levels of reality among which we may move in the educational setting, schooling most frequently leads to alienation rather than to freedom. Deprived of a personal history or socially meaningful context in which to act, in need of constant supervision and surveillance, the student is a stranger in a foreign land.

KNOWLEDGE IN THE PEDAGOGICAL RELATIONSHIP

This innocent and ignorant child is the product of three interlocking discourses—scientific, professional, and popular. Together they locate an ideal childhood in a far-off place and designate the educator as responsible for controlling exposure to the world as adults know it. Proponents of compulsory education hoped to define a single, coherent world in which students would ultimately take their place as compliant, responsible citizens. But adults know many worlds, and our knowing is not disinterested (Habermas, 1968). Knowledge may be defined narrowly as information that is processed and easily retrievable, or more broadly as cultural capital to be employed in making value-laden decisions. Thus behaviorists concern themselves with measuring the amounts and types of information to be inculcated, while educational philosophers have traditionally asked questions about the kind of knowledge deemed to be of most worth. Critical theorists have taken as their focus the problem of the socioeconomic interests served by the knowledge promoted in schools. But what exactly is the nature of the space between childhood ignorance and adult knowledge? Is it bridged through the accumulation of knowledge, qualitative changes in cognitive structures, or caring interpersonal relationships?

Curriculum theorists have recently turned their attention to psychoanalytic theory not, as in the past, to track the psychosexual development of the young child but rather to learn more about its epistemological underpinnings. Here knowledge is viewed not as an entity, something to be possessed, manipulated, or controlled, but as a structural dynamic. Felman (1982) points out that it is the pedagogy of Freud and Lacan, rather than theory per se, that most effectively instructs us about the possibility/impossibility of teaching anyone anything. In their work, teaching emerges as a possibility only if teachers can help students gain access to what they already know. Its impossibility rests in the assumption that students already know everything they require and teachers know nothing. Knowledge might be said to be a form of remembering, ignorance only a question of forgetting. The teacher's function is characterized as making ignorance present to the student. From this perspective, ignorance is not a passive state, an accidental by-product of our drive to know. As Lacan (1975) maintains, we all have a stake in defending against knowledge, a "passion for ignorance" (p. 110). With knowledge we are implicated, forced to assume a relationship to the information and to its source that may be unsettling, distressing, or transformative. The texts that resist interpretation are the real locus for learning. I want to know why J.D. was able to outlive the expectations of his nurse and her inadequate explanation of his "case." What enabled Michael to remain so close even as he drifted so far away? How did Bill learn so much about dying, become such an effective caregiver to the living?

If we assume that a teacher cannot know in advance what must be taught and if knowledge has no predetermined exchange value but works only as an internal structural dynamic, what conditions promote learning? To answer this question, it is necessary to turn to the archetypical pedagogical situation, learning a first language, to see that coming to know is only made possible by the presence of someone who is presumed to know. The child strives to communicate with the caregiver in charge. The possibility of the knowing subject brings the possibility of transference, as the one who is presumed to know becomes the object of desire. Cognition and affect, love and knowledge are inextricably bound together. The authoritative posture of the adult only establishes the condition under which learning can occur by virtue of suggesting that there is indeed something to be known. Without the affective investment of the learner, who is presumed to be ignorant, in the teacher, who is presumed to know, there can be no learning.

A psychodynamic model reverses our assumptions about knowledge and ignorance, drawing our attention to what our students do not know or cannot learn, just as John Holt (1964) was drawn to the wrong answers and "mistakes" of his students during the 1960s. It places our own knowing/not knowing more directly at the service of the student. At the same time, the ambiguity created about the locus of control in learning greatly shortens, if not totally erases, the distance between student and teacher. I would argue, however, that some space must be preserved for the construction of a socially and personally meaningful curriculum. When life in classrooms is reduced to the student–teacher dyad, there is no accounting for the world that exists outside of that relationship. Left to follow the student's agenda, a technician of resistances and defenses, the teacher is provided with no normative guides for evaluating the curriculum, no way to assess the connection between schooling and society. While psychodynamic insights interrupt our assumptions about the knowledge/ignorance dynamic in critical ways, we must inquire further into the relationship between the structure of our relationships and the content of the curriculum if we are to fulfill our social responsibilities. Where do we locate ourselves in conversations with students that promise the closeness born of shared existential questions while still claiming a distinctly pedagogic function?

Grumet (1988) answers this question by drawing on her experiences as a mother and teacher and her knowledge of psychodynamic processes. Attending to the curriculum and to life in the home that precedes and gives shape to life in the classroom, she reads early development through object relations theory, the mother–infant pair becoming the literal and metaphoric model of the teacher–student dyad. Like the absent spouse or transitional object replacing a temporarily missing parent, the curriculum completes the triadic pattern of family relationships. The parent who is less directly involved in daily care offers the young child a first means to escape an omniscient primary caregiver and to find a new source of independence and power. The material world is a place in which to express the frustrations, fears, and anxieties inherent in our growing independence from the primary caregiver. Through language we learn to assert our intentionality, to become subjects, and to establish a separate identity, even as we enjoin others in the search to fulfill our desires. At the same time as the child seeks to know and be known through material and linguistic production, the adult also welcomes a respite from the all-consuming work of child rearing, turning to the world to reestablish a separate identity. Engagement with the world functions to expand and support our first relationships while establishing the salience of appropriate distances. For without distance we cannot see the other, nor can the other see us.

At first blush Grumet appears to collapse differences between home and school, parental nurture and professional pedagogy. But closer inspection suggests critical distinctions. For one, student and teacher have a time-bound relationship that takes place in the context of a group, while parent and child establish and transform their relationship over the course of a lifetime with greater privacy and opportunities for reinterpretations. Moreover, at school life is abstracted, fragments selected for re-presentation through signs and symbols, traditional disciplines, and discrete subject matters. At home children learn alongside adults as they engage in immediately purposeful activities. Knowing about the world, acting on it, provides the warmth of clean clothing, the nourishment of tasty food, and the safety of familiar shelter. All our senses are involved in this knowing, not just the intellect or powers of reason that are rewarded in schools. It is this kind of body knowing that Dewey (1899/1959) attempted to restore to the curriculum so long ago by breaking down the isolation of the school from home and community. He envisioned a school where sewing and weaving, woodworking and metallurgy, art and music, cooking and gardening were daily occurrences. The school as workshop and resource center is a place where children actively experiment with materials—planning, executing, and evaluating their work—making palpable the basic life-sustaining activities that are obscured from view in a complex, industrial society. Schools built on a factory model with legions of quiet, passive, and unchallenged students preclude the messy touches, excited sounds, fragrant smells, and active movements indicating that learning is occurring through the body as well as the mind and that adults and children are constructing meanings together rather than simply memorizing what others have said.

Educational reformers have also tried to interrupt the objectification occurring in large-scale institutions by bringing student and teacher closer together to create more personally relevant curricula. But humanistic psychologies often assume a false equality between student and teacher that makes the pedagogical relationship an end in itself, excluding the world to which we must ultimately turn and the accumulated experience of the adult. Taubman (1990) characterizes this as the neo-Freudian model of teacher-analyst, the one who cares, and juxtaposes it to the philosophical model of Plato's Socrates or the master of knowledge. It is the former who immerses him- or herself in the lives of students and the latter whose professionalism is defined by a commitment to the subject matter and strict adherence to the formal curriculum. Taubman seeks to define a midpoint between the extremes of teachers who disingenuously make no knowledge claims that might separate them from complete identity with their students and the teachers who establish their authority in absolute forms of knowledge. But the midpoint between submergence in our students' lives and surrender to the world of formal knowledge is not easily charted in a linear fashion because it reflects the layered, triangular organization of our primary relationships. The joy of the curriculum comes through mutual participation, building trust and understanding as we reconstruct experience. The school is less a site in which to seek the truth than a place to enjoy the multiple pleasures of the text, the meaning of that reward contained in the structures of our caring relationships.

The formulation of a dichotomy between the one who knows and the one who cares is seductive, and Taubman's text affords me singular pleasures through his willingness to share his own intentions as a teacher, including the nervous moments spent in front of the mirror before his first day of classes or the quandaries raised by socializing with adolescent students during the 1960s. These scenes touch me deeply. They also touch off in me a set of ideas that draw me out of the high school in which they are set and into the world of early childhood, where my own struggles to achieve the right distance first began.

In Taubman's terms I and my colleagues at the small progressive school where we taught identified ourselves as people who cared, who wanted to be close to children, to understand their life worlds. These experimental schools were designed in the early twentieth century to be laboratories for the scientific study of children's growth, with particular emphasis on the social and emotional aspects of development. The teacher's primary role was to observe and record information about the developing child, building a curriculum based on the objectively gathered data. The method is described in detail by Antler (1982) and is best summarized in the 1919 report from the Bureau of Educational Experiments, later known as Bank Street College of Education:

> We are working on a curriculum, checking it by our growth records; and working on how to record growth, evaluating our records by the children's reactions to our planned environment. . . . We were perforce recording growth of parts of children; but we were living with whole children as that each half of our thinking constantly served as a check for the other half. (Antler, 1982, p. 571)

Yet by midcentury we had lost confidence in ourselves and sought legitimation in the words of a new kind of master. Trained to listen to and observe young children for signs of developmental deviance, our claim to professionalism was based not on knowledge to be imparted to students but on the knowledge that informs the pedagogical gaze. The early childhood ethos, as I later recognized, was one that all too easily reduced epistemological issues to concerns with psychological surveillance (Walkerdine, 1984). The subjective desire to be a caring, if not loving, educator was transformed by a flight into the objective world of scientific research. In sum, we had become practitioners of scientific nurture.

I use this oxymoron to underline the discrepancy between the identity that leads us to immerse ourselves in the world of the child and the language we find to describe our work and its impact on children. I also use it to suggest some difficulties in translating Taubman's insights into the idiom of early childhood education, where the possibility of curriculum construed as a body of knowledge outside of the child's immediate experience is far more difficult to imagine than in the hubbub of the American history classroom where Taubman locates himself. Perhaps the real question is less about the age differential between his students and mine than about the work of curriculum making, the politics of knowledge. Although he introduces curricular possibilities that lie outside intersubjective knowing, they are defined by the Socratic search for truth, a search that takes place far from the dailiness of our lives with children (Alston, 1991).

Truth in the Distance, Care in the Foreground

While Socrates tells us that the search for truth is illumined by ignorance, feminists turn our attention to the social ground that gives meaning to ignorance. Absent from the canonical texts, often excluded from the public domain where official truths are produced, women have begun to interrogate the very commitment to searching for truth, a commitment that bears little relevance to their lived experience. Gallop (1982) depicts the feminist scholar Luce Irigaray struggling to be the teacher who respects the indeterminacy of knowledge. Invited, as an "authority on women," to lead a philosophy seminar, Irigaray (1977) begins by recognizing her doubled not-knowing: "I don't know how to conduct some *renversement* [overthrow/reversal] of the pedagogic relation in which, holding a truth about woman, a theory of woman, I could answer your questions: answer for women in front of you" (p. 120). She does not want to be an authority speaking a single truth for all women. She does not know such a truth, nor does she know how to speak about her not-knowing. A radical response to the repression of feminine desire in Western philosophical discourse involves writing the unpredictable, undefinable subject rather than simply inverting the masculine position or asserting an equality that affirms the phallic "economy of sameness."

Gallop contrasts Irigaray's wish to take part in a seminar in which all the participants share their questions equally to Freud's lectures on women that reduce the plurality of women to a coherent, single theory. Irigaray does not have the coherent theories or simple answers that would allow her to become part of the traditional trade in knowledge about women. She refuses phallocentric knowing and definitions that would fix plurality, close off questions, predetermine answers. She seeks an open dialogue that allows the otherness of her students to emerge, in effect initiating the *renversment* of the traditional pedagogic paradigm.

The difficulty of fostering open dialogues, acknowledging uncertainty, and respecting multiple perspectives cannot be minimized. It disrupts contemporary liberal models of education, which are grounded in the Platonic paradigm celebrating intellectual development, rational self-control, and autonomy. In contradistinction to Enlightenment educators like Rousseau, who argued that women need their own forms of education to succeed in the domestic world, the Greeks assigned no theoretical significance to gender even as they enshrined characteristics "naturally" associated with men. The tasks of the domestic sphere were to be carried out by women and other untutored members of the lower classes. Education was directed to preparing the elite to function in the public realm, where precedence was given to mind over body, reason over emotion, individual difference over social connection. The Greek ideal equated knowing the good with doing the good, and this knowing was conceived in the most abstract and theoretical terms.

Jane Roland Martin (1986) counters that it is not love of the intellect and abstract forms of truth that are required to ensure our survival in the coming years but rather a more earthly love, defined by traits associated with the feminine in our culture—caring, concern, and connection. If increasing family and community violence are taken as accurate indicators of our ability to communicate these values in the domestic world, then fostering capacities for generative love must become central to the public pedagogic agenda. We need not eschew intellectual achievement in order to include the feelings, attitudes, and values reflecting future possibilities. A gender-sensitive approach to education recognizes differences as they occur, values the relational characteristics Rousseau only attributed to woman, and promotes multiple ways of knowing regardless of the student's gender.

Nel Noddings (1992) illustrates how the substitution of generative love for the love of truth might transform our pedagogical practices from a singular focus on reason and the role of intellect to issues of motivation and the skills and attitudes necessary to sustain caring relationships. She rejects the Greek assumption that right knowledge is sufficient to right behavior, because it does not take into account how responses of a given individual may vary with context and age. Acknowledging that linguistic rationalization may become more sophisticated over time, Noddings resists the equation of moral behavior and intellectual articulation embedded in many approaches to moral education (Kohlberg, 1981). In place of stage theories, even those grounded in feminist premises (Gilligan, 1982), Noddings advocates moral education based on an ethic of care, which includes modeling, dialogue, practice, and confirmation. Belying the value that Socrates assigns to what is not known, the classic scenario implies that ignorance is inevitably associated with wrong-doing, knowledge with ethical behavior. The love of truth brings with it a disdain for ignorance.

Feminists consistently raise questions about ignorance and absence, especially absence of the body in the systems of those who imagine a single notion of truth. An ethic of care respects the body, arises out of an appreciation of embodied knowledge, and rejects the mind/body, intellect/affect, heart/hands dualisms that dominate contemporary education. In this process an ethic of care sets aside the same distinctions that have created the innocent and ignorant school child of our imaginations, the child we would protect from knowing about sex, death, and HIV/AIDS. It asks us to consider the ways in which we are connected to the child and how those connections are mediated through the curriculum.

The Professorial Body as Text

I am riveted to the *Lesbian and Gay Studies Newsletter* announcing a paper, "AIDS, Confession, and Theory: The Pedagogical Dilemma," to be presented at an upcoming conference. Only too aware of his declining health, Thomas Yingling (1993), the paper's author, joins with feminists seeking to return the body to pedagogical discourse. He writes of his decision to tell his graduate students that he has AIDS, a process that will transform his body into the class text to be read for signs of endurance, disease processes, and treatment effects. Yingling comes out in an academic setting of "fairly aggressive readers" in order to exercise greater control over how his disease is constructed and reconstructed. It is a move out of the specular mode, the fantasies of others witnessing his already evident physical deterioration, and into a confessional mode. Always the teacher, he realizes the pitfalls of the confession even as he hopes that it will raise questions about how we align bodies in the classroom, schedule learning in the university, value disembodied knowledges.

Declaring an AIDS diagnosis is a pedagogical act in any context, teaching others about the specificity of the disease, asking them to consider risk in a new way. In the academic world it changes the discourse as the body itself becomes a site of knowledge, not just an occasion for it. Yingling is concerned about what happens when the subject of knowledge assumes a body, wondering aloud if it is no longer eligible to be imagined as a subject-that-knows. His attempt to purchase agency in shaping the text of his disease has the potential for objectification and distancing. He may be misjudging the proper distance, touching his students in inappropriate ways and places, causing them to turn away from rather than toward the professorial body.

My interest is piqued by Yingling's abstract. Although I am neither HIV-positive nor think primarily about adult learners, I, too, have struggled with the confessional mode and tried to understand how HIV/AIDS can inform our pedagogy. I am drawn to this subject who knows, to this knowledgeable body. In order to get still closer, I seek out the full text of the announced paper. Not finding Yingling's address, I write to the newsletter editor. Her response directs me to the chair of the panel "he was supposed to be on." But why *supposed* to be on? Didn't he get to the conference, or perhaps the editor is simply unsure? I am beginning to have intimations of other meanings. Feeling anxious and unsettled, I look for my long-ago-filed copy of the newsletter, reread the abstract, and see that Yingling's name is followed by a pair of brackets enclosing the dates 1951–1992. Dates in brackets are dates on a tomb stone, dates of death. I am stunned. All of the carefully considered analysis, desire to avoid the specular, ends here with these brackets, these dates. I have barely begun a conversation only to find it abruptly terminated.

I dutifully write to the panel chair requesting the full paper. I know now this is a futile exercise and that the paper was never completed. I try to imagine what it was like for Yingling to write even this abstract—really too long for an abstract, more the length of an extended summary, and finally all that remains of the paper itself. In between bouts of which opportunistic infections, managing what drugs, supported by how many loved ones did he plan to travel to an academic conference, to finish a paper, complete the text? I do not know the answers to these questions, will never see the body of Yingling's text, but its themes haunt me. They echo my own efforts to understand the function of distance in caring relationships, to relate personal and professional histories, to take account of the body as well as the mind in our pedagogical practices, and to educate others about HIV/AIDS.

And what of the HIV/AIDS seminar with which I began this chapter? In retrospect, I can see that my anxiety about the session was unnecessary. The teachers did not need instruction about the disease; no additional information was required. Rather both they and I needed to focus on their not-knowing, to understand the resistance to addressing the difficult issues raised by HIV/AIDS. Given the salience of ignorance to our educational projects, why do we not learn its lessons? Here I think we need to attend to the public as well as the private meanings of ignorance and the ways they affect our ability to hear students' questions.

THE SOCIAL POWER OF IGNORANCE

Wexler (1990) deconstructs the multiple meanings of ignorance and its political function, linking it to our conceptions of time and social progress. In its weak sense ignorance has been used to refer to an absence, a dark region that awaits illumination by the inevitable triumph of knowledge. Time thus brings the progressive elimination of ambiguity; knowledge assures certainty and control. Unknowing, tentative children will develop into mature, wise adults. The Enlightenment drama in which the superiority of reason conquers the evils of the unknown has no space for ignorance. The alternative, if minority, tradition uses ignorance in its strong sense with quite different effect. Here it is understood as a form of knowledge, not error. It is characterized by the suspension of certainty and openness to experiment. The child is greeted as a newcomer with unknown possibilities. Ambiguity, complexity, even anxiety are the conditions of learning, teaching an interpretive rather than legislative project.

The dominant pedagogical mode in our society is based on ignorance in its weak sense. The world is divided into two camps: the knowing and ignorant, developed and undeveloped, capable and incapable. Questions about HIV/AIDS undermine the mutual pretense with which children and teachers fulfill their socially prescribed roles. The presumption that children are ignorant and innocent is belied by their concerns about a disease that we wished they did not know about. Most poignantly, parents with HIV/AIDS and parents of children with HIV/AIDS frequently try to avoid naming a diagnosis about which their children may already be aware (Tasker, 1992). Questions are posed by those who are knowledgeable enough to ask, not by those who are uninterested or unknowing. In turn, the assumption that adults are informed and knowing is challenged by a subject matter that places in doubt our time-honored belief in the power of science to provide solutions to human problems and in the ethics of its practitioners. HIV/AIDS also tests our reliance on socially constructed categories to keep us safe from a virus that shows no respect for such human distinctions. We rush to reassure children that HIV/AIDS will not happen to them. It is a disease of certain adults, adults who are far from their own lives.

Children's questions about life and death, pain and pleasure, behavior and intentionality are most realistically answered in terms of the ambiguity, complexity, and anxiety that characterize a commitment to ignorance in its strong sense rather than the rational certainty of ignorance in its weak sense. A commitment to ignorance in a strong sense means becoming familiar with its various forms. Wagner (1993) clarifies the terrain of the unasked question by advocating that researchers consider how educational interventions reduce ignorance rather than promote truth. Those who seek truth assume that knowledge is both constituted and therefore limited by empirical evidence and universal criteria of validity and reliability. They understand what they know and what they do not know, the research trajectory takes them across an already identified field that simply awaits more detailed exploration. Wagner refers to these unexplored areas as blank spots. They reflect questions already posed for which we seek answers. They tell us about the status of our existing knowledge. In contrast, blind spots, more easily located when ignorance is assumed to be the starting point of research, emerge when totally new questions are raised by our work. They reflect what we do not know well enough or care enough to ask about. By drawing our attention to blind spots, Wagner wants to subvert the myopia that can develop from a narrow focus on blank spots, causing us to miss the larger blind spots.

Any field of knowledge is defined by a unique combination of blind spots and blank spots that structure our collective ignorance. Old news in one arena may reflect the latest advances in another; for example, the importance of social context and qualitative methodologies in anthropology may be revolutionary when applied to education, or the long-recognized power of the small group in early education may be quite revolutionary when applied to industrial settings. Similarly, the regulative functions of child psychology may reflect a blank spot on the larger map of critical theory but a blind spot in early childhood education. A shift from truth to ignorance may redirect us from the blank spots on the existing map of knowledge to the blind spots that define the borders of the map itself. For some, the reluctance to answer children's questions about HIV/AIDS may be read as a blank spot in the map of pedagogical knowledge, waiting to be filled in with targeted information and social-skills training, while others may experience it as a blind spot demanding a reevaluation of our purposes and goals in education. In either case, Wagner makes it more difficult to turn away from ignorance.

Ignorance makes us uncomfortable. It democratizes our relationships with children. Waksler (1991a) identifies the social purposes served by ignorance by using adult memories to study the ordinary, everyday difficulties of simply "being a child." Interested in experiences that children themselves might define as the "hard times of childhood," she locates these moments—the mandated swimming lessons, enforced naptimes, unwelcomed separations from a sibling—at points when we lose control over the physical, social, and moral world. They reflect a social structure in which children themselves lack power or knowledge of the rules considered necessary for appropriate conduct. Beyond telling us about the unintended messages of our actions and similarities across the ages, the hard times of childhood reveal how much we do not know about children, an ignorance that Waksler does not find accidental. Rather, she theorizes, it allows adults to act in routine ways that do not take into account the child's perspective. We believe ourselves to be altruistic agents and children willing participants in a painful drama of misunderstood intentions.

Waksler's immediate concern is less with increasing children's control over the material circumstances of their lives than in provoking adults to rethink the advantages and self-interest in not seeing children's hard times, in not hearing their questions about the adult ordering of the world. Do we consider the discrepancies among what we want, what children want, and what we think children want? These distinctions become especially blurred when we speak in terms of children's needs and ourselves as disinterested professionals. Most nursery school teachers speak the language of individual needs. I remember only too well my frequent response when confronted by the oppositional behavior of one of my young students. The words ring in my ears even today: "You *need* to sit down now," "You *need* to be alone for a while." My demands for compliance were always couched in terms of what children needed to do. In retrospect, I think this was an attempt to mask what in fact was the coercive imposition of my will by drawing attention to the child's lack of restraint or internal control. This might also be read as a substitution of power for authority.

Rodham (1973), discussing children's status under the law, notes that nineteenth-century social reforms were often based on adult perceptions and needs regarding children. She argues that adult moral prescriptions and political demands are voiced as children's needs and interests but cannot necessarily be construed as children's rights. The language of needs veils our uncertainty about what is right for children (Woodhead, 1990). We manage to cloak decisions based on personal values and specific cultural locations in a vocabulary that appears factual, universal, and timeless. To speak of the other's need is to speak of an objective description that is driven by an emotional imperative. For the child is understood as unable to recognize that which makes such evident common sense to the adult. The empirical and evaluative are combined so as to assure us that the needs are intrinsic to the child rather than socially constructed in our daily interactions and encoded in the pedagogical canon. The teacher's claim to truth lies not in the ambiguously negotiated realm of intersubjectivity but in the objectivity of the scientific gaze that obliterates both the observer and the observed.

At our weekly staff meetings and at endless parent workshops, we would talk about what children needed, here cast as a matter of curriculum. The need for play, social interaction, or learning by doing were uppermost on the agenda for children of sophisticated, middle-class, urban families. Seldom did we stop to wonder whether those needs attributed to the children might more accurately be found in ourselves, the culture of the school, or the community. Such considerations would suggest the more fragile, situated nature of the discourse in which we engaged and the power arrangements on which it was built. The discourse, which at that time had not been infused with the vocabulary of multiculturalism, only reinforced a polarity between the interests of the individual and of the group. Steeped in a plethora of psychological theories explaining children's development and studies documenting their growth, we reproduced what seemed to be an inevitable conflict between the personal and the social, the private and public worlds of childhood.

By definition, difficult questions cut across arbitrary social categories, interrupting the accepted inequalities that structure our pedagogical relationships. They force us to turn away from the primary mode of instruction, explication, in which the infantilized, dependent student awaits enlightenment as it is measured out by the teacher, and to turn toward more narrative forms of communication. The act of storytelling assumes an equality of intelligence in its interlocutor rather than a superiority of knowledge. In moving from the hierarchy of explication to the more democratic participation of interpretation, we also move from ignorance as a vacuum to be filled by knowledge to ignorance as the light that illumines knowledge. This is to recognize that we are best instructed by ignorance rather than knowledge, by the questions that are not asked as well as the ones which are. Perhaps, after all, what we most fear are the unspoken questions, questions that define the epistemology of the closet with which gay men and lesbians are so familiar and which I address more fully in Chapter 7.

THE LIABILITY TO CARE

I began this chapter with Bill's story and our mutual attempt to modulate the distance separating health and illness at the same time as my work in AIDS education led me to reconsider the spaces that divide students and teachers in our schools. Exploring the social definitions of children as ignorant and innocent and adults as knowledgeable, I have come to understand how these assumptions about knowing/not-knowing structure our ability to hear children's questions. For when children raise questions about HIV, they not only interrogate a particular adult, they also interrogate our entire system of binary oppositions and the personal identities embedded in them. When they do not raise these questions, they tacitly accede to the mutual pretense that assures their place in the world as the unknowing child. They thus display their own command of the social system, enabling adults to play the familiar part of the knowledgeable one without embarrassment.

The production of ignorance is critical to strengthening the social fabric and to the hegemony of those who have mastered its many meanings. If anything, AIDS teaches us about the social power of ignorance. It is nothing less than our glorification of knowledge as certainty and the vilification of ignorance as error that has contributed to the public paralysis with respect to this disease. Ignorance becomes the rationale for inaction, the failure to find a cure or to secure absolute certainty about the risk of transmission confirming that we really understand nothing of value about it. Through legal exclusions, social ostracism, and the gloved hand of the professional caregiver, we have learned to remain distant from those who are in need. There is a willful ignorance about the disease, a desire to keep the guilty at a distance in order to protect the innocent.

I do not think the barriers we create between sick and healthy are so very different from the walls we erect between adults and children. Segregated in age-graded classes, children are cared for by professionals whose touch is increasingly regulated by guidelines defining the conditions under which they may be alone with adolescents, hold the young on their laps, or come in contact with body fluids. The body of the other is rigorously policed, mysteriously private, the ultimate unknowable. Our touch has been professionalized, the distance dictated rather than achieved. Finally, these spaces we have created between our lives and the lives of our children, between those of us who are healthy and those who are ill, are symptomatic of a larger attempt to deny the liability to care, which is the human condition. For if to exist is to be responsible, answerable to ourselves for what we do and who we become, then to exist with others is to be liable to them. The failure to respond to our children's questions only reflects a momentary flight into irresponsibility that belies our need to care for and about the existence into which we are thrust at birth. It is only through understanding more about our own ignorance and recognizing the knowledge implicit in the questions of our students that we can join in a common pedagogical project, bridging the distance between their worlds and ours.

CHAPTER 6

Curricular Languages:
Queerying Feminist Perspectives

Ideas come to us as the successors to griefs.
Marcel Proust, *Remembrance of Things Past*

Between us and them: between child and adult, healthy and ill, gay and straight. This is the space we try to span with language. Structuring the distance with stages, ages, and developmental processes, we fill the gap with familiar markers, addressing the void that was the object of our very first attempts to communicate with others. Our research and teaching may be understood as an extension of these most primitive cognitive attempts to respond to the silence of being. To insert ourselves into the world through language is to insist that we can fill the silence, we can hold off death. In this sense pedagogy, the nurture of possibility, functions oddly like mourning, our memorializing of the past; both draw the individual out of self-absorption and into the collective space of community. Death creates the occasion for intersubjectivity and is the motor driving our desire to engage with the other or, as Helen Schlegel pithily comments in E.M. Forster's *Howards End* (1908), "Death destroys a man: the idea of Death saves him" (p. 239).

Feminist scholar Evelyn Beck (1988) writes about the struggle to feel at home in language, a project through which she has turned her personal history into a professional journey. As a Jewish child fleeing Vienna with her family in 1938, she had to learn and relearn many mother tongues, placing in doubt the assumption that language provides a spiritual homeland even for those in geographic exile. As an adult, returning to the city of her birth, invited to give a major public address in German, she finds herself emotionally and practically challenged. The childhood terrors of saying the wrong words, potentially fatal words, haunt her preparations even as she acknowledges her affiliation with the language of her birth. Although her research

136

has dealt with themes of the outsider and the literature of oppressed minorities, it is only when confronted with her own linguistic history that she recognizes in a visceral way the anxieties that can prevent women from giving voice to their experience. She fears she will be unable to express herself, will not have anything of importance to say, will have nothing to say. Thus she understands the ambivalent relationship of all women to the language of patriarchy, a language they have learned to distrust but whose power they cannot deny. It is a language that separates women deeply from their lived realities.

Although Beck has learned to express her multiple identities in many languages—scholarly, vernacular, and aesthetic—I read her story as one of loss and displacement. The threat of annihilation frames her exile from a mother tongue. Nothing is permanent after an encounter with death. Death shatters coherence, life as we have known it, rending what had first appeared as the seamless fabric of experience. It is this very fragmentation that also opens for examination issues once concealed. Often, out of our despair, we are willing to take new risks, attending more closely to what the Jewish tradition refers to as *tikkun olam*, repair of the world.

Language is always borrowed. Even as we try to imbue it with our own meanings, it manages to retain the lingering flavors of others who have come before and used these words, those phrases, that sentence structure. Language is deeply social. In the early 1950s Simone de Beauvoir (1972) identified the unique rift between language and the woman speaker, commenting: "Representation of the world, like the world itself, is the work of men; they describe it from their own point of view, which they confuse with absolute truth" (p. 161). But many women have tried to invent new forms to give voice to their experience. Evelyn Beck joins a tradition including poets like Audre Lorde and Adrienne Rich, novelists like Jane Rule and Dorothy Allison, theoreticians like Monique Wittig and Nicole Brossard, historians like Lillian Faderman and Esther Newton. Their commitment has become part of a larger project to make present the lives of all those absent from the canon. It is consistent with but not always the same as the postmodern interest in difference and marginality. In the field of education it has been realized largely through the introduction of narrative methods into research, teacher preparation, and curriculum development (Schubert, 1991). It is hoped that by producing more language and telling different stories, everyone will have a greater stake in the educational process.

My initial interest in narrative was not pedagogical. It began with an effort, reproduced below, to grieve in a more public way for someone who had died of AIDS. Like the lover who spends days frantically searching for the most flattering clothing, I have passed months exploring the language that would best reflect the paradoxes of my experience. And like the eager suitor who seeks the advice of trusted friends, I have frequently turned to feminist

colleagues to assist in persuading the reader of the authenticity of my arguments. It is their assumption of an interrogative stance toward the language
of patriarchy that serves as a model for those who would resist the limits of
academic categories in order to name the underground streams that feed our
experience.

Impelled to tell our story, we are of necessity forced to find a language
adequate to its message. Language is a primary way we learn to know and
not to know ourselves. The epistemological assumptions embedded in language signal its critical implications for pedagogy (Huebner, 1975b) and guide
us in answering the classic educational question: What knowledge is of most
worth? In our culture, feminists argue, language privileges difference over
sameness, separation over connection, abstraction over specificity (Pagano,
1990). They ask: Who is the speaker and what kind of language is being
spoken/not spoken? They inquire into the epistemological significance of the
sex of the knower (Code, 1991). I want to inquire into the connection between this gendered analysis of language and my experience as a gay male
speaker. What kinds of similarities and differences between feminist and queer
perspectives might enrich our reading of the curriculum? Isn't the presumption of heterosexuality limiting for everyone, not just lesbians and gay men?

To learn to grieve is to learn to give voice to our sense of loss, to speak
within a communal context. Living in and through the AIDS crisis I no longer
have the luxury (was it ever a luxury?) to deny my membership in the community that stands to hear my plaint. Nor do I want to discount the ways in
which my gay identity may inform my educational perspective. Finally, then,
I want to understand how this newly achieved voice might be heard by that
other critical community in which I live and work, the community of progressive educators. It is our very participation in different worlds that offers
the potential for mutual influence and the possibility of transformative practices. I begin in the world of childhood, with memories of myself as a young
boy and my father as a middle-aged man, going to synagogue on the High
Holidays.

STANDING FOR MICHAEL

I have recently returned from summer camp and am newly measured,
assessed, and outfitted for the coming year. Unlike the American New Year,
which is primarily an adult holiday that I learn to associate with artificial
merriment and the chill of winter, this fall celebration is both more cerebral
in its focus on introspective questioning and yet connected to nature's
rhythms, as it marks the end of one agricultural cycle and the beginning of
another. Still retaining the healthy glow of summer, I stand next to my father

as he sways back and forth reciting the Hebrew prayers with a speed and fluidity that is the wonder of everyone in the family. It is a secure, warm place to be. My father is preoccupied, engaged with the ritual of atonement yet never too busy to respond to a child's query or provide advice on the appropriate moment to slip out of the crowded synagogue to join the group of peers that re-forms every year. Then we are strange to one another for only a few moments as we make our awkward overtures, sharing tales of vacation exploits and anticipatory concerns about the new school year.

Like my father, I am conscientious in my observance of the rituals and attend religious school until I am 16. When I am an adult, long after I have announced my dissociation from any religious practice, my father will still entreat me to attend services to listen to the shofar, the symbolic welcoming of the New Year. But for me the mystery of this holiday is not concealed in the shrill plaint of the ram's horn; rather it is contained in the overarching request of the suppliants to be inscribed in the Book of Life. According to the ancient texts, on the first of the holidays, Rosh Hashanah, it is written who will live and who will die, who will be sick and who will be well, who will prosper and who will suffer, and on Yom Kippur, nine days later, this fate is sealed. We are given a little over a week to plead our case, to search our souls, to ask for forgiveness and make amends for our transgressions.

My child's mind grasps neither the metaphorical language nor my father's absolute belief in a deity who distributes justice. My father is more a man of God than of poetry. He does not help me to make sense of this bibliographic request. If there is an inscription, then someone must be the inscriber; if there is an inscriber, there must be a book; and if there is a book, then there must be a place where it is kept. And how can one authority know everything about everybody? No, my feelings in the synagogue are not about God or books or sin. They are about being with family, being in a community, and being in a world that is ordered and orderly.

What I do understand, perhaps because it requires no leap of the imagination or of faith in a nonhuman being, is the time for mourners to rise and be recognized in the sight of the entire congregation. As children, we are forewarned not to remain during the Yizkor service. We are not to see the adults in their vulnerability, and they in turn are to be allowed to express their grief without embarrassment. We are forever curious about this time yet relieved that we do not need to witness such a reversal of roles. If, as happens on some rare occasions, my father fails to signal our departure in time and we are caught inside, we find the intensity of emotion unsettling, frightening. It is safer to know sadness at a distance than to see it firsthand.

*   *   *

My father moved to New York City in 1935, at age 24. He married my mother a year later. As a child I was fascinated by his roots in a small western Pennsylvania town. I could not imagine him living in a place other than the one I knew. Person and context were one and the same. Periodically I would query him about how he came to live in New York. Although he provided numerous explanations, all unsatisfying in some unknown way, the most unsettling was his desire to escape the anti-Semitic slurs that punctuated his growing up. He wanted to raise a family safe from the taunts and epithets of his youth.

Thus I was raised in an urban, predominately Jewish enclave free of explicit displays of anti-Semitism, if not from my father's continuing fear of potential persecution. Because anti-Semitism was not part of my daily life, it seemed a distant, vague, and ultimately incomprehensible threat. The Holocaust was never mentioned, although its images were all too clearly engraved in my memory when, as a young child, I was taken to the Yivo Institute with other members of my small Hebrew school class. There we saw photographs of concentration camp survivors, products made of human body parts and assorted documents of devastation. It was a trip I would not forget.

Tied in some mysterious way to the suppressed memories of the Holocaust was the more explicit anxiety over the precarious new state of Israel. Weekly we purchased labels to affix to the picture of a tree. At the end of the year our completed pictures were redeemed for an official certificate. A tree would be planted in our name. But why were trees so important? How was I connected to such an arid and foreign country?

When I was 6 or 7 my mother took me and my brother to the sailing of a friend who was emigrating to Israel. The singing, dancing, and excitement were infectious and titillating, again reminding us of a revered but strange place. I would need to wait 10 years, until the summer before entering college, to understand more about my connection to Israel. Then I would spend three months working on a kibbutz, learning directly about the perils of life in a country surrounded by hostile neighbors, the difficulties of agriculture in the Middle East, and the pioneer spirit that I had first observed as a child.

Ironically, it was soon after returning from Israel that I stopped going to synagogue. This was also the moment that I began to accept my homosexuality. The synagogue, with its emphasis on family, children, and survival in the Diaspora, seemed irrelevant. I was neither angry nor bitter. The Sabbath sermons were simply not addressed to me. My life was elsewhere, with others, in a different world. And that is how it remained until recently, until AIDS.

Now sadness cannot be held at a safe distance as in childhood. Now I have been impelled to find ways to express the grief that has become a recurrent motif of my life. I have learned to say Kaddish, to participate in the Yizkor service, to be part of a new community of survivors. Let me explain.

*   *   *

In the last several years I have begun to attend a gay synagogue. I go to say Kaddish along with the other mourners, to remember friends and lovers with the Hebrew and Aramaic words that permeated my childhood. I go to be among those who, like myself, have been written out of the traditional Jewish script that emphasizes reproduction within the context of the heterosexual family and stereotypical gender roles. I am pleased to be surrounded by gay and lesbian couples and single congregants, amused that the young children still provoke the same responses ranging from admiration to tolerance to impatience with their often distracting presence. I am especially touched by the seats reserved for elderly parents who invariably arrive late, taking their time to make the trip from the suburbs or uptown Manhattan to this Greenwich Village location. Thrilled by the sound of our singing and chanting as we breathe new life into old forms, I find myself alone in thought, together with others whom I do not know.

I want to write that the gay synagogue is the fulfillment of a childhood fantasy, but this would be an anachronistic reading of my own imagination. For although I was only too aware of my interest in particular boys during the grade school years, mesmerized by the way that Bobby rolled his jeans, Jimmy wore his T-shirt, and Danny combed his hair, a more explicitly genital eroticism was only to emerge in junior high school. This was the 1950s, after all, long before Stonewall, a time when the very bravest of our forefathers and foremothers, members of the Mattachine Society in Los Angeles and Daughters of Bilitis in San Francisco, were beginning to fashion a notion of gay people as a unique minority, an oppressed group with its own identity. I am proud of what we have accomplished in so few years, no longer defined by a doctor's diagnosis, defining ourselves through the culture that we are building.

Even with all my political awareness, I had not thought to say Kaddish for Michael as I prepared to go to synagogue that first New Year's after his death. But as I found a seat, carefully chosen for its unobstructed view of the pulpit, and put on the prayer shawl, I knew that when the time came I would rise along with the other mourners to recite the ancient prayer for the dead. I wanted to stand for Michael, for myself. With this recognition I was also gripped by fear, my hands began to tremble, and I searched obsessively through the prayer book for the exact moment at which the Yizkor service would begin.

I did not understand my own response. Was it simply the public statement of grief that I would be making, or was it something more primordial that caused these tremors—to be a man mourning the loss of another man with the same words that had been used for centuries to sanction the loss of a heterosexual spouse or blood relative? In a single moment I was not only to affirm my particular relationship with Michael but also my participation in the larger community of lesbians and gay men. Words once used to celebrate the resolutely heterosexual meanings of Jewish tradition were now to be used to sanctify my own recalcitrant sexuality, my desire for the boy at the neighboring desk in Hebrew school and the older teenager who included me in a handball game on Saturday afternoon. But there is still a moment of uncertainty, a sense of transgression against the ancient law, against my own loving but rule-abiding father.

By reciting Kaddish for Michael, by uttering his name in public, I am not only asserting that we can read old traditions in new ways, that we can choose to create an identity that was literally inconceivable 30 years ago; I am also fulfilling my status as an adult in a way that I have never done before. For it is adults, not children, who are official mourners, charged with the task of memorializing the dead and linking the immediate loss with the larger history of the culture.

In this context, redolent with childhood memories, I am grieving for my lost self as well as for Michael. I am unprepared for this kind of work. The service has become a time to examine how well I accept myself and the life I have chosen. I am made sad and thoughtful by my memories of Michael but, strangely, not unhappy. I find comfort in an inexplicable closeness to my own father, feel myself becoming my father, as I claim my place in this new kind of congregation.

THINKING THROUGH OUR FATHERS

In "standing for Michael" I also stand with Evelyn Beck in the pursuit of linguistic authenticity. I, too, seek to understand death, although a particular death, through reconciling with a homeland from which I have been alienated. Mourning is an act of individual resistance against the losses that frame our lives. For me, it has also meant a return to a community of my childhood. Participation in the gay synagogue allows me to feel reconnected to my family and its history as well as to my own biography. I am connected to the present, to the larger family of Jewish lesbians and gay men responding to the realities of HIV/AIDS. I realize that for some readers, references to the Jewish culture and religious ceremonies of my childhood may be as foreign as descriptions of gay society and mores. But it is at this very intersection of identities that we are constructing something new, a home for future generations of lesbians and gay men. Perhaps it is this fusion of identities and temporal moments that draws me to the synagogue. It is a place where I can be completely present; the past and future are with me. In the gay synagogue I find neither denial nor hopelessness, but rather a will to unify the narrative fragments of my own life story.

"Standing for Michael" teaches me that beyond the creation of new forms through which to express our grief—candlelight vigils, community memorials, quilt projects—we must continually monitor the internalized homophobia that blocks access to our feelings of loss and confirms their inevitability. For we, too, are part of the same culture that has associated homosexuality with illness, long before the advent of HIV/AIDS. Notions of death have been at the core of historical constructions of same-sex desire. The aura of death and self-destruction surrounding the prototypical gay man with HIV/AIDS—Gaetan Dugas, Patient Zero in Randy Shilts's (1987) *And The Band Played On*—is foreshadowed by his nineteenth-century predecessor in Oscar Wilde's (1891/1985) *The Picture of Dorian Gray*. The self-centered hedonism of the Shilts character is only a contemporary version of Wilde's inaugural presentation of gay identity, in which the Hellenic ideal of the beautiful youth is equated with the prospect of inevitable death (Nunokawa, 1991). Alternatively, the story of Patient Zero can be read as a resurrection of the homosexual vampire—sexually exotic, alien, unnatural, oral and anal at the same time (Hanson, 1991). Bram Stoker's *Dracula* and Freud's homosexual incite a similar homosexual panic, confirming the fragility of heterosexual identity. HIV/AIDS provides further opportunity to reassert the binary divisions structuring our knowing of homosexuality, compounding the scientific and moral rationales that buttress the power of the male, heterosexist perspective.

Internalized homophobia may take distinct forms among gay people. Odets (1990, 1994), a clinical psychologist, writes that because of the magnitude of loss within the gay community, the uninfected find it difficult to experience and express a full range of emotions. HIV/AIDS not only confirms the identification of same-sex desire with illness, it also silences the healthy by making survival a source of guilt, renders expressions of emotional need unseemly in the face of the critical care required by so many others.

Given the press of events and absence of adequate rituals, it has been only too easy for activists to tell themselves that mourning is a form of self-indulgence (Bronski, 1989). Living in the midst of a health crisis, we need immediate forms of collective action, not prolonged bouts of individual introspection. Those who came of age within the movements of the political left take their cues from Joe Hill's injunction, "Don't mourn, organize," and Mother Jones's "Pray for the dead, but fight like hell for the living." And it is right to be concerned with the way that sentimentalizing the past can keep us from engagement with the process of changing the present.

But some suggest that militancy can also function as denial, directing our attention to external sources of violence, blinding us to its internal sites of eruption (Crimp, 1990b). It is easier to see the destruction caused by the hostile legislator, uncaring medical establishment, and apathetic government bureaucracy than to know the violence of our own intrapsychic conflicts. Indeed, mourning itself may be construed as a primary act of violence, a protest against his absence, the void left by death. Mourning begins in speechlessness, the unutterable, unimaginable dissolution of meaning, and ends in the recovery of voice as we locate the words through which we can reinsert ourselves into life. Language is all that remains to us, the only means to represent the absence, to speak to the absence, and in so doing to reconstitute the self. Mourning, then, is work through which we restart meaning, finding our way back into language and into the human community.

Crimp urges us to examine the harm we do ourselves, the care we deny our damaged psyches and bodies, when we do not acknowledge and live through our losses. This is not to minimize the difficulties of mourning when individual losses are compounded by the threat HIV may pose to our own lives or the guilt over survival we experience when faced with a multiplicity of deaths. Crimp is only too aware of the melancholy touched off in a community when there is a rupture of an entire way of life. But he does insist on the necessity of mourning for repairing that which has been broken, for making ourselves whole, for restoring meaning. Militancy cannot be equated with mourning, nor should mourning be construed as capitulation. Rather, we must find room for both militancy and mourning in our lives, grounding our personal experiences of loss on a foundation of public hope for recovery. Individual sorrows modulate our collective defiance; collective defiance enables us to imagine the future.

But this reading of my text in terms of recent gay history is only one out of a world of possibilities. Presenting "standing for Michael" as part of a longer paper to a gay/lesbian studies colloquium, I am moved by the question of a young student sitting in the first row. After a long, awkward silence seeming to signal an end to discussion, he hesitantly asks if I go to synagogue with my father now. I am taken aback. No, I do not go to synagogue with my father now, do not have the desire to go; but asked to consider what it would be like, know the possibility is fast fading from view. What is behind the question? Is the student seeking some form of closure not provided by the story, a tidy resolution that would suggest that my father and I had come full circle? To paraphrase Virginia Woolf, is he beginning to think through his own father, to assess a transitional moment in their relationship? Identifying closely with my father apparently allows others to identify the father in me. No theoretical interrogation of the text, this student's query goes to the heart of my own narrative intentions.

In public mourning I announce my sexuality and at the same moment imagine myself as the loving child at his father's side. In this way I continue to write about passionate attachments, discovering that pain is embedded in the very meaning of the Latin *passio*, "to suffer." Perhaps I should not be surprised to find solace next to my father, in a religious context where it has been said that passion reflects the transfiguration of individual pain. Although the spiritual and erotic are not far apart in the writings of some religious mystics and ascetics, I have not often turned to the study of ancient texts in order to seek consolation. Like some gay men, I have come to understand the erotics of grief in quite another way (Bronski, 1988). Surrounded by continuous loss (when are we not in mourning?) and concern for the sick, sex has taken on new meaning as an arena in which to be safely vulnerable. The French have always referred to orgasm as "la petite morte." In sex we tease death, mimicking its final rattle while we expire in each others' arms. But now the residue of our lovemaking, the dull white droplets that remain on his chest before we ever so carefully remove them, is an unwelcome reminder that the rehearsal hall has all too frequently been transformed into the scene of the performance. Even as we lie on beds in which others have been nursed and, yes, died, we seek to break through the isolation of grief in moments of sexual affirmation. Gay activists have been eager to assert that being gay is not just about what we do in the bedroom, but they have been slow to add that what we do there may be the only thing that enables us to survive.

I came to the gay studies colloquium thinking about issues of community and voice, politics and identity. My student-listener teaches me something quite different about fathers and sons. And in so doing, he asks me to consider how the more familiar role of teaching informs the less familiar role of telling. In a brief but illuminating essay, Moger (1982) reassuringly suggests that curriculum and story have similar structures, each proceeding through the stimulation of desire. The author and teacher seduce the reader/student into wanting to know, promising to deliver the certainty that would itself terminate desire. Drawn to the classroom or book in search of truth and beauty, we find frustration and ambiguity. Our interest in the story is maintained through its mystery, the complex motivations of the hero, the unexpected turn of plot, the indecipherable outcomes of the actions. The author stimulates and provokes, calling forth more questions than answers, functioning like the good teacher by giving and withholding, promising and postponing, titillating and calming. Although piqued by the suggestion that we can achieve certain knowledge of the storied world, desire only arises in the space between the known and the unknown. It is about the search not the prize, the pursuer not the pursued, the possibility of going to the synagogue with our fathers now or ever.

Pedagogy, too, works best when it concerns itself with the evocation of desire rather than the possession of knowledge. Explanation leads to fulfillment. Satisfying the appetite, it kills desire. So we want our students to grasp the questions that inform their search for meaning, questions that tell more about the desiring self than the object of our desire. The multiple meanings of the curriculum reside within us, not in the text. The world makes sense because we each build an interpretive matrix to insure its meaningfulness, not because there is a predetermined order in things themselves. Knowledge as an expression of desire is self-referential, called into being by the problematic, not the given, the question not the answer, the ambiguous not the certain.

THE FUNCTION OF NARRATIVE KNOWING

The gay synagogue is as much a challenge to the official story of Jewish identity as an attempt to become a part of it. There is both assimilation and accommodation, normalization and transformation of the traditional narrative of our lives. Bruner (1990) writes that narrative is the primary mode through which we make the unique, the experience lying outside of the cannon, comprehensible to ourselves and to others. Through the sharing of story we not only recognize difference, we also make it congruent with the prevailing world view. Narrative brings stability to our social life by accommodating and explaining the unusual, voiding its destabilizing potential. Bruner illustrates his argument with examples of the power of the noncanonical to provoke narrative telling in young children. Young children begin to use narrative only as they are ready to mark the unusual and leave the usual unmarked.

Children are not the only ones who mark the unusual. Grounded in the sociology of knowledge and relying on Schutz's social phenomenology, Berger and Luckmann (1967) describe how various social elites, including scientists, religious leaders, and politicians, explain the exception, normalizing the strange in order to preserve the status quo. They also examine how the recipe knowledge embedded in everyday language assures uninterrupted social functioning and maintains group solidarity:

> Language provides the means for objectifying new experiences, allowing their incorporation into the already existing stock of knowledge, and it is the most important means by which the objectivated and objectified sedimentations are transmitted in the tradition of the collectivity in question. (p. 68)

Berger and Luckmann suggest that it is our language structures that determine what we know and what we see. Bruner (1990), focusing on the individual child within the family, asserts that social meaning precedes and makes possible linguistic expression. The acquisition of language reflects our mastery of the folk psychology ordering our social worlds. This folk psychology, our taken-for-granted assumptions about human intentions and behavior, is organized narratively, not conceptually, placing our storytelling rather than our propositional thinking at the center of the socialization processes. Language learning is motivated less by a need to construct logical explanations than by a desire to grasp social meanings. We want to assure our place in the world of others and reassure ourselves that the others will be there when we need them.

Bruner's understanding of language learning in the service of narrative development helps me to locate the expression of grief, our stories of loss, in the context of community, a fundamental process of resocialization. At the same time, I can not help but recognize the regulative function of his telling as well as of my own. In his story there is no place for difference, no speaker other than the unsexed child seeking a role in the family drama. He is the objective scientist recording this accomplishment in a value-free language. The noncanonical has no substance, does not reflect powerful political realities or inequitable distributions of economic resources. It is the process of learning per se, not *what* we learn, that holds Bruner's attention. But I am interested in how differences survive and thrive as well as how we are socialized to the status quo. What sense can we make of a folk psychology that defines us as inferior because of our gender, race, ethnicity, or sexual orientation? What difference does difference make? What words can tell of a love that dares not speak its name?

As a gay reader, I know the critical role that narrative can play in the formation of identity. Growing up with an absence of positive role models and of a socially sanctioned community of reference, I frantically searched for the written words that would describe my plight. Books and media, rather than family and neighbors, are frequently the only way in which gay people see their lives and longings reflected. Without local images, often forbidden to create our own texts, we have depended on the representations of others to fill the gap between "finding" our gay identity, the first recognition of difference, and "developing" an identity through which we integrate this difference into a fully realized life. Some gay people first identify their sexual orientation in literary representations, while for others novels, poetry, scientific studies, and media portrayals are critical to defining the possibilities it holds (Bergman, 1991). To be sure, these narratives, from the scientific discourses of Krafft-Ebing, Havelock Ellis, and Edmond Burgler to the literary fictions of Oscar Wilde, André Gide, and Marcel Proust, have sent a complex message about the meaning of sexual difference, about the necessity of concealment and fear of revelation. Historically, gay writers became masters in coding and decoding, uniquely attuned to what texts can and cannot do. In the absence of explicit statement, a concern with form and style, a facility with parody and the creation of camp, was nurtured as the very means to represent the sense of gay selfhood.

With the Stonewall revolution and the establishment of new gay and lesbian markets, the quantity and quality of representation has dramatically changed. The spread of HIV/AIDS has further contributed to the production of technical, social science, and fiction writing by gay people. Most importantly, writing has become an act of cultural and political urgency through which the dishonest fiction of the closet might be replaced with the honest fiction of an identity in formation. Robert Glück (1991) comments:

> A new self, like a new aesthetic form, like any new approach to art, is something of a scandal. . . . New forms, new content, demand a new way of being, of representing your own life, just as new vocabulary calls forth its meanings in your life. It is at this starting point that an art movement, or a political movement, has moral life. The appearance of a gay self in fiction can rarely be naive—even now. It will be tested and taken as a demand as much as a description.

Glück is part of a loosely defined school—including Bruce Boone, Kevin Killian, and Dennis Cooper—who write the "New Narrative." There are many other groups of writers *within* the community giving voice to multiple versions of the gay self, from the African-American men who make up the collective Other Countries to the women who write for numerous small publishers such as Naiad Press and Kitchen Table: Women of Color Press. This fiction emerges from and is addressed to the very community that makes scandal possible. That is, in the past classic and closeted gay writers defined the scandal of homosexuality, the transgressions and taboos of the outsider, in terms of the nontransgressive community, consolidating and normalizing its power over us. In contrast, much of contemporary writing "appeals to its own community, operates within the social logic of scandal, thriving on the other side of the heterosexual aversion" (E. Jackson, 1991, p. 114). Narrative not only socializes the outsider into the values and norms of the larger community, the process described by Bruner and by Berger and Luckmann, it also functions within communities to define new identities and ethical standards of behavior.

LANGUAGE AS GENDERED EXPERIENCE

The significance of representation in the formation of gay identity and the manner in which these representations have changed underline the power and the politics of the text, an understanding of which begins with a gendered analysis of language. Feminists have long debated the transformative possibilities of language, only too aware of the distances between language and experience, one community of speakers and another (Martusewicz, 1992; Nye, 1987). Feminists in education assert that the relationship between language and knowledge, knower and known, child and the curriculum is always mediated by gender. Pagano (1990) explores the pedagogical ramifications of the different ways that males and females come into language. If, as psychoanalytic theory claims, language is the infant's first attempt to resist the absence of the primary caregiver, to substitute the symbolic for the actual, to give voice to desire, then males and females will have differing relations to that which they would represent. When raised by women, boys must find images for one who is totally other and girls must seek to call forth one whom they resemble. Both try to compensate for their exile from the maternal body, but from its beginnings knowledge of the other for boys is about difference and distinction whereas for girls it is about affiliation and similarity.

In Lacan's version of these developments, language learning is linked to structuring the ego and obscures all prior knowledge of the caring body. Identity and symbolic knowledge result from separation, loss, and unfulfilled desires. Language is about substitution for the female; women are its objects but never its subjects. Kristeva (1980), also looking through the lens of French psychoanalytic thought, maintains that signification has two distinct aspects. The symbolic, the dominant and assumed mode of communication, is constituted by sign and syntax and the laws of social representation that shape our public identities. The semiotic is the presymbolic mode of knowing that derives its energy from the fetus's experience in the womb and the infant's attachment to the mother. Rarely audible, the semiotic may be heard in the child's uncensored nonsense or the mad person's incoherent ramblings. Semiotic forms of meaning are dependent on the maternal body and have potential for challenging the paternal function of the symbolic.

In contrast to American object relations theorists, who suggest that changes in our asymmetrical child-care arrangements might alter our gendered identities (Chodorow, 1978), Kristeva appears to be less sanguine about the possibility of change. There is an inevitability about psychic distortions and language confusions initiated during the mirror stage of development when, as she writes, "The symbolic destiny of the speaking animal . . . *seals off* . . . that archaic basis and the special jouissance it procures in being transferred to the symbolic" (1980, p. 241, emphasis in original). This fatalism is driven by the perceived power of the unconscious and the splitting that occurs with the intervention of the symbolic order. The patriarchal nature of the symbolic would appear to place the female at a disadvantage that is not ameliorated by her closeness to the semiotic. Yet for some, it is this very fatalism, the normalization of failure, that constitutes the heuristic power of psycho-analytic theory. Feminism and psychoanalysis share an understanding that there is a resistance to identity at the heart of psychic life, and it is this resistance that can best be marshaled in the service of change.

> What distinguishes psychoanalysis from sociological accounts of gender (hence for me the fundamental impasse of Nancy Chodorow's work) is that whereas for the latter, the internalization of norms is assumed roughly to work, the basic premise and indeed the starting point of psychoanalysis is that it does not. The unconscious constantly reveals the "failure" of identity. Because there is no continuity of psychic life, so there is no stability of sexual identity, no position for women (or for men) which is ever simply achieved. Nor does psychoanalysis see such "failure" as a special-case inability or an individual deviancy from the norm. "Failure" is not a moment to be regretted in a process of adaptation, or development into normality, which ideally takes its course. . . . Instead "failure" is something endlessly repeated and relived moment by moment throughout our individual histories. (J. Rose, 1983, p. 9)

As an educator, Pagano pursues the elusive nature of female identity through the novels of the Brontës and Virginia Woolf, Doris Lessing, and May Sarton. These are voices that stay close to the literal, to the maternal body, and to the material world. They depict the opposing, conflictual forces in women's lives at the same time as they open possibilities for resymbolizing our stories as students and teachers. That these narratives are so powerful attests to the dominance of androcentric language in our culture and, as Grumet (1988) suggests, to the patriarchal project that masks the inferential nature of paternity. Language has become a tool to assert difference and certainty and to exclude those for whom connection and ambiguity are part of their first experience. The language we teach, the curriculum to which we subscribe, does not allow for representations of experience in which affiliation is given equal value to differentiation. Grumet decries the way that female teachers have served a curriculum that delivers the child to the father's world. She describes the paradoxical role of the female teacher who must deny her lived reality in order to survive in an educational system that valorizes the figurative over the literal, the mind over the body, the simple over the complex. I would add here my concern for the ways in which we all assist in giving our children up to a heterosexist world that precludes a fuller exploration of human sexuality.

Grumet and Pagano do more than point to the limitations of the curricular language currently in place. They also suggest the elements of a new language that would recognize the dilemma of the female teacher caught between the sterile language of male academics and the less valued but equally truthful poetics of the female body. Grumet argues that woman can initiate a new and powerful dialectic between the domestic world of nurturance and reproduction and the public space of formal education. Pagano, too, insists that household language and the language of the symposium can become complementary aspects of the pedagogical discourse. Although women participate in the symbolic order that defines them as other, they can resist co-option into the patriarchal project by remaining close to the literal and imaginary. The role of the feminist intellectual, whether male or female, is not limited to disrupting the discourse of the patriarchy. Rather the feminist is one who draws strength from the pregrammatical, pre-Oedipal world of the text itself even as he or she acknowledges the value of the symbolic and conceptual. The intent is to avoid equating the female with a subjective, sentimentalized male version of the feminine without obliterating the masculine position. Differences in gendered experience are neither denied nor romanticized but fully articulated, so that they might become the basis for authentic conversation. Without distinction there is no possibility of connection.

In teaching young adults, I have been struck by how easily feminist analyses of education may be misinterpreted by both male and female students. Confusing the feminist scholars' descriptions of what is with their own passionate beliefs in what ought to be, my students blame the messengers for the message. New teachers, with heightened concerns for agency and authority, read history as destiny and reject the former in the hope of controlling the latter. They are ready to see individual potential in their most difficult students but not their own role in framing the geography in which this potential is mapped. Thus they are able to believe in their own efficacy while at the same time maintaining a commitment to universal, transhistorical ideas about childhood that absolve them of responsibility for its construction. The classic early childhood tension between nurture and nature spills over into discussions of essentialist and constructivist positions with regard to gender and sexual orientation.

But political expediency suggests the need for a middle ground between a determinist essentialism that fixes identity in biology and a social constructivism that relativizes knowing, hampering engagement in the real struggle to interrupt existing power alignments. Constructivist and essentialist positions may be more complimentary than contradictory, each speaking to different audiences and serving distinctive purposes (Bergman, 1991). For example, Code (1991) consistently questions essentialists who alternatively present women as possessing increased capacities for gentleness, goodness, nurturance, and sensitivity and as less intelligent, independent, objective, rational, and competent than men. At the same time, she recognizes the historical significance of essentialism in establishing the legitimacy of the feminist voice and accepts the essentialist/constructivist tension as part of the terrain of feminist thought that both recommends and resists appeals to absolute differences. But she herself disavows the idea of discrete feminine and masculine realities, incommensurable languages, because it can blind us to the discursive construction of meanings within the existing structures of power and dominance. Instead she adopts Alcoff's (1988) concept of positionality, identity construed as "relative to a constantly shifting context, to a situation that includes a network of elements involving others, the objective economic conditions, cultural and political institutions and ideologies" (p. 418). Subjectivity is relational, read in terms of multiple positions— not a single, unified, androcentric norm.

JOINING FEMINIST CONVERSATIONS

Joining feminist conversations is never easy. For a man it may be especially difficult. Can he ever be inside a feminist conversation, or is he, by definition, always a marginal participant? Stephen Heath (1987) asserts that "men's relation to feminism is an impossible one" (p. 1). Women are the subjects of feminism, its initiators, makers, and force. Men are the objects of feminism, part of the problem, carriers of the patriarchal power system in need of transformation. Although a feminist perspective is not a given of a woman's experience but one that is learned, when men attempt to become a subject in feminism they practice a form of colonization through which they appropriate difference in the service of their own hegemony. Despite our best intentions at understanding, the existential realities of difference must be respected. Irigaray (1984) summarizes, "I will never be in a man's place, a man will never be in mine. Whatever the possible identifications, one will never exactly occupy the place of the other—they are irreducible the one to the other" (p. 19).

Heath suggests that feminism, living with difference rather than denying or resolving it, makes men feel unsafe and unsettled because it requires the undoing of given identities. Hence men's reactions to feminism, ranging from violent rejection to sympathetic patronizing. Others, seeking to mitigate anxiety and reestablish the security of the known, try to get close to the source of discomfort, affirming Roland Barthes' insight that "you study what you desire or what you fear" (quoted in Heath, 1987, p. 6). Heath urges men in feminism to adopt an attitude of admiration, defined by the qualities of reverence and esteem that follow upon the recognition of difference. Admiration motivates us to learn to write and act in response to feminism so as to be neither antifeminist nor supportive of old, oppressive structures.

I join feminist conversations as a man working in a field where women predominate. It is not difficult for me to acknowledge the many ways I have benefited from the dominant androcentric discourse. Illich (1979) points out that in its origins, education of the young was a purely feminine practice, quite different from teaching:

> *Educatio prolis* is a term that in Latin grammar calls for a female subject. It designates the feeding and nurturing in which mothers engage, be they bitch, sow or woman. Among humans only women educate. And they educate only infants, which etymologically means those who are yet without speech. To educate has etymologically nothing to do with "drawing out" as pedagogical folklore would have it. Pestalozzi should have heeded Cicero: *educit obstetrix— educat nutrix*: the midwife draws—the nurse nurtures. Men do neither in Latin. They engage in *docentia* (teaching) and *instructio* (instruction). (p. 69)

In Western society it was only with the creation of a taught mother tongue, during the sixteenth century, that education became institutionalized, a male prerogative. Through this devaluation of the vernacular, politicians sought to limit access to the cultural capital that could insure material success and intensify the centralized power of the state. Language, like religion, came to be mediated by a male bureaucracy. The commodification of language and the resulting confusion between education and instruction allowed the school to become a primary site for the inculcation of a gendered power structure.

What Illich (1979) misses in his historical account of the relationship between language and capitalism is that it is women who most frequently bring children into language, who possess a primal verbal (biological) fertility that men cannot seem to forgive (Schleifer, 1990). The institutionalization of language instruction can be read as central to the psychological movement through which men sought to heal this linguistic wound, by transforming ordinary language into the subject of a hermetic discourse. Thus distanced and uncontaminated by the vernacular, the male speaker turns the *materna lingua* into a new *patrius sermo*. Privileged to see beyond the ordinary surface of language, he seeks to disclose a lost but pure patronymic, patriarchal speech. Language becomes a means to secure control over the material economy of goods and services as well as to stabilize an internal economy threatened by female productive/reproductive capacities.

Educational languages have long celebrated technical, empirical forms of knowledge that lead us to believe we can achieve mastery over the environments in which we live and work. In the past, researchers, mostly males, have found the language of teachers, mostly females, vague, lacking in specificity, and unscientific. For example, Lortie (1975) was disappointed because an analysis of interviews with teachers showed "a low proportion of words which are not commonly used; since the interview dealt with teaching, it should have elicited a technical vocabulary" (p. 73). Philip Jackson (1968) further criticized teachers for their "tendency to rely on spontaneous expressions of interest and enthusiasm of their students rather than on scientific or objective measures" and for their "conceptual simplicity" (p. 144). Dreeben (1970) called for the development of a more highly defined "technology" of teaching as the only means of increasing the level of professionalism.

Contemporary research on teacher thinking addresses this denigrating view of the teacher. There is also a minority tradition, predating a specifically gendered critique of language, that has long been skeptical of the technical ideal. Huebner (1975a) described five areas of valuing—technical, political, scientific, aesthetic, and ethical. He argued that schools have focused on the first three forms of valuing, that the language of school people is concerned only with control and certainty. Educators have failed to develop a language that would allow them to move into the ethical and aesthetic realms of experience. Denton (1970) advocated the creation of language that would permit educators to talk of education as a first-person experience, concerned with individuals rather than institutions. The language of ordinary experience, in opposition to "steno" (institutional) language, attempts to capture the all-at-onceness of lived realities. Habermas (1968) also distinguishes between pure language—the language of empirical, scientific investigation—and ordinary language, the everyday language through which people strive to communicate with one another. Too often, contemporary educators try to substitute the former for the latter, belying the complexity of pedagogical tasks.

These critics suggest that curricular languages play a limiting function in schools, denying the lived experience of teachers and students and reinforcing the omnipresent themes of modern life—control, conformity, efficiency, and speed. In contrast, they believe that not all experience can be categorized, explained in terms of cause and effect, and evaluated with true/false criteria. Language can be a tool to liberate and open possibility, to describe the multiplicity of experience, to give space to the personal without equating it with the irrational, to accept doubt and uncertainty as legitimate forms of knowing.

Giving Up Heterosexuality

To liberate, to open possibilities for men in feminism, for men in education, inevitably means an extended examination of difference as it is written in various forms of psychoanalytic theory. Barthes (1982) assures us of the necessity of such a passage: "The monument of psychanalysis must be traversed—not bypassed—like the fine thoroughfares of a very large city, across which we can play, dream etc.: a fiction" (p. 412). Stephen Heath's (1987) own journey leads to a surprising conclusion:

We should take seriously at last the "hetero" in heterosexuality, which means the heterogeneity in us, on us, through us, and also take seriously the "sexuality," which means, I think, giving up, precisely, heterosexuality, that oppressive representation of the sexual as act, complementarity, two sexes, coupling. (p. 22)

Give up heterosexuality! My heart says "yes" but my head says this is not about embracing homosexuality but about eschewing the binary thinking that distances us from one another and from our own desires. The suggestion of giving up heterosexuality comes closest to asking what it means to be a gay man in feminism. For in addition to the early childhood context, I join feminist conversations as a participant in the struggles between gay men and lesbian feminists.

In the 1950s and 1960s, many gay men and lesbians seemed blissfully ignorant of each other's existence; the growing self-consciousness of the 1970s ushered in a period of open hostility over issues of intergenerational sex, "fringe" sexualities, and the place of feminist concerns in the movement. This was a time when some men tried to terminate popular stereotypes of gays as gender inverts by projecting a "hypernormal" image, suggesting that we were just like everyone else except for what we did in bed. Unfortunately, this attempt to isolate sexuality from issues of gender distracted many from the new feminist dialogues. It was also undercut by the gender play of a gay culture populated with supermasculine clones, drag queens, butch/femme lesbians, and s/m practitioners of both sexes. Only in the last decade, with the critical role that lesbian activists and service providers have played in responding to the AIDS crisis, and with the more open discussion among lesbians about the spectrum of their own sexuality, have men and woman begun to work together in more productive ways.

In the 1990s gay men and lesbians co-habit a world alongside their queer siblings. These younger brothers and sisters have abandoned the vocabulary of gay rights, adopted in the first flourish of the sexual liberation movement to claim a newly discovered political status and to escape from the medical diagnosis of homosexuality. They have tried to construct a more militant and equalitarian movement with greater visibility for lesbians, bisexuals, and transgendered people. But as a community defined from the outside by the gender of our object choices, we can still be confused and embarrassed by individuals for whom achieving the appearance, identity, and/or biology of the opposite sex may be of greater interest than the sex of their partners. Others may make us uncomfortable because they choose to explore their female or earth-associated characteristics in radical faerie circles, or to parody stereotypical notions of gender by stridently mixing both male and female associated articles of clothing, a practice called "gender fuck."

Gay artists and writers have also played an important role in decon-structing gender as we know it (E. Jackson, 1991). They depict nonphallic masculinities in which the traditional erotics of penetration have been re-placed by multiple sites of pleasure, destabilizing the fixity of dominant and submissive roles that has characterized heterosexual relations in the patriar-chal mode. Such explorations grow out of our experiences as gay men and may be seen as part of a subtle shift in gender discourses away from a concern with the im/possibility of men in feminism and toward a reconceptualizing of masculinity in a nonpatriarchal way (Klein-Davis, 1993). Although this work on male identity (Boone & Cadden, 1990; Silverman, 1992) is fraught with the dangers of recolonizing the geography secured by feminism and has too seldom combined a Foucaultian sociopolitical analysis with an in-depth psychoanalytic perspective, it is essential to re-visioning stereotypical gender identities.

While these challenges to traditional gender categories flourish, and theoretical debates between gay men and feminists, lesbian and otherwise, persist (Owens, 1987), they occur in a space that seems far removed from the realities of life in young children's classrooms. And I remain uneasy when I join feminist conversations as a gay speaker, perhaps because my concerns are with young children and because questions of sexuality, more so than gender, make everyone uneasy. I would argue that we all too easily conflate sexuality and gender rather than honoring them as parallel axes of analysis, distinct yet inextricably linked. Gayle Rubin (1984) clarifies the strengths and limits of feminism:

> I want to challenge the assumption that feminism is or should be the privileged site of a theory of sexuality. Feminism is the theory of gender oppression. . . . Gender affects the operation of the sexual system, and the sexual system has had gender-specific manifestations. But although sex and gender are related, they are not the same thing. (p. 307)

Is it possible to teach as a feminist and a gay man? What does it mean to give up heterosexuality in the classroom? James King (1993) writes about his discomforts, embarrassments, successes/failures in becoming a feminist teacher. As the leader of a graduate seminar in education, he proposed using an oral history project to stimulate critical reflection on gender. Although he was successful at building participatory structures within the seminar, King's students refused to engage in a more politically oriented dialogue about the lives of the women they had interviewed. He learned that the potential for critique, process examination, and deconstruction of the "naturalness" of the text is not necessarily realized in whole-language or other student-centered pedagogies.

King is not the first to comment on how these strategies produce a reinscription of stereotypical female subject positions (Gilbert, 1989). However, he reads his particular failure as reflecting a defensive use of feminist theory, the rift that develops with his students mirroring a rift within himself regarding sexual identity. That is, feminism is used as a substitute difference, as close as he can come to the difference he does not publicly name. As he develops a stronger gay identity, King eventually sees that gay/lesbian experiences might also serve as the basis of critical pedagogy. But his position in feminism is made more complex. As a gay man, he is not only an oppressor, framing the problem of an oppressed group, women teachers, but also a member of an oppressed group, with a problematic relationship to the category of "male gender" in our culture. While affirming his current commitment to feminism, he sounds the call for a discourse of queer pedagogy.

A QUEER PEDAGOGY

Increasingly, progressive thinkers have made heterosexuality uncertain, a phenomenon to be researched and understood rather than assumed or ignored. In recent work Chodorow (1992) subjects our taken-for-granted assumptions about heterosexuality to new scrutiny, believing that the origins and vicissitudes of "normal" heterosexual development have not been sufficiently described in the psychoanalytic literature that has given attention to the development of perversions and homosexualities. And Heath's call to give up heterosexuality echoes Adrienne Rich's (1980) earlier recommendation that "like motherhood, [heterosexuality] needs to be recognized and studied as a *political institution*" (p. 637).

Two complimentary streams of research seek to realize the promise of Rich's mandate. The first, constituted by feminist educators, describes the experiences of girls and women in schools and suggests alternative practices that would liberate both sexes from categorical assumptions about gender (Jipson, 1992; Noddings, 1992). The second, comprised of queer theorists, seeks to understand what it means for teachers to be explicit about their sexual identities in the classroom and how to integrate lesbian and gay subject matter into the curriculum (Cruikshank, 1982; Garber, 1994). The majority of work in both feminist and lesbian and gay studies focuses on high school and college teaching. Here it appears easier to expatiate heterosexist practices because the curriculum is explicit and the challenge of coming out somewhat less threatening. In classrooms with young children the curricular implications of lesbian and gay studies are less immediately obvious and coming out is more difficult, since young children are seen as directly at risk from adults assumed to be sexually predatory. However, I would argue that it is exactly in early childhood education that we can best see the connections among professional languages, gender stereotypes, the production of heterosexuality, and the incipient beginnings of a queer pedagogy.

Walkerdine (1990) studies how children, especially girls, are constituted as subjects in the child-centered discourse of contemporary English pedagogy. Through the assumption of a totalizing, omniscient gaze, the nurturant teacher helps to produce the fiction of a "natural" child developing freely within the safe confines of the early childhood classroom. With its roots in the Enlightenment tradition, the Piagetian perspective that informs this gaze enshrines the child as an active learner in constant pursuit of knowledge, eschewing work for play, open exploration for rule following or role modeling. The focus on reason over emotion, structures of knowledge over information or social meaning, mind over body supports the fiction of childhood innocence. The child's interests are in conquering the material world through the increasingly sophisticated use of intellect rather than in exploring the desires and intentions that structure our erotic life. Sexuality enters the classroom only at the interstices, to be suppressed and denied.

The discourse of child-centered learning embedded in our spaces and educational practices—room arrangements, materials, reporting mechanisms, evaluative tools—leaves female children in contradictory and conflicting positions. If "the child" learner is constructed as active, seeking mastery over the environment through the use of reason, then girls are consistently taught the value of passivity, skills of social negotiation, compromise, and repression of feelings. Although initial success in schools reflects socialization to following rules and maintaining social harmony, later academic failures are said to fulfill the prediction of objective studies showing women as less capable of the logicomathematical thinking valued in our culture. Using as an example a scene from a nursery school, in which a female teacher is unable to respond effectively to the active resistance displayed by a group of young boys, Walkerdine suggests how female teachers reinforce the image of feminine passivity. The contradictory position of the female teacher identified by Grumet (1988) is again confirmed. Walkerdine (1990) comments:

> It is the female teacher who is to *contain* this irrationality and to transform it into reason, where it can do no harm—a transformation which turns physical violence into the symbolic violence of mastery, the law. And in each case, the woman as container soaks up and contains the irrationality which she best understands. (p. 24)

The teacher of young children facilitates learning through her keen powers of observation and the scientific knowledge of child development that informs her vision. Her knowing is always in the service of the individual children she watches, but she is not a knower herself. That is, when early childhood educators define their work as the application of the science of child development, they *a priori* commit themselves to the idea of the developing child. This is an idea premised on the location of certain capacities within the individual and therefore within the domain of psychological knowing. Other capacities are assumed to be totally determined by material circumstances and therefore not amenable to pedagogical influence. The children we inscribe in our pedagogy are individuals with capacities that mature over and against the world into which they are born. Factors external to children may shape development and ultimately influence their educability but remain outside of the teacher's control. What the teacher can do is monitor the child's "natural" development. We can look for indicators of the understandings and concepts that underlie the acquisition of knowledge. Structuralism leaves the educator an observer of the child's growth through predetermined stages. The goal of education is not the transfer of information to groups of children or promotion of social transformation but the fostering of individual development. Knowledge becomes development, development the aim of education.

Despite the ever-growing body of child development knowledge, our surveillance of children is never complete. Within the dominant language of a natural, universal, and gender-neutral childhood, doubt and resistance persist. We attempt to regulate sexuality and desire, the reproduction of heterosexual norms, through covert communications about appropriate feminine and masculine behaviors and aptitudes and through the overt products of popular culture. For example, Walkerdine examines how young girls are prepared for entering into heterosexual practices, and more specifically the ideology of romantic love, through comics targeted for their consumption. She argues that girls do not passively identify with the female role models offered but rather struggle to resolve conflicts and contradictions in their own social worlds through the adaptation of formulaic responses. Finding the knight in shining armor appears as the solution to an otherwise unmanageable set of desires and problems.

Walkerdine does not directly address same-sex desire but by deconstructing the inculcation of heterosexual norms, she problematizes sexual identity altogether, portraying heterosexuality as a shaky and partial achievement at best. She reminds us, too, that silence in classrooms is often about gender; that gender ideals are equated with heterosexuality; and that heterosexual norms in our culture assume an active, knowing subject who is male and a passive, facilitative object who is female. Walkerdine links these fictions of childhood to the child-centered pedagogical discourse of early educators, which appears to privilege active over passive, child over teacher, and male over female. In opening for our consideration questions of desire among children and between children and adults, she suggests a new way of understanding the effects of schooling and challenges the traditional, masculinist critique of mass education based on reproduction theory. For in their discussions of class, hegemony, and ideology, male scholars do not address the reproduction of patriarchal values in schools and the manner in which these are presented as "genderless" (Khayatt, 1992). Thus schools not only teach us how to be good workers but also how to be good men and women and to engage in normative sexual practices.

In our culture, good workers are those who abide by a gendered division of labor. Men do not enter women's fields and women do not engage in men's work without raising suspicions about their motives. Men, both gay and straight, avoid early childhood education because of the shadow it casts on their sexual identities (J. R. King, 1994). A queer pedagogy encourages gay and lesbian teachers to come out, erasing the threat of disclosure and accusation that makes the primary classroom inhospitable to all men. The participation of more men in early childhood education brings the promise of improved salaries by transforming "woman's work," with its artificially low wages, into a gender-neutral field.

From the perspective of gay teachers, however, coming out is less about these issues of policy than about the quality of daily teaching. Drawing on feminist definitions of primary teaching as caring, as integrating curricular subjects and interpersonal relationships (Nais, 1989; Noddings, 1992), James King (1994) argues that teachers, like children, must have the freedom to be totally present in the classroom. Queer pedagogy embraces the ability of men to practice the connected knowing, the nonhierarchical relationships that are associated with women in Western society.

> Being there for children means freedom to be there as a whole person. How we construct ourselves as persons for our students is a purposeful act. Teachers who are comfortable with who they are, are able to "be there." Those who are preoccupied with life issues outside the classroom are less able to center on children and their needs. (J. R. King, 1994, p. 6)

A queer pedagogy not only allows students to learn about a broader range of relationships, it also means they learn from teachers who model an authentic presentation of self, teachers who bring all of themselves to the classroom. Becoming queer subjects, lesbian and gay teachers are more likely to place queer subjects on the agenda of early learning, including discussions of discrimination, gay families, human sexuality, and HIV/AIDS (Chapman, 1992; Wickens, 1993). Thus homophobia and heterosexist stereotypes are confronted through transforming the curriculum, the quality of pedagogical relationships, and the composition of the work force itself.

Despite these extensive claims, I would suggest that a queer pedagogy is neither so radical nor so far away as it might at first appear. It begins with our willingness to read and write from responsibly identified positions, a lesson learned from feminists. Queer pedagogy is close to feminist pedagogy but does not involve its direct appropriation. Rather, we must read feminist theories and practices in a double register, appreciating them within their own contexts and engaging dialogically with them to stimulate thinking about our own lives. Queer pedagogy draws on the long history of gay/lesbian sociopolitical analysis, grounds its epistemological assumptions in the experience of the closet and the unique importance of representation to those who do not grow up with role models or mentors. It is as relevant to heterosexuals as to homosexuals, for as Paula Giddings (1984) says, referring to the ignorance of most white Americans about the history of African-Americans in the United States, "Whoever does not know *our* history, does not know their *own*."

CHAPTER 7

How Do We Know? And Other Questions of the Closet

It is perfectly monstrous the way people go about, nowadays, saying things against one behind one's back that are absolutely and entirely true.

Oscar Wilde, *A Woman of No Importance*

I once thought I knew a lot about the closet. Now, I am not so sure. Growing up in New York during the 1950s, I was certain that my first explorations of the city's gay neighborhoods were to be kept hidden from family and friends at all costs. Like the young hero of *Remembrances of Things Past*, I had two separate walks that were equally enticing but corresponded to entirely different moods. The first, most often a daytime excursion, took me to Greenwich Village. Here I was attracted by the many outward indications of political and social rebellion, while secretly seeking signs of sexual resistance. The second walk was a more purposeful, carefully mapped nighttime tour of Third Avenue, during which I tried to identify with middle-class and middle-aged homosexual men, while erotically drawn to the young hustlers who plied their trade on the streets. I doubt either the hustlers or their tricks had difficulty reading the excruciating ambivalence that informed my movements. But what of the others on the street? Does it matter?

These walks tell of my adolescent drive to know other homosexuals and to be known by them. They also tell of my need to keep this search secret. Although lived with a sense of isolation and some desperation, my history resonates with the history of urban gay life; with Oscar Wilde's London, Walt Whitman's Brooklyn, and Arthur Rimbaud's Paris. It is a history through which we have learned to encode personal desire in a language that can be spoken in public spaces and to decode the messages sent to us by others. We are socialized into a community that has always conducted its private affairs

162

in front of/behind others. I spoke the language of the closet long before it was labeled or became academically fashionable.

With time and the growth of the gay liberation movement, I was increasingly comfortable with more emphatic announcements of sexual identity than were viable in the era prior to the Stonewall riots. Of course the possibilities for "passing" at age 14 or 15 have a way of disappearing at 30 or 40. Or perhaps they just require a vigilance I was no longer prepared to adopt. However, as a gay man working with young children, the intrusiveness characterizing many educational institutions posed a particularly strong challenge to my new identity. How can I forget the kindly, well-intentioned teacher who drew me aside that first year of teaching to inform me that I had been seen at lunch locked in intimate conversation with my friend Lou, an obviously effeminate high school English teacher. My would-be mentor suggested the need to be more circumspect in my public associations if I intended to continue working in the kindergarten.

Gossip serves a critical function in communities, defining the norms and informing us when they have been transgressed. I do not know if any parents had also seen me talking with Lou, but I soon came to believe that if they allowed themselves to think about my life outside the classroom, they, too, would know the unspeakable truth of my gayness. So I worked hard to keep the truth silent. We all felt safer that way.

However, I soon began to realize that the inevitable tension of private voices in public spaces is one that permeates the early childhood discourse. The first school experience is typically one in which parents and children begin to make regular and systematic decisions about what to reveal and conceal from the professional caregiver. This is also a time when professionals make critical judgments about a child's family and their own needs for information about it. Though recently receiving considerable attention, the sexual orientation of teacher, parent, or child is only one of many identity issues negotiated in the school context. For example, a proliferation of curricula addressing issues such as substance use, child abuse, and HIV/AIDS has created new opportunities for students to offer information that may place them and their families at risk for various kinds of social service interventions. Teachers find themselves in a quandary as they confront the limits of governmental interventions and the ethical issues raised by breaches in confidentiality.

It is not my intention to assess the specific policy implications of such curricula, but rather to underline the growing pressures schools place on children, parents, and teachers to tell or not to tell the truth of their lives. For everyone schools are places that invite exposure, provoke the desire to hide, and stimulate the development of differentiated social personae. They are complex institutions through which we want to know, want to be known, seek not to be known, by a plethora of helping professionals.

In this chapter I explore the fine line between knowing and not knowing that makes the closet a central theme, if not *the* central theme, of gay life. I also suggest that the closet tells us about more than just gay and lesbian lives. It can be an essential metaphor for understanding the way that classrooms and schools function in our culture. Fuss (1991b) summarizes the concerns that are basic to gay and lesbian studies and by extension to anyone concerned with social identity:

> Questions of epistemology ("how do we know?") enjoy a privileged status in theorizations of gay and lesbian identity. How does one know when one is on the inside and when one is not? How does one know when and if one is out of the closet? How, indeed, does one know if one is gay? (p. 6)

SOL, JIMMY, AND MY PARENTS

Indeed, how does anyone know anything about identity? How do we manage *not* to know about another's identity? According to Sedgwick (1990), the closet is made of glass, a spectacle which everyone can view as well as a vantage point from which its inhabitants can view others. Our secrets are always open secrets, secrets whose knowledge is mutually silenced by agreeing "to conceal the knowledge of the knowledge" (D. A. Miller, 1988, p. 206). In her autobiography, Audre Lorde (1982) writes about growing up in New York during the 1950s and moving among multiple identities—African-American, lesbian, student, poet—each with its own defined boundaries. In the African-American community and among straight women, her lesbianism was unacceptable, while the lesbian community refused to acknowledge her racial identity. She is especially well positioned to know about open secrets and tells the following story about two coffee shop owners whom she saw every day for eight years on her way to work or school and with whom she developed the closeness bred of such routines.

> On the last day before I finally moved away from the Lower East Side after I got my master's degree from library school, I went in for my last english muffin and coffee and to say goodbye to Sol and Jimmy in some unemotional and acceptable-to-me way. I told them both I'd miss them and the old neighborhood, and they said they were sorry and why did I have to go? I told them I had to work out of the city, because I had a fellowship for Negro students. Sol raised his eyebrows in utter amazement, and said, "Oh? I didn't know you was cullud!"
>
>   I went around telling that story for a while, although a lot of my friends couldn't see why I thought it was funny. But this is all about how very difficult it is at times for people to see who or what they are looking at, particularly when they don't want to. (p. 183)

Recent attempts to rewrite American military policy highlight the on-going nature of open secrets in American life. Prior to these revisions, most knew about gays and lesbians in the military but few talked about it. With the legal pressure brought to bear by gay people discharged from the ser-vices, everyone now acknowledges their existence, even their superior per-formance records, although many still resist public recognition of this real-ity. Thus policies such as "don't ask, don't tell, don't pursue" not only institutionalize homophobia but also codify history as policy by returning to the time when we all agreed not to see. But once gays are in view, the closet door slightly ajar, we cannot seem to close it properly, despite the best efforts of all branches of government.

Some argue that homosexuality is not like a readily observable but so-cially unmentionable physical characteristic, a "secret that always gives it-self away" (Foucault, 1978, p. 43). To insist on the closet as an open secret is to undercut the idea of the closet altogether, denying the reality of hidden secrets. It is probably true that some children may be unaware of gay fami-lies, as suggested by opponents of the Rainbow Curriculum in New York City, just as some adults may not have recognized that I was a gay teacher. But did Sol and Jimmy not see the color of Audre Lorde's skin? Did my own parents not know I was gay? They ask why I have chosen this particular Friday night dinner to announce my homosexuality. Implicit in their emphasis on the word *this* is the understanding that they have known about my sexual orientation for many years, could not help but have known, had unknow-ingly introduced me to my first lover at age 15 and witnessed that relation-ship coalesce and dissolve over a 10-year period. They knew and I knew, but we both agreed to maintain the silence. Why break the silence now? Why ever?

I tell them out of respect, because I do not want them to see my picture in the newspaper under the headline "gay activists arrested . . . " or "cele-brating gay pride . . . " and because they remain the only people in my life with whom I have not had this discussion. But in this instance, by shattering the glass closet, I have also disrupted a deeper set of interpersonal arrange-ments that functioned to maintain the fiction of the innocent child, without adult desires or the possibility of an independent, sexually fulfilling relation-ship, who continues to be protected by the institution of "normal" parent-hood. Why break the silence now? Why ever?

In one sense my declaration and my parents' response affirms that we live in a culture in which sexuality is perceived as central to individual iden-tity, truth, and knowledge. They want to know if, as a result of this newly shared information, we will be closer, more intimate. I do not think coming out is about seeking happiness or connection but about claiming our own lives, finding a ground on which to stand. Closets are for hiding and organizing the unsightly mess out of which we select the elements to clothe our public image. Coming out places principle over practicality, since being public often exposes one to increased prejudice and discrimination. It places dignity over shame. There is nothing to hide.

Or so I think now. That first year of teaching I did not come out and therefore helped to perpetuate the unspoken homophobia that frames the closet. However, my pride would not let me suspend all communications with Lou. I simply began to censor the degree of intimacy that I permitted myself to display during school hours. Like the lesbian teachers in rural Canada described by Khayatt (1992), I judged the practical consequences of a public gay identity to be more negative than positive. Like my Canadian sisters, I, too, sought a balance between maintaining a sense of personal integrity and concealing just enough so as not to provoke the heterosexual world. Here is how one lesbian teacher describes her position:

> People know. People suspect and are often pretty certain of what they suspect, but it's not until the knowledge becomes actual fact that they really are concerned. Kind of contradictory in a way. It's OK to suspect, but it's not OK to know. But had they known, it would have had a great bearing on my relationship with the people I saw socially (most of whom are teachers). It would have had a bearing on the way they viewed me, and I'm certain it would have had a bearing on my teaching career. Exactly what it would be, I can't say, but one is always afraid that that's going to happen. (Khayatt, 1992, p. 234)

In effect this teacher lives in a glass closet. For the game of hiding involves two, the one who hides and the one who does not see. The former produces the right cues and clues and the latter learns to read them in a correct way. The lesbian teacher attempts to create a safe environment, and her colleagues become complicit in her hiding to avoid knowing something that would make them uncomfortable. To properly play her role she must not "flaunt" her sexual orientation, the definition of *flaunt* being relative to every community's norms of behavior and applied to anyone who challenges them. The lesbian teacher strives to appear conventional through avoiding compromising or risky situations. The mechanisms of concealment range from social distancing of faculty and students, geographic distancing from the school setting, and curricular distancing from potentially controversial issues related to gender and sexual identity, to changing the gender of friends and lovers in ordinary conversation and a preoccupation with modes of dress and presentation of self in everyday life.

While studies of how gay/lesbian families negotiate the school setting have been initiated (Casper, Schultz, & Wickens, 1992), most research describes the costs of identity-management strategies—self-hatred, nonacceptance, frustration, isolation—among gay teachers (Harbeck, 1992). Interviews with lesbians in the academy reveal that the public/private dichotomy used by a majority of faculty to rationalize the invisibility of gay people privileges some lives over others (Bensimon, 1992). Although public space is perceived as desexualized and degendered by most faculty, in fact heterosexuality is assumed and structures social expectations. Lesbian teachers are thus forced into hiding for fear of personal or professional rejection, and the inequalities experienced by all women are obscured. The ideology of dual spaces actually creates the unnatural or abnormal—life lived in the closet.

But the figure of the closet is inevitably coupled with the trope of "coming out." Accounts of teachers claiming their gay and lesbian identities within the classroom document the power and pedagogical transformation these radical acts make possible (Garber, 1994). The structure of our closets demands that the confession of personal identity become a consideration in each new encounter. We are never in or out but always in the process of reconstructing a continuum that is made up equally of our daily choices for silence or for expression. No matter how often I speak publicly as a gay person, I must declare that identity every time it is to be acknowledged. Identity is produced in relation to others, not in isolation.

Finally, the closet is a function not of homosexuality but of compulsory heterosexuality. Every time I come out, I affirm the existence of the closet and the heterosexual world that becomes my audience. Coming out brings with it the destabilizing potential of the erotic even as it reproduces the oppressive social categories from which we seek liberation. The challenge is to balance the instrumental use of existing categories in the contemporary political context without foreclosing new possibilities. How do we avoid succumbing to our own resistance?

In the ethos of this community we escape from the closet in order to claim political and social recognition. National Coming Out Day is promoted with a Keith Haring drawing of a lone figure triumphantly bursting out of a closet door. While coming out is the essential political act for the individual, keeping the secret of another's sexual orientation has been constitutive of the community itself. Mohr (1992) contests this ethic of keeping the secret. He suggests that to maintain such a compact is to become complicit in a definition of self that is derogatory and degrading. We have no ethical commitment to self-hatred and no right to secrecy. To identify someone else as gay may reveal a secret not known to others, but it does not describe his or her private life in any more detail than labeling someone divorced or married. There is no shame to being gay, and there are as many ways of living one's gayness as of living one's heterosexuality. This is the distinction between the right to privacy—to be protected from invasive prying into what is accomplished out of sight—versus the right to secrecy, to naming the fact of gayness. It is the living out of our lives that demands privacy; to keep the fact of our gayness a secret is only to perpetuate oppression. There is nothing to hide.

Crimp (1992) would add that real political change, challenging institutionalized homophobia, depends on collective political struggle, on identity politics—not on isolated acts of heroism. While individual struggles to come out of the closet are to be lauded for the way they shift the local terrain, encouraging celebrities to come out or assertively outing them may not be an effective political strategy. In specific instances, outing famous people can backfire by confirming stereotypes (e.g., Roy Cohn and Rock Hudson). Moreover, outing confirms that homosexuality per se is a nasty secret rather than directing attention to the real secret, homophobia, and the way it is enforced by the media.

In relationship to my own parents, I doubted that coming out would bring the closeness they desired. We were all too skittish of intimacy at any level. What I am less doubtful about, however, are the ways in which we have come to pose essential knowledge as sexual knowledge, ignorance as sexual ignorance. Beginning with the biblical announcement that the tree of knowledge bears only the fruit of shame, through the increased naming and refusal of sex between men and between women in the nineteenth century, the ultimate sexual secret has been the homosexual secret. Drawing on the canonical texts of Melville, James, and Proust, Sedgwick (1990) documents how a growing historical emphasis on homosexual/ heterosexual categories affects us all, arguing that "an understanding of virtually any aspect of modern Western culture must be, not merely incomplete, but damaged in its central substance to the degree that it does not incorporate a critical analysis of modern homo/heterosexual definition" (p. l). She distinguishes between those who see this dichotomy as relevant only to a small minority of people on the sexual fringe and those who accept this universalizing principle. The former believe the closet belongs only to those who live within its confines whereas the latter understand the closet as a pervasive structure of our culture, marking every critical set of categories—

> secrecy/disclosure, knowledge/ignorance, private/public, masculine/feminine, majority/minority, innocence/initiation, natural/artificial, new/old, discipline/ terrorism, canonic/noncanonic, wholeness/decadence, urbane/provincial, domestic/foreign, health/illness, same/different, active/passive, cognition/paranoia, art/kitch, utopia/apocalypse, sincerity/sentimentality, and volition/addiction. (p. 11)

Although the distinctions associated with homosexuality run across the culture, Sedgwick maintains that the closet itself is never devoid of its specificity with relationship to homosexuality.

Sexuality, once confined to our reading of individual Oedipal dramas, now enters the early childhood classroom embedded in our basic epistemological assumptions, tainting subjects that once seemed far from its touch. Like gender, race, and class, sexual orientation can no longer be ignored as one of the critical tools for unpacking the meanings transmitted in the pedagogical encounter, and the closet itself must be considered with regard to our assumptions about differences between adult and child. Sedgwick asks us to think of the closet as more than the hiding place from which some may emerge. For her it is a set of unspoken compacts informing every aspect of our society that may be opened through a discursive deconstruction of its narrative sources.

To be clear, the claim of gay scholarship is not that everyone is capable of enjoying homosexual relationships or constitutionally bisexual—though this may or may not prove to be the case—but rather that "homosexuality and heterosexuality are definitional parts of, definitionally precede, or provide the core cultural paradigms for other distinctions that radiate throughout society, chief among them gender" (Mohr, 1992, p. 258). It should also be noted that not all cultures construct gender—and by extension, sexual orientation—in terms of irreconcilable oppositions. In attempting to re-imagine gender and family in contemporary America, Schultz (1993) explores the Native American tradition of the berdache, explaining:

> Here is a man who may dress as a woman. Who most often takes on many of the occupations and behaviors of a woman, and who is sometimes sexually oriented toward another man. For many Native cultures, this individual is a man-woman. (p. 3)

In a world that emphasizes connectedness and relationship, the berdache embodies the in-between-ness of man and woman and is generally seen as extremely talented and gifted (Williams, 1986).

Mohr (1992) argues that in modern America the concept of homosexuality itself, not the gay person or a set of specific behaviors, defines the very nature of personhood. Until recently, military laws and immigration codes purportedly seeking to defend the country have done so through excluding gays and lesbians. Similarly, in *Bowers v. Hardwick,* the Supreme Court excluded gays from the right to private consensual sex through proscribing sodomy when it occurs between members of the same sex but not between people of different sexes. Homosexuality is used to mark the limits, to set the threshold criteria for membership in the larger community. It is as if the margins that define the page have become the text itself, a process confirmed by the historical record, which indicates that the modern homosexual was invented prior to the heterosexual (J. Katz, 1990).

Unfortunately, any satisfaction in this historical precedence of homosexuality as a social category evaporates in Judith Butler's (1990) analysis of gender as performativity. Although she makes clear that homosexuality is neither secondary to or derivative of any heterosexual norm, she also makes it difficult to discover any logical or temporal order for the emergence of one category or the other:

> Hence, if gay identities are implicated in heterosexuality, that is not the same as claiming that they are determined or derived from heterosexuality, and it is not the same as claiming that heterosexuality is the only cultural network in which they are implicated. These are, quite literally inverted imitations, ones which invert the order of imitated and imitation, and which, in the process, expose the fundamental dependency of "origin" on that which it claims to produce as its secondary effect. (p. 22)

Through the light and smoke of Butler's verbal pyrotechnics we can discern her basic argument: All heterosexual gender identities are imitations, approximations, for which there are no orginals. They do not express preexisting or deep psychic realities, as traditional psychoanalysts contend. Rather, needing constant repetition for their realization, gendered identities are precariously constructed and easily placed at risk by the failure to repeat the requisite performance.

It is impossible to say that heterosexuality precedes homosexuality, since there are no original categories but only copies. Gay and lesbian identities, heterosexual norms and hegemonic culture are inextricably bound together, each producing the other as it reproduces itself. Indeed, as I suggested in Chapter 5, the classic gay narratives make no presumption of authenticity. They are narratives about hiding and concealing, about the invention of multiple identities through assembling bits and pieces from the lives of others. It is not happenstance that theft and forgery are essential subtexts in Wilde and Proust, Gide and Genet; after all, we are always trying to speak the unspeakable. There is nothing to hide.

With these ideas in mind, I return to the parents of the children I taught, to my own parents' surprised distress at my coming out, and to Sol and Jimmy's resistance to knowing that Lorde was "cullud." Perhaps all their genuine caring belies the instruction they have received about difference. Perhaps, too, their preferred ignorance, like their knowledge, is allied to a specific regime of truth, one that privileges conformity over distinction, the Caucasian over the person of color, the heterosexual over the homosexual. Regimes of truth establish fields of force, exert controls over thought and behavior, our knowing and not knowing. Sol and Jimmy, my parents and the parents of the children I taught, are purposefully ignorant. Ignorance is not the opposite of knowledge but rather an integral part of the same dynamic system, and it needs to be studied in all its multiplicities and extensions. The ground for such a claim has been prepared by Foucault (1978):

> There is no binary division to be made between what one says and what one does not say; we must try to determine the different ways of not saying such things. . . . There is not one but many silences, and they are an integral part of the strategies that underlie and permeate discourses. (p. 27)

Ignorance is negotiated as we actively conspire not to address certain topics, maintaining a foundational set of open secrets. It is these secrets, with their critical information about acceptable and scandalous behavior, that provide the structural underpinnings of social life and the thematic material of cultural production. Silence is itself a performative speech act and becomes essential pedagogy, a way to remain not implicated, to teach nonresponsibility.

How often have I heard teachers rationalize their failure to talk about AIDS by observing that children did not raise questions about it. But since when have children spontaneously asked about the colonial experience in America or how to measure the area of a right triangle? These are subjects we have no difficulty imposing on the curriculum. Indeed, an academic journal rejected an earlier version of this chapter because of my failure to "prove" that children have questions about HIV/AIDS, as if their prior knowing or articulated knowledge is the only ground on which our instruction can proceed. When did responsibility for breaking silences pass from adults to children? What is there to hide?

MY FAMILY'S CLOSETS

I once thought I knew a lot about the closet. Now I am not so sure. Literary critics such as Sedgwick (1990) and Butler (1991), legal scholars such as Mohr (1992) and political strategists such as Crimp (1992) analyze the epistemology of the closet and the ethics surrounding coming out in a way that would not have been possible 35 years ago as I wandered the streets of Manhattan or 10 years later when I began to teach. This theoretically ophisticated work, grounded in the contemporary gay experience, raises questions about the categories that frame our social identities. Yet when I recently had occasion to explore two of the closets of my own childhood, I was immediately struck by quite another phenomenon: the urban attic as repository of personal, familial, and cultural artifacts. The contents of these closets not only reveal events my relatives may have once actively sought to

hide, but also others that were made secret simply by the passage of time, by
the lack of attention given to that which remains out of sight.

*   *   *

There is much that I might say about opening the door of an apartment
that has not been occupied in months—my aunt's apartment, the apartment
of an 87-year-old blind widow. I am struck by the windows without cur-
tains or shades, taken down for repairs but never replaced, the overstuffed
domestic furniture of the 1950s, the clothing casually strewn across the bed,
the half-empty jars of creams and emoluments on the dressing table and sink
counter. But all this, so redolent of the daily life that no longer occurs in these
rooms, seems self-explanatory compared to the mysteries that lie behind the
closet doors. To enter these miniature rooms without windows is to enter
the inner sanctum, the heart of the home. To stand in the middle of the hall
closet is to take possession of a space of which, as a child, I could claim only
the minutest glimpse. For when one arrived at this apartment, the visit always planned, never of the moment, preparations were long underway. The
closet was opened only momentarily, the door just enough ajar so that the
hostess could slip in to retrieve an extra serving bowl, gravy boat or hot pad.
For who would ever think of inviting you, a guest, into the closet?

Now as an adult I am drawn to this very same closet. Perhaps it is a
fascination with the once forbidden, or simply that it seems to tell so much
more than the apartment itself. My aunt's closet is the closet of a bourgeois
housekeeper, someone who has given a great deal of time and thought to
organizing, maintaining, and preserving the objects that announce a life of
substance. Here there is clearly something to watch over, protect, and count:
sterling silver bowls, the smaller sizes carefully nestled within the larger, each
in its own felt bag to prevent tarnishing; stacks of formal Wedgewood china;
dozens of glasses that were never covered and have become dim with dust;
vases of every shape and size still awaiting the flowers purchased weekly, to
stand on the entrance hall chest and welcome their owner home. That is a
routine long ago abandoned, never to be revived by my aunt, now perma-
nently languishing in another closet, a nearby nursing home.

Although my aunt's closet can be read as a vault of traditional values
and gender roles, it also hints at significant social changes. For it contains
the boxes of papers, documents and diplomas, bills and bank statements,
insurance policies and legal contracts that go beyond what might be required
of one who depended on others to manage her affairs. These are texts that
in another era would have been sequestered in a more distinctly male preserve—the patriarch's desk, file, or office—a terrain once well demarcated

from that which held the supplies to sustain the household in its private nurturant and public host functions. They signal to me that my aunt was someone who in her own way pushed the limits, leaving a small town in western Pennsylvania to attend an Ivy League college in 1920, moving to New York to become a self-supporting professional, marrying late, without children, and in her widowhood taking on her husband's stockbrokerage business.

These are accomplishments that deserve recognition. They are conventional in that the college chosen was a women's institution and the professional role played was that of keeping accounts in order that men might make critical decisions. However, they are more radical when viewed within their historical context; at that time, the majority of middle-class woman neither entered college nor lived alone and supported themselves. So I must be careful to weigh my judgments about a life that sought security in the accumulation of household goods against the life lived through negotiating a male-dominated world of work.

There is a part of me that does not want to know my family's closets. It has not been my choice. I have entered my aunt's closet because she is dying, because there is no one else to see to the disbursement of goods, to the passing on of that which will remind some distant relation of their connection to the deceased. But once the ensemble is disturbed, these things removed from the closet for the last time, they will lose the sense of permanence that accrues through years of existing within a given context. Still made of the same silver and gold, porcelain and glass, onyx and crystal, they now remind us of what is not, their hardness and definition contrasting all the more with the impermanence of human life. Eventually they will be imbued with other meanings; no longer the objects *of* my aunt's landscape, they will have become objects *from* her landscape. In time the unthinkable may happen, and they will lose any connection with their place of origin, weighed down with many new associations.

Inherited objects, carefully extracted from dusty closets, lovingly lifted out of bureau drawers and serendipitously saved from junk-filled attics, also ask to be known even as they resist yielding the secrets of their history. It is their very demandingness that makes them part of our lives. We seek explanations and invent imperfect, deceptive interpretations that offer a gloss of understanding. We are not quite satisfied with these half-truths, nor are the children, who are most insistent in their questions about the past as we attempt to explain the special qualities of grandmother Sarah's personality, of Uncle Jay's critical life decisions, of cousin David's social milieu. We are sorry that we failed to listen more carefully to the stories imparted by our own parents and frustrated by the limitations of memory.

*   *   *

Like my aunt's, my father's closet gave off a familiar musty odor from its faded, peeling green walls and shelves stacked with countless cardboard boxes. I remember these boxes, once packed with reams of tissue paper, under which were hidden my father's eagerly awaited new suit, always a disappointingly somber gray; a dress for my mother to wear at my brother's high school graduation; a sport jacket that would see me through several years of family functions; or button-down shirts with that perfect roll to the collar, providing a particular Ivy League assurance to the wearer. The boxes are dark blue with yellow trim, brown with black lettering, white with red flowers. They signal permanence, less through their sturdy construction than through the signature names written across their covers: Brooks Brothers, Saks Fifth Avenue, Lord & Taylor, B. Altman, Di Pinna. Even as I say the names of these once-famous stores, they call forth memories of a childhood in which things seemed to matter, in which objects themselves seemed to hold the promise of a managed and manageable life.

Piled high with old suitcases, cartons, and assorted paintings as this space is, there is no way to enter it, no way to take control. Nor is the 80-year-old man who anxiously awaits your evaluation of the project so eager to relinquish that control. As you reach out to grab the first stack of canceled checks bound by a crumbling rubber band, he tells you with irritation that these are unimportant; they can wait until after he is dead to be put in order. I am unnerved to think of my next foray into these discrete areas of chaos that are to be left untouched at present. Nevertheless, he impatiently insists that there are other priorities now. He is right. This is a moment to remain focused. I am conscious that the energy will dissipate quickly as the morning draws on. But focused on what? Why am I in my father's closet?

I tell myself that I am here to help him locate the wills, insurance papers, powers of attorney that will be required if the impending operation does not go well. I am made uneasy by this task of becoming the dutiful son, leaving behind my more favored role of disdainful rebel, in order to complete the process through which we become caring parents for our own mothers and fathers. The work is accompanied by recurring comments about my father's failing eyesight and the ambiguous diagnosis of the physician who will attend him. But it is I who have become the surgeon this morning, aggressively cutting into the abyss of papers to find an imposing leather portfolio with an embossed heraldic emblem. Yes, I am instructed after my brief description, those are the life insurance policies. I am surprised by the plural. No, each is worth very little, I am reassured. Buy them when you have money, borrow against them when you do not. And mostly he did not have money, and mostly he was concerned about how we would survive without him: how he might, in death, become the stable provider he felt he had failed to be in life.

And here, jammed into the red leather letter container, edged in gilt, that sat on my father's desk while I was growing up, is an old photograph. It is a formal studio portrait from the late nineteenth century of my father's grandfather and his wife. Although this photograph resembles others I have seen in museums and books, I examine it closely as evidence of my own history. When I turn it over, I am surprised to find a note in my father's handwriting scrawled across the back. He asks that I read it. Written on the occasion of our move from one apartment to another, a turning point in our family saga, it describes his sense of connection to the past and high hopes for the future. I am embarrassed by the directness and naivete of the writing. He was 46 years old, a year younger than I am now.

I have finally moved into the closet, into his life. I can not help but wonder if he has ever been in my closet? Would I ever allow him comparable privileges? The closet, I am learning, promises intimacy as well as history, and I am a person who has been shy of such moments of vulnerability and self-revelation. Perhaps I should not see any more, have already seen enough, am drawn to see more. Do I really need to read the letters that my grandfather, who died before my birth, sent to my father when he was a freshman at college? Letters that I am surprised to learn were typed by a secretary. He was a far more successful businessman than I had imagined. And do I need to see the 1929 inventory of his business, my father's all-important college diploma, or even the small simple statement from Lenox Hill Hospital dated April 12, 1944, nine days after my birth at that institution. Curious, how someone else's closet can tell so much about us.

For months after the great excavation of my father's closet, I get calls from him at odd times of the day and night. Where did I put the wills? Do I remember the account book that held the stock certificate numbers? Where is my mother's birth certificate? He is always sure to remind me, as if it were possible to forget, that he could not see anything then, when we worked together. In his voice I hear an unspoken pleasure in the success of the operation, the gamble of a lifetime, as well as a slight reproof. I tell myself that the reproof is not about being careless with valuable possessions but about the very act of disturbing the sedimented strata that had been so carefully laid down. It is as if, by changing the physical space of the closet, I threatened to change the past itself, to undermine his ability to control time. But by inviting me to assist him, he has also acknowledged that he is no longer able to manage alone, is overwhelmed by the layers of experience that we are forced to peel back in search of the critical documents. My new role in his life points to the demise of his bodily powers. I have been indicted for meddling with his history, indicted for being a part of that history.

OBJECTS PROMISING SURVIVAL

Again I find myself writing about memory, about trying to remember, about being mindful. Ironically, it was the illness and death of my peers rather than the frailty of my father that first brought to the fore the significance of our mortality and the way it might inform our sense of social purpose. It is they who have helped me to make the distinction between chronological memory and the deep, chaotic memory that sporadically disrupts the surface flow of events. Like every writer, I want to get it right, overwhelmed by the need to tell my story even as I am sure that no one will possibly understand its meaning. I am haunted, too, by the fear that my efforts will contribute to the further romanticizing of illness. Trying to work in the space between private memories and public accounts, the writing process itself has become more than a matter of biographical record keeping, more than an attempt to memorialize the past. As I seek to make sense of the disparate parts of my life, writing has become a ceremony of connection, a ritualized attempt to sustain the links between past and present, to project a future in an impossible time.

But these forays into my family's closets are also ceremonies of connection. As I read the inscription on the back of my great-grandparents' photograph, as I place it in my father's hands, even though he can barely see it or me, we turn toward one another. We meet in that moment as we have not met before, connected in and through this remnant of the nineteenth century. I am aware that all of our particular history—the intense attachment of infancy, open hostilities of adolescence, and residual conflicts of adulthood—is obliterated as we contemplate the distant past. It is as if there has been a bracketing of our natural attitude, an instantaneous refusal of our taken-for-granted relationship. So distanced are we from the subjects of the photograph that, if it had not been for his own midlife markings on the back, I might almost believe that we had suddenly become equals in our quest for knowledge of the past. My feeling is one of neither sentimentality nor vulnerability, but rather of respect for a fellow voyager who is further along on the same journey. I cannot help but wonder if my father is trying to look for images of himself, his father, or even of me. And for whom or what am I looking, in this transitional object that links my great-grandparents to their immediate social world, their past to my present, myself to my father?

It is a basic insight of phenomenology that we know others only through our joint participation in the world. Consciousness is always directed toward something or someone, always intentional. Merleau-Ponty (1964) reflects, "If I am consciousness turned toward things, I can meet in things the actions of another and find in them a meaning, because they are themes for possible activity for my own body" (p. 117). And it is Merleau-Ponty who teaches us that knowledge of the self and others is about the corporeal and postural schema through which we attempt to understand the world. We are not known to ourselves nor do we know others as closed psychological systems. We are open systems accessible to each other through the gestures that bind us in a common project. I discover others in their conduct, as they move in the world, as they live out a particular relationship to it. My knowledge is always mediated through the world or, more precisely, through the intentionality of others. But how do we make sense of a world from which the other is absent, a world seemingly devoid of the shared intentions that allowed me to feel so close to my father? What meaning does my aunt's closet hold? In what context might I more properly set down her carefully stored possessions?

Although closets appear to tell stories of absence, they might easily be read as narratives of intensified presence, each object calling forth a new effort to reconstruct the past. The door stands open, beckoning us to remember that which we have forgotten, to recognize that which we do not want to know, to reclaim territories long ago abandoned to the rule of the unconscious. Like explorers moving through a dense forest of memories, we clear sites for temporary encampments, spaces in which to rest as we rebuild the imaginative fictions that support the past. Like the first taste of the madeleine to the narrator of *Remembrance of Things Past*, or the lingering smell of smoke in the furniture that reminds Rufus of his recently dead father in *A Death in the Family*, the sight of objects from our past can become powerful stimulants to the unfolding of childhood memories and offer pathways to those no longer present. It is not the specific events they evoke—the Thanksgiving dinner of 1954 to which a set of distant cousins traveled for the first time, or the lavish 1957 anniversary party signaling financial success—that remain so vivid, but the emotions associated with them: anticipation, security, a sense of place.

Smith (1991) writes about these remembered emotions as the source of pedagogical understanding. Although memories of particular events may be given causative explanations, he is more interested in the way they are suggestive of the continuity between past and present. It is our ability to capture the qualities of past moments, as they are inscribed in the body, that most effectively informs our insights into what the present may hold for children. Nostalgia is not an end in itself but rather functions in the service of imagining and realizing our notions of a good childhood. For within our remembrances are images of children, their activities, modes, and postures. A vivid connection to our personal past makes possible a richer interpersonal present.

These objects from the closet offer an especially vivid connection to the past. They are not just symbols that stand for something else; rather they are parts that stand for the whole, fragments of the past itself. They allow us, as adults, to review with serenity a time that was fraught with its own uncertainties, displacements, and terrors; a time when we often tried to manage our inner turmoil by recourse to objects of another sort. As children, we seek reassurance from the object that can stand in place of the absent caregiver, that remains despite the rupture of time caused by a disappearance, that endures the way people cannot. We cling to the new box of crayons, familiar blanket, or tattered doll with the intensity of life itself, for without it there is no possibility of return, no future. The transitional object is a talisman against death, holding the promise of survival in a world where painful separations must be sustained with ever greater frequency and duration. We learn from earliest experience to substitute material goods for human interactions, hoping to find in them the other who is even then far away, hoping for permanence and security as we learn the realities of flux and change. It is our resistance to this instruction that lies hidden at the back of our individual closets and is signified by the enduring monuments of civilization. There is always the impossible hope that they will not fail us as we must inevitably fail one another.

POWERFUL SILENCES

It is this very matter of hopefulness that also draws us to children. Phenomenologists describe the sense of futurity, the continual disclosure of possibilities, that defines childhood. Children teach us about hope. Max van Manen (1986) writes:

> "I wish I could be young again but know what I know now." Many of us are nostalgic about our childhood, and not because we want to be children again. What we really want to do is to be able to experience the world the way a child does. We long to recapture a sense of possibility and openness—a confidence that almost anything is possible. . . . All kinds of things are possible when one is young, and the reward for both parents and teachers is the presence of hope. That is what a child can teach us. It is what a child must teach us if we are to be true and good parents and teachers. (p. 15)

If we are to learn the lesson of hopefulness that children have to offer, then we must be close to them, accepting the common ground we all share regardless of age. It is this search for connection that causes me to turn away from stage theories of development that assure an absolute distinction been child and adult. Merleau-Ponty (1964) describes how our adherence to the Piagetian conception of cognitive structures sacrifices the immediate, visceral knowledge of self and others that we possess before being overwhelmed by language and rules of perception. Hierarchical stages posit an artificial separation of childhood from adulthood. Merleau-Ponty points us to continuities rather than differences, the child as neither absolute other nor as exactly the same as ourselves. Such continuity comes from assuming the centrality of preconceptual knowledge, knowledge that is neither objective nor subjective but that emerges through direct participation in the world. This is knowledge that allows us to know both the child in the classroom and the child within ourselves.

It is not easy to attend to this knowledge amidst the cacophony of contemporary educational jargon. This preverbal, semiotic knowing requires that we set aside the scientific and technical understandings of teaching that express our interest in the manipulative grasp and control of classroom life in order to hear the instruction offered by silence. Earlier in this chapter I explored the negotiated silences through which we avoid the discussion of issues that make us uncomfortable. Here I point to the comfort of shared silences through which we can also experience relationships. For just as silence can imply hostility, anger, and disapproval, so can it signal deep friendship, emotional admiration, and love. We may scold a child with the stern look or nod of the head or express empathetic appreciation through mindful watching.

We live in a culture that obligates us to speak, to verbalize the slightest disturbance in our emotional lives, to find the polite but often hollow formulas for resolving differences, "to use our words rather than our hands." We celebrate the caregiver who interacts, extends, and elaborates the utterances of the child as precursors to rational argumentation and pathologize silence as absence (Walkerdine, 1990). We teach in whole-language classrooms, where a strategy for teaching reading has replaced a philosophy of education, where individual textual production has been substituted for direct experience with materials, and where children learn to couch responses to each other's work in the meaningless reframe, "I like the way you. . . . " In other cultures and times, among Native Americans, in ancient Rome and Greece, in Japan, the multiple meanings of silence are honored and taught to children.

T. Tatetuso Aoki (1992) suggests that listening to the silent call of teaching means giving up our romance with the uncannily correct in favor of the elusively true. He illustrates the power of listening filled with care, and the embodied doing and being that are pedagogical thoughtfulness, by recounting June Aoki's story. She tells of the displacement and confusion caused by the government-directed closing of her Japanese-language school during World War II. She describes the silent watching of her teacher, his eyes filled with sadness and hope for his students, as they leave on that final day.

Forty years after the event in question, June Aoki asks Mr. McNabe, her former teacher, what he was thinking as he watched his students depart and he replies simply, "That was a sad day." As I read this story, I recall my own attempts to communicate with Michael after he had lost the use of words, and with Bill when he pronounced his terminal diagnosis. I think about how Mr. McNabe bears witness to this student's unjust exile and my own attempts to testify to the suffering of others, to the painful presence of absence in my own life.

Sinclaire (1992) writes from a teacher's perspective about the silent connections that bind us to our students. Vianna, a sixth-grade student who had been sexually abused as a young child, seeks advice as she proposes attending a Halloween dance in a sexually provocative costume. Her questions cause Sinclaire to reflect on her own struggles in coming to terms with a social world that frequently gives inconsistent and contradictory messages to adolescent females. Remembering these troubles, moments of intense personal embarrassment and confusion, she responds to this student in trouble even as she tries to stay out of trouble with school authorities for exploding accepted home/school prerogatives. Sinclaire stays close to Vianna's feelings of helplessness, as well as her own sense of inadequacy to affect her students' future, through recalling moments of childhood powerlessness. She describes her own pain, and her father's indifference, when he returns from a hunting trip with a deer strapped to the top of the car, concluding:

> As a teacher, I identify with the image of the child who longs to bring the deer to life as I wish I could restore Vianna. It is a futile act for I cannot erase what has happened to her. I cannot be Vianna's parent to spend my time exclusively with her. All I could hope to do is to help her understand what has happened and impart what I could from my own experience. . . . Vianna must struggle to find her costume, her true identity, and I must watch over her while she does so, standing back enough to leave her room to discover herself so that she might begin again to grow. (Sinclaire, 1992, p. 14)

Although she ultimately loses contact with Vianna, Sinclaire bears witness to Vianna's life and her own attempt to honor the memories that have bound them together.

IF LOOKS COULD KILL

Not all closets resemble the urban attics of my past, filled with memories of childhood and thoughts of familial connections. Nor is it their particular contents that necessarily tell the most significant stories about our social identities. The closet itself has a history with roots in the organization of social knowledge. The dictionary informs us that the word *closet* comes

through Middle English from the Middle French *clos*, "enclosure." Originally it referred to a small room or apartment, a space to which the king
and/or his counselors retired in order to conduct secret interviews and to make
politically charged decisions.

I cannot help asking myself how it is that an enclosure meant for temporary reflection became a permanent home to so many. When was the closet
transformed from a refuge in which to gain insight (as in, "he was closeted
with his advisors for many hours") to a place in which one simply *is* (as in,
"he lived his entire life in the closet")? While royalty were able to withdraw
to a distinctly private space before making public pronouncements, the
modern individual appears condemned to a continuous struggle with when
and how to stay in/come out of an increasing number of closets. For some
this struggle is framed in terms of how to avoid harm, for others it is a matter of sustaining a sense of integrity in a fragmented world, and for a few it
is about promoting social transformation through shifting public discourse.
Whether one is in or out, whether the issue is addiction, religion, or sexuality, the concept of closetedness itself has become central to defining personal
identity. But many, myself included, are sometimes confused by this new and
unstable geography, have become preoccupied with demarcating the boundaries between private and public territories, find ourselves living in the borderlands that alone permit our multiple, overlapping identities to coexist
without need of explanation.

The closets I know best tell stories of the body. The closet defining my
life as a gay adolescent tells of my desire for other men. My aunt's closet,
though quite different, was the storehouse for the goods that sustain the body
and provide for its comforts. The occasion itself for entering my father's closet,
his imminent surgery, underlines his growing frailty. The contents reveal the
younger, energetic *pater familias* still enjoying the strength that informed the
athletic accomplishments of his youth. My family closets speak to the impermanence of life as well to the possibility of communication between generations. In this sense they are not so different from the closets of my youth
in which I sought to hide my gayness, to make it go away, while simultaneously communicating to others who would be sympathetic. The closet
sounds a death knell to a public identity even as it promotes a secretive form
of community life. Those who live within its confines may distance themselves from some, while they affiliate with others who share the particular
insights and privileges of the closet. Coming out can mean going into a culture
with its own conventions and norms.

During the last decade the spread of HIV has added further meaning to
this connection between the closet and the body's viability. Many HIV-positive
people choose to remain closeted and some gay men may feel the need to
hide their sexual orientation as well as HIV status. To be openly gay is to claim

membership in a community under siege, to be automatically suspect with respect to HIV. It is to take up the position of one who knows about death and illness as well as about sexuality and pleasure. Heterosexual friends ask how we endure the constant losses. I do not know. I do not want to know. I am ignorant. To be public about one's gayness is to be vulnerable in new and unexamined ways. To be public about one's HIV status brings with it an additional set of concerns. They are not the same. At first infection, HIV is like gayness—there are no observable signs. Eventually, HIV is more like race—the indications unmistakable to anyone who wants to know. There is no way to hide.

Who better to tell this particular coming out story than someone for whom fictions about death, the fiction of death, has become the pedagogical project itself, the teacher who would announce: "I have AIDS"? Like Thomas Yingling (1993), Michael Lynch (1990) contemplates the risks inherent in the confessional mode in order to gain greater control over how his students perceive him. He also speaks with the same vocabulary as Moger (1982) about the patterns of giving and withholding that constitute the seduction of teaching. But for Lynch the temptation to withhold information is not about adherence to traditional codes of professional behavior that titillate interest in personal life even as they presume to protect students and teachers from one another. Rather it is an attempt to avoid being consumed by the gaze of students who would bring all the apparatus of the sentimental deathbed scene into the classroom. For if to teach is to be watched, and watched closely, to teach with AIDS is to be watched for the signs of imminent death.

I cannot help monitoring my own response to Lynch as I hear him tell of his indecision. His once thick, muscular body is now reduced to a paperthin shell. He is hunched over the table, apologetic for being too weak to stand, his handsome face so entirely emaciated and lined that it is no longer recognizable. I concentrate with great difficulty in order to find gestures and intonations that I can recognize. Despite frequent interruptions for water, his voice is clear and strong. I hear him claiming the right to construct his own literary deathbed framed by references to Cather, Twain, Dickinson. His words do not send me to the tomes (tombs) of the literary giants but rather back to my own text to ask if I have not usurped another's place by turning his death into a source of narrative, uttering words about an utterly senseless situation. Satisfied that I have spoken only for myself, unsatisfied that the one I presumed to know would approve, his love and authority so thoroughly with me even now, I return to the living Lynch, who, in describing his own ambivalence about involving others in his deathbed drama, poses the very same questions that have preoccupied my own thinking about pedagogy:

Last December 5, at the last meeting of the Willa Cather seminar where I flirted and skirted the announcement all term, I wanted to announce this talk (Last Onsets—Teaching with AIDS). But I could only bring myself to announce the first half of the title. How could I hit them with the second half, the AIDS marker half, when they were just about to write their course evaluations?

This concealing/revealing and hinting/coding may remind us not just of the basic structures of teaching, but also of the structures of the closets that pervade our culture. In a culture of identities, the textures of withholding and revealing can become all-encompassing. So can the textures of wanting to guess, and wanting above all not to see. (p. 14)

I am left wanting to peer into those closets, for, like Lynch, I somehow believe that they will enable me to understand the patterns that structure my teaching and writing and through which I attempt to engage my student/ reader. I am also left knowing that the time of "interesting deathbed scenes," which Richard Howard locates in the late nineteenth and early twentieth centuries, is not yet over. Now, too, I am more conscious than ever that it is my own love and loss propelling these researches, a final effort to stay the distance between living and dying.

CHAPTER 8

The Politics of Identity and the Differences Inside Me

... for nothing seems more certain than that homosexuality is
contagious.

Willard Waller, *The Sociology of Teaching*

Some weeks are worse than others. I can remember a time when I could count
on one hand the number of funerals I had attended. Now I have lost track.
Jim's memorial service is on Sunday. It is held in the tastefully decorated
meeting room of the suburban hospital of which he was a board member.
An innovative, successful member of the business community and an outspoken advocate of environmental causes, Jim had become a respected member of the local power structure. Two hundred people stand through a carefully orchestrated series of remembrances. As I turn from side to side and
see so many who have threaded their way through our lives, I miss Jim. But
my reverie is broken by the growing realization that, while speaker after
speaker refers to Jim's commitment to liberal causes as well as the dignity
with which he managed to live with AIDS, no one has mentioned his active
participation and generous contributions to gay rights organizations. Within
this setting it is acceptable to talk about the disease that took Jim's life, but
not the sexual orientation with which he struggled to come to terms and
through which he expressed so much of his identity. Jim is presented as the
good burgher, unsullied by sex, love, or the politics of desire.

On Tuesday, Allen's funeral reflects a similar form of denial. Like Jim,
Allen had been an activist: the founder of a gay synagogue and a consistently
successful fund-raiser and public speaker for the AIDS agency of which he was
a client. Allen had a warm, endearing nature that attracted many friends.
He was gentle to a fault, his anger too easily directed inward, causing him to
slip into prolonged periods of depression. But Allen's mother did not hold

back, and the memory of his funeral is haunted by the violent wailing of this woman, who, when escorted into the sanctuary for the final service, collapsed sobbing over the casket, crying out for the son who had been taken before his time. And what of the life described by the rabbi? He told of a half life, at best. For while there is no denying that Allen was an unusually loving and loyal family member, he was also a man who loved other men. Because of this love he responded to the needs of a community in crisis, exercising civic courage in his outspoken attempts to educate others about the disease that was killing him. The remarks, delivered with dignity and solemnity, nonetheless infantilize a 45-year-old adult by denying his membership in the political, social, and erotic community of his choosing. In the end, those present are asked to make contributions, in Allen's honor, to the local animal hospital.

On Thursday the final service of the week provides the greatest surprise of all. John had already been diagnosed with AIDS-related complex when he was hired as an educator, at the AIDS agency where I was director of public information services. He was able to work for two years before an increasing series of complications finally caught up with him. He never wanted to stop, and confronting him with this reality was one of the most difficult jobs I had ever had. It was clear that from John's point of view, he was being deprived of the very context in which he could most effectively struggle against the disease. He was to be left now with only his failing body, the site of ever more radical and useless medical interventions.

A tempestuous relationship with his large Italian family informed much of John's life with his lover Daren. And by the time of his death, there was little communication between Daren and John's parents. Making connection with the priests at the Catholic church where John had been baptized as a child, Daren drew them into their life to comfort John and legitimize the relationship. At the high mass before the burial, three priests speak of the strong bond between John and Daren, a bond that sustained John through his ordeal and enabled them both to confront HIV in their personal and professional lives. Many friends climb the steps to the pulpit to echo these thoughts. I am moved by these public acknowledgments of John's accomplishments, but at the same time I am only too aware that all the insistence underlines the denial and alienation that framed much of his life. It is the willful silence of John's parents and five siblings, whom I have met in one or another of John's many hospital rooms, that belies the articulateness of the speakers. This silence is pregnant with words not heard from anyone during this solemn rite of passage, words of my own youth, words of another rite of passage, terms of derision now recycled as labels of pride: *sissy, queer, faggot.* Denial and recognition are part of the same system, not so very different after all.

These funerals are difficult for me. They resonate with complex emotions. I attend in the official guise of the AIDS agency for which I work. Each person has made a contribution to the agency's success; each person has also been a client. But I am present as a friend, too, flooded with memories of particular interactions and events. Most often I leave as a gay man, incensed by the way we are remembered, the way our stories are told. For our biographies are written as if to suggest that we have never loved anyone but parent or relative, worked for any but the most respectable of causes, experienced desire for anything more radical than the domestic comforts of hearth and home. Should I be surprised that the orators find praise for those roles with which we all feel safe—the concerned citizen, the loving child, the caring friend? How frequently do we attend a service that memorializes the ardent lover, radical activist, or conscientious gay/lesbian community member? These are the specifics that shape our lives and express our civic, familial, and interpersonal commitments, as well as other more traditional roles.

But mourners seek reassurance in the normative, meaning in that which is familiar. At the moment we confront the transitory nature of existence and the arbitrariness of fate, we are comforted by the outlines of a life that helps us to reaffirm the world as we want to know it: a world of constancy, of fixed and predictable behavior. Indeed, the prototypical biography, Xenophon's encomium of the Spartan king Agesilaus, is one that seeks to erase any sense of the particular in favor of the generic pattern that defines a public life. The career portrayed is modeled on the lives of the demigods from which the great myths are drawn. These twentieth-century eulogies, like the classic encomium, are not about individuals so much as they are about approved, socially sanctioned life trajectories. Their subjects become unintelligible to me when represented as icons, models of deportment. What is lost in this process, what has been lost in this death, is the life lived through the body. We are not asked to hear that these were men who desired other men, who struggled to claim a territory in which to express their desire, and who fought to create public spaces—houses of worship, community centers, and political organizations—in which they could feel safe and proud. Nor are we asked to hear of the social and erotic transformations that they precipitated by confounding taken-for-granted boundaries between public and private spheres of activity. To hear praises of these accomplishments, to hear of the specific relationships and interests that frame the dailiness of our lives, we must turn to the literature of testimony (Lynch, 1989; Monette, 1988), to the elegant elegies and gritty obituaries that have proliferated in the gay press and publications of people with HIV/AIDS.

I have come to these ceremonies to remember but find myself alienated from the process that so distorts the people I knew, angry because the silences make me feel shame about what is not spoken. I suspect that we are enduring the ultimate form of cultural violence when our lives are sanitized. Afterwards, we cluster outside the meeting rooms, funeral homes, and churches to share our own memories, confirming the sexual identity in which our lives are grounded. Always acknowledging the consanguinal family as it passes, I am aware of the distances that separate our worlds and our awkward attempts to bridge them. Can it really be that they do not know the truth of the lives they have come to remember? Why do they consider reference to sexual orientation a dishonor—would it deny the deceased's role as instructive icon and model of deportment? Or perhaps, after all, the carefully crafted silence serves the same function as an official announcement, validating the centrality of sexual identity to the modern idea of the individual.

In this chapter I want to understand their silence and my own desire to speak. This means exploring the history through which we have fastened our erotic impulses to categories defining sexual orientation. As an early childhood educator, I am interested in how these notions about adult sexuality are linked to our beliefs in childhood innocence and ignorance. As a gay man, I am impelled to ask additional questions about how these characterizations of children as without knowledge of sexuality are reinforced by popular stereotypes of the homosexual as pederast preying on the young. To disentangle the images of gay men and children that power homophobia, the funereal silences against which I rail, we would need to re-imagine our own sexuality and the protective powers we believe central to our relationships with children.

PUBLIC, PRIVATE, AND SOCIAL IDENTITIES

The idea of sexual identity is neither universal nor atemporal. In Western culture it brings together two previously discrete realms of human behavior. Our ideas of private and public are grounded in the absolute distinctions of the Greek city-state; all that happened within the domestic sphere having to do with sustaining life, producing the necessities of existence, and reproducing the species was equated with the private. The public sphere was one in which free citizens debated the merits of various political acts, and differences were welcomed as signs of community health, not illness. In contradistinction to the private world that was hierarchically structured and constrained by the demands of nature, the public world was democratically organized to allow for free speech and the emergence of individual identity. To be sure, this democratic process was open only to the privileged few and supported by the labors of many. For it was the domination of woman and the slavery of conquered peoples upon which the entire structure was built. There is little record of how those who maintained the private sphere and made possible the luxury of a public world understood their own experience. Nevertheless, the Greek ideal of citizenship, in its assumption of respect for pluralism and community, reflects an ideal against which we can measure contemporary society, where differences are frequently denied and the possibility of freedom is so diminished.

According to Arendt (1958), who tells this story most thoroughly, the once autonomous realms of public and private activity have been collapsed in the modern nation-state. We are left with what she disdainfully refers to as the social. This collapse reflects both the demise of forums for public discussion and the increasing provision of essential goods and services by government itself. The social is neither public nor private. It consists of the accumulated rules of behavior that impose an unceasing burden of conformity on the individual and a concomitant desire to rebel against these constraints. Where once character was a matter of public record, shaped and tested in the crucible of democratic debate, war, or other agonistic contests, it is now expressed through personal interactions hidden from others. Because of the omnipresence of the modern state in domestic life, we have no private spaces of retreat. We are left to seek temporary relief from the strictures of society in moments of intimacy that provide a limited sense of self at best. Our search for closeness is born of the romantic resistance to conformity and to the leveling produced and demanded by the social.

In the contemporary world, the classic ideal has been inverted; moments lived in private take the place of acts undertaken in public and are the new signifiers of character and identity. Without the protection of a truly private domain we scramble to hide, to find space in which we feel ourselves to be in control, safe enough to lose control. Deprived of forums for creating public identities, we have become preoccupied with declaring/not declaring the identities formed in private. We believe our truest selves are expressed in moments of intimacy, behind closed doors, rather than in public arenas. The closet, framed by normative standards of behavior, might best be described as a social space, neither as private as we might wish nor as public as we might fear.

Arendt, a political philosopher, uses concepts such as public, private, and social as if they were transhistorical phenomena rather than socially constructed concepts relevant to specific moments in time. The importance she attributes to citizenship and the loss of identity experienced by stateless persons bears witness to her experience of Germany in the 1930s and her own flight from that totalitarian regime. However, to flesh out our understanding of sexual identity, we must turn to those who write the history of the body and the regulative apparatuses through which the tyranny of the social is maintained (Danzelot, 1979; Foucault, 1978).

At first blush, this history of sexual identity may appear to be of little direct relevance to early education. But on closer inspection it emerges as central rather than peripheral to our interests. First, the debates it has fomented between essentialists and constructivists further illumine problems in the historiography of childhood described in Chapter 5. For example, the essentialist strategy central to the project of groundbreaking sexologists like Magnus Hirschfeld (1946), Richard von Krafft-Ebing (1931), and Karl Ulrichs (Kennedy, 1988) was similar to that employed by nineteenth-century child savers. The former argued that homosexuality was not a sin of willfulness or indication of innate depravity, but rather a natural aberration to be accepted as part of the spectrum of human behavior; the latter rationalized their work by asserting essential, universal aspects of childhood that they undertook to protect. Unfortunately, these arguments from nature also confirmed both the homosexual and the child as special beings, members of discrete populations, who could be observed, classified, explained, and ultimately controlled.

In the latter half of the twentieth century, sociologists left behind this fruitless search for the origins of homosexuality, establishing themselves in the terrain that can be broadly defined as social constructivism. Using different strategies—social/symbolic interactionism (J. H. Gagnon & Simon, 1973; Plummer, 1975), labeling theory (McIntosh, 1981), and the new social history (Weeks, 1981)—these researchers described homosexuality as a function of the rich interplay of social forces occurring between individuals and among populations. Parallel changes in historiography and developmentalism led others to look at the ways that childhood has been constructed over time and at how individual children build their knowledge of the world (James & Prout, 1990a). Although the constructivist perspective has more fully saturated progressive gay politics than our thinking about children and childhood, it continues to be challenged and debated (Epstein, 1987; LeVay, 1993).

In addition, the history of sexual identities reveals how the expansion of the medical, psychological, and pedagogical discourses of the nineteenth century pathologized the homosexual and the child as suffering from the same need for immediate gratification of undeveloped, egocentric impulses. In the process of naming that which is not immediately apparent—sexual practices, psychological pathologies, intellectual capacities—the new professionals produced an ever-expanding and infinitely complex taxonomy of human potential, while insuring their own power to pass authoritative judgments on its meaning. But where exactly is this story of the pairing of child and homosexual written, and how can they be disengaged so we might respond to each with greater dignity and respect?

SEX, HOMOSEXUALITY, AND THE PETITION TO KNOW

David Halperin (1990), for one, describes the construction of sexuality as an autonomous domain of personal identity. Halperin argues that while it is possible to assess and classify sex acts prior to the nineteenth century, it was only then, with the assumption of "sexuality" as a singular drive, that they were elevated to a basic organizing principle of character. At other times and in different cultures, sexuality was treated in a more matter-of-fact way, a mode through which people might experience themselves as meaningful actors but not necessarily one in which they claimed their primary identities. The emergence of heterosexual and homosexual types, people defined by the gender of their object choice, and the concomitant structuring of the closet awaited the formation of a discrete region of sexual intentions.

Drawing on the history of the Greek city-state, Halperin contrasts our belief in sexuality as a natural instinct that can be expressed unfettered by social commitments with the way classical cultures considered sexual protocols to be constituted in and through the politics of the state itself. That is, far from construing sexual interactions as expressive of a deep self, they were understood as an essential part of the socioeconomic arrangements they were designed to uphold. In Athens, sex was assumed to take place only between an active and passive partner, each expressing his or her dominant or submissive social role. Sex was not about mutuality and collaboration, the goals so frequently championed in modern sex manuals and sought through various therapeutic techniques. Nor was sex considered to be a place of refuge where one can leave behind the constraints imposed by an overbearing society and come in contact with an inward disposition, an essential truth. Rather sex affirmed political distinctions and reinforced social distances, legitimizing the differential status of the actors and the entire social order.

The Athenian discourse was structured by a singular focus on phallic penetration. It was the social inferiority/superiority of one's sexual partner, not his or her gender, that was of primary significance. A citizen (i.e., an adult male) could choose equally among youths, women, and slaves, the specific object being a question of taste, a matter of no more significance than whether one preferred one kind of food or another. To talk about sex acts between men in such a context is historically accurate; to refer to these as behaviors undertaken by homosexual persons is an anachronistic imposition of an irrelevant category.

For such a system to work, it was critical that those who were judged to be socially inferior were also described as sexually inert, lacking the wide-ranging, object-specific desires of the free citizen. But Halperin insists that although active and passive partners experienced sex differently, no one believed there to be different kinds of "sexuality"—that is, differently structured psychosexual states or modes of affective orientation. Not until the nineteenth-century introduction of heterosexual and homosexual types was this universalism challenged by the supposition of two opposing sexual orientations, two different ways of being in the world. It is Foucault (1978) who most aptly describes the appearance of the modern homosexual:

> The psychological, psychiatric, medical category of homosexuality was constituted from the moment it was characterized . . . less by a type of sexual relations than by a certain quality of sexual sensibility, a certain way of inverting the masculine and the feminine in oneself. Homosexuality appeared as one of the forms of sexuality when it was transposed from the practice of sodomy onto a kind of interior androgyny, a hermaphrodism of the soul. The sodomite had been a temporary aberration; the homosexual was now a species. (p. 43)

Foucault, by juxtaposing the sodomite with the new homosexual, defining the former as one who engages in discrete aberrant acts and the latter as a person with a unique psychological structure, implies that this story can be told solely in terms of gender inversions, reversals, and contradictions. But a more thorough investigation of the nineteenth-century medical literature suggests otherwise.

Although the concept of inversion was prevalent throughout the century, it was only in the last quarter that the centrality of object choice itself was introduced into the discourse. The invention of the homosexual actually coincides with a shift away from concern with gender transitivity and toward the biological sex of one's partner. The homo/heterosexual dichotomy gave birth to a new set of sexual taxonomies based on object choice alone, leaving other distinctions—predicated, for example, on age, active/passive role, or conventional/unconventional activities—without categorical significance. Primacy was given not to what one does but to whom one does it with.

But Foucault does more than document the invention of the modern homosexual. He charts the progress through which sexuality achieved its ascendancy in our lives. While Halperin (1990), the classical scholar, unearths the meanings of sexual practices in the ancient world, Foucault (1978) describes how we have come to believe that sex tells the truth of our lives, speaking over and against specific "bodies, organs, somatic localizations, functions, anatomo-physiological systems, sensations, and pleasures; something else and something more, with intrinsic properties and laws of its own" (p. 152). And so I, too, am caught in the historical moment. I cannot accept the silences at memorial services, believing that some essential aspect of my friends, of myself, has been denied, even as I understand these "essential" qualities and the categories through which they are inscribed as socially constructed. In our world sex is constituted as a secret, hidden meaning that, once uncovered, is revealed as the omnipotent cause of who and what we are. How can I tolerate silence?

> Between each of us and our sex, the West has placed a never-ending demand for truth: it is up to us to extract the truth of sex, since this truth is beyond its grasp; it is up to sex to tell us our truth, since sex is what holds it in darkness. But is sex hidden from us, concealed by a new sense of decency, kept under a bushel by the grim necessities of bourgeois society? On the contrary, it shines forth; it is incandescent. Several centuries ago, it was placed at the center of a formidable *petition to know*. A double petition, in that we are compelled to know how things are with it, while it is suspected of knowing how things are with us. (Foucault, 1978, p. 77)

This *petition to know* announces Foucault's challenge to the traditional view of the nineteenth century as a period of repression during which our essential sexuality was denied, blocked, and without expression. In contrast, he asserts that beginning in the eighteenth century, a proliferation of medical, pedagogical, and psychiatric discourses began producing new forms of knowledge, framing sexuality as textuality. Sex was transformed from a matter of sensation and pleasure, law and taboo to a problem of truth that could be interrogated through science. Governmental and private agencies deployed the new texts in the interest of controlling populations.

The Western world does not produce *ars erotica*; it practices *scientia sexualis*. The art of initiation and the masterful secret are replaced by the personal confession. A relational strategy once confined to religious penance, the confession now characterizes expectations of personal disclosure between parent and child, student and teacher, patient and psychiatrist, delinquent and expert.

Linked to science and the confession, sexuality extends its influence as the basis of knowledge/power. That is, the new knowledge of the body permits more subtle and intensive regulative techniques. Power that functioned through law and prohibition, liberty and sovereignty, now becomes an effect of knowledge and the new technologies of the self promoted by psychologists, psychiatrists, social workers, and educators. The direct exercise of force and the use of punishment are replaced by the normalization of behavior and surveillance of the body. Once public and visible, power now hides and is invisible. With Foucault we move out of the great halls of state and public tribunals and into the university and school, hospital and clinic, where knowledge is produced and reproduced. We also move into the bedrooms and examining rooms of friend and neighbor.

Foucault names perverts, the heterosexual couple, women, and children alike as critical sites of scientific investigation and textual inscription. The psychiatrization of perversions has several results: categorizations of the abnormal, the normalization of reproductive heterosexuality, and the creation of various corrective technologies. The socialization of procreative sex brought with it a new interest in birth control, to insure the regulation of population growth. The medicalization of the female body was justified in the name of responsibility to family and society. The hysterical pathology of women was considered to be the result of the constant agitation of sexual excitement. Women were simultaneously saturated and emptied of sexuality, as sex and reproduction were designated constitutive of the female body itself.

Like women, children were also in danger of succumbing to their own sexuality. Prone to premature indulgence, requiring constant observation by parents, teachers, and doctors, children were the enemy of the war launched against onanism. As with the project to control female sexuality, Foucault claims that the attempt to protect children from masturbation did more to sexualize the child's body than to deprive it of erotic expression. Referring to the new textbooks, manuals, and studies, Foucault (1980a) says:

> But their *effect* was to din it into parents' heads that their children's sex constituted a fundamental problem in terms of their parental educational responsibilities, and to din it into children's heads that their relationship with their own body and their own sex was to be a fundamental problem as far as *they* were concerned; and this had the consequences of sexually exciting the bodies of children while at the same time fixing the parental gaze and vigilance on the peril of infantile sexuality. (p. 120)

In fact, through a "secret causality," the long-term effects of masturbation, this war did as much to problematize the adult's sexuality as the child's.

The perverse adult, Malthusian couple, hysterical woman, and masturbating child were thus turned into privileged objects of knowledge, visible targets through which sexuality could be controlled. This process was not about the exclusion of individuals but rather their specification and incorporation into society. The field of sexuality was expanding and growing in importance even as the techniques for surveying its contours were refined. Pedagogy helped to identify childhood sexuality, medicine to map the sexual physiology of woman, psychiatry to normalize the perverse, and demography to control populations. In this process, sex was secularized, removed from the realm of religion and aura of sin, and placed under the protection of the state, in the service of the social body.

This is not to suggest that the secularization of sex was complete, or that the new focus on object choice—signaled by the location of homo/heterosexual desire within mutually exclusive, transhistorical categories—displaced earlier belief systems. In the late twentieth century it is the coexistence of multiple vocabularies for talking about sex that provides insight into its social construction and opportunities for disruption of the system in which it is embedded. The priest, the doctor, the educator, the psychiatrist, and the lawmaker offer simultaneous pronouncements about the meaning of sexual behavior that can be conflicting, overlapping, and contradictory. This complex linguistic landscape is mapped daily by everyone from the New Right evangelists, who continue to reproduce the image of the sodomite as sinner, to the television talk show hosts, who frame the homosexual as gender invert when politely and not so politely probing their guests to determine which partner of the gay or lesbian couple plays the husband's role and which the wife's.

History links women, children, and homosexuals in the same nexus of unfulfilled desires. For it is the emergence of the mental health perspective that announces the psychological needs of children and the unique abilities of woman to fulfill them and at the same time defines the homosexual threat to normal development. The homosexual, embodying everything that the child is not, allows us to see what the child is—innocent and without desire, a blank slate on which we may write at will. Women are charged with protecting this (their own) innocence from the powerful desires of those who would seduce them away from and out of their "natural" heterosexuality. In Chapter 4 I explored the nineteenth-century rationale for the introduction of female teachers, which was based on the belief that they shared with young children a greater vulnerability, emotionality, and access to the nonrational than men. Because they were presumed closer to children and children's ways of knowing, women would be better able to communicate and control them. This history suggests the efficacy of looking at Foucault's discrete sites of sexual knowing as part of a fine web of interrelated meanings.

In the twentieth century, developmental research has reinforced the sanctity of the mother/child dyad, while simultaneously suggesting that the partners in the dyad have conflicting desires and interests (Singer, 1992). The imagined tension within this couple most often surfaces in policy debates regarding child care. A mother's need and/or desire to work outside the home is frequently juxtaposed to her child's need for a single, responsive caregiver. A mother with independent interests threatens her child's chances of normal development. Idealized and vilified, glorified and potentially improved, mothers are ultimately exploited; fathers are assigned a minor supporting function. Knowledge about mothers and children cannot be separated, must be read in tandem.

Foucault describes new forms of power operating unobtrusively through the professional discourses that establish behavioral norms; Singer alerts us to how these same invisible technologies are communicated from parent/mother to child. In the isolated but closely bonded family, discipline is exercised not by direct prohibition but by emotional manipulation. That is, the child-centered pedagogy of the middle class conceptualizes the mother/child couple as existing outside the constraints of the real world. Because household work and the mother's wishes are seen as contrary to the child's interests, power is experienced by the child as arbitrary and individual rather than as a reflection of material circumstances. But power exercised through bonds of love and diversion of attention is also a source of uncertainty about discipline and separation for the mother. When power is neither visible nor legible, and harmony is assumed to be the norm, then its potential for misuse is heightened.

Singer suggests that the function of power at an interpersonal level must be connected to a clearer identification of power in the broader social arena. This means challenging the structured maternal inadequacy built into our false ideal of an intensely emotional but socially isolated mother, endlessly responsive to her child's needs. Such an ideal has dominated our research efforts and perpetuated the illusion that mothers can protect their children against the hostile world outside the home. We assume mothers offer a disinterested love and that the outside world cannot offer any emotional support. Equating love with family and power with the external world, we look to programs outside the home to ameliorate social ills and to create a more just society. But the ability of education to effect such transformation is questionable and leads to unrealistic expectations among adults. Rather than emphasizing the future social benefits to accrue from education, we might better focus on the immediate quality of life experienced by all children. To this end we need to replace universalizing developmental philosophies—which deny the power relations between the sexes, classes, ethnic groups, and generations—with analyses of contemporary child-rearing practices using multiple perspectives, including those of the actors themselves.

PERVERTS AND CHILDREN: WHO KNOWS DESIRE?

Questions of power in and around adult–child relations also call attention to a less benign dyad than mother–infant: that of pervert–child. Although the latter is a connection from which we ordinarily prefer to shield ourselves and that is more difficult to extricate from the Foucaultian schema, it, too, is an inevitable outcome of the petition to know. After all, isn't it our most fundamental belief that perverts are linked to children insofar as they are permitted to overpower their innocent victims, the effects of their domination spreading like an unstoppable infection? Willard Waller (1932), a classic educational sociologist, makes clear the diseased nature of the gay teacher, "for nothing seems more certain than that homosexuality is contagious" (p. 147).

Here we must interpret the popular ideas that fuel homophobia against the scholarly histories of sexuality. Stereotypes are far from harmless and reflect a good deal more than the absence of accurate information. Their resistance to correction through the testimony of science attests to this. Originating in cultural ideology, stereotypes reveal the belief systems by which people live (Mohr, 1992). For example, the stereotype of gay men as sex-obsessed child molesters preserves the belief in family innocence. It enables us to locate potentially unregulated and unruly desires outside of the home. Sex is a simple, reproductive activity, not a destabilizing, pleasure-oriented play of complex emotions. The stereotype of homosexuality as the mismatch between a person's biological sex and his or her self-perception—gay men want to be and act like women, lesbians would be men—reinforces the belief in traditional gender roles. The threat posed by the notion of choice in gender identification is derided and disarmed, made ridiculous and unnatural. Homophobic stereotypes are critical maintainers of the social fabric, assuring the economic and biologic reproduction of the family through adherence to appropriate gender roles.

The gay teacher comes into the contemporary classroom conscious of these stereotypes and walking in the shadow of the nineteenth-century homosexual. Our historical predecessors, not yet the self-indulgent "clones" of gay liberation who spread physical disease, are the powerful members of the underworld whose contagion is moral corruption. In the standard text, the older, incurable, "true" invert is driven to choose a younger, passive (need I add, innocent) victim as the object of his attentions. This narrative tells a contradictory story: Homosexuality is both a repugnant practice and one to which it is all too easy to succumb. In the end no one is safe, least of all the child, the apotheosis of the defenseless victim.

In the United Kingdom, the most recent version of this story is codified in Section 28 of the Local Government (Amendment) Act passed in 1988, which states:

(1) A local authority shall not
   (a) intentionally promote homosexuality or publish material with intent of promoting homosexuality;
   (b) promote the teaching in any maintained school of the acceptability of homosexuality as a pretended family relationship.
(2) Nothing in subsection (1) above shall be taken to prohibit the doing of anything for the purpose of treating or preventing the spread of disease.

Watney (1991) points out that the fear of promotion combines a traditional belief in the vulnerable child seduced by the powerful pervert with a new theory of representation. Section 28 has been interpreted to ban representations in any medium that depict gay relationships as equivalent to heterosexual families, tacitly acknowledging that homosexuality is a social identity that does not simply flow from some natural/unnatural wellspring of desire. Media images are capable of doing the work of seduction once left to perverted old men; this leaves open the opportunity for gay people to use public representations to their own pedagogical advantage. The challenge of cultural representation is that it humanizes by individualizing the gay experience, making it less abstract and more mundane. Such representations undermine the purpose of Section 28, which is to project the premodern image of the homosexual as a sinister other and to secure childhood innocence by protecting it from its own desires. Whether through traditional or modern methods, "it is the imagined vulnerability of heterosexuality that is most significant, together with the assumed power of homosexual pleasure to corrode the 'natural' order of social and sexual relations" (Watney, 1991, p. 392).

Talking Abuse/The Abuse of Talking

It is the yoking together of these apparently oppositional images—of childhood innocence and worldly dissipation—that fuels the ultimate moral panic, sexual abuse of the child. The escalating concern about child abuse is evidenced by multiple day-care scandals, stringent new hiring regulations in educational settings, and the appearance of shelves upon shelves of books to sell both prevention strategies and after-the-fact therapeutic interventions. Tracing the history of family violence from its "discovery" in last half of the nineteenth century to its "rediscovery" during the 1960s, Linda Gordon (1988) places our current preoccupation in historical context: Family violence, which was originally defined as an issue of cruelty to children requiring the charitable efforts of child savers, was subsequently transformed into a problem of child neglect needing the intervention of professional social workers or a medical crisis requiring a physician's diagnosis and treatment. Most often, young people suffer from ambiguous forms of neglect rather than from direct assault. The waxing and waning of interest in the topic reflects pervasive anxieties about the health of the family; violence is often the result of power arrangements within a given relationship.

Best (1990) describes the recent focus on abuse in terms of a broad spectrum of threats to childhood that began to emerge in the late 1960s: child pornography, satanic cults, adolescent prostitution and runaways, missing children. The fears for our own children, natural symbols of the future, were a projection of a more general anxiety over the future of society sparked by the civil rights movement, the Vietnam War, and Watergate. We identified with the child's vulnerability and marked visible adult targets—the abusive parent, sexual pervert, pathological criminal—as scapegoats for our broader social concerns. This scapegoating allowed us to avoid more intractable problems such as poverty, health, and education, and served as a springboard for congressional hearings and political rhetoric on the subject of "our most valuable resource." In fact, little was done to effect the programmatic changes that would actually make a safer world for children.

The child abuse panic permits the outsider, the deviant, to highlight the normative ideal. The ideology of the innocent child, developing free from adult interference but always under close protective surveillance, is punctured most radically by the image of the intrusive, adult deviant. The menacing adult underscores the defenseless child. Press accounts frequently refer to the potential dangers of the unknown adult, when the majority of crimes against children are perpetrated by people they know. The problem itself has grown from the battered child syndrome of the 1960s, to child abuse (incest and child molestation) in the 1970s, to child abuse and neglect in the 1980s. Finally, physical, sexual, and emotional abuse are confounded, permitting the issue to be transformed from a subject for criminal investigation to one for social welfare intervention.

However, it might also be argued that the panic reflects more than a projection of economic and social anxieties onto the fate of children. It also serves to instruct us about the line between licit and illicit behavior, which reinforces the family as the locus of safety, the place where appropriate desires are shaped by two loving, heterosexual parents. The lesson is clear: Legitimate desires are not sexual desires; sanctioned emotions do not include jealousy or anger. Erotic attachments to children, erotic attachments of children, must not be admitted, admitted only in the presence of a trained professional, admitted for the purposes of control and abnegation. Abuse is the result of abnormal development, development that can be regulated through the caring pedagogy of the family circle. By heightening a focus on individual pathology and the role of parents in producing acceptable psychological characteristics, the moral panic diverts us from the intense emotional fabric of the isolated, nuclear family in which the majority of abusive situations originate.

The proliferation of media stories about the abuse of children in early childhood settings is more than a conservative resistance to professionalized care. It is part of a larger compulsion to control and rewrite sex in a way that distances the child from the adult and removes both from the passionate desires that might inform behavior. The child is ignorant, innocent, and pure, and the adult is knowledgeable, guilty, and sexual. The moral panic serves to reinforce normative sexual stereotypes, to teach us anew about the significance of heterosexual, monogamous domestic arrangements. Bersani (1988), in describing the sexual aversion-displacements that have intensified with the HIV epidemic, suggests the way that these have been realized through the increased interest in incest and abuse:

Adult sexuality is split in two: at once redeemed by its retroactive metamor-
phosis into the purity of an asexual childhood, and yet preserved in its most
sinister forms by being projected onto the image of the criminal seducer of children. "Purity" is crucial here: behind the brutalities against gays, against
women, and, in the denial of their very nature and autonomy, against children
lies the pastoralizing, the idealizing, the redemptive project I have been speaking of. More exactly, the brutality is identical to the idealization. (p. 221)

Kitzinger (1990), analyzing newspaper accounts of child abuse, documents its depiction as an attack on childhood itself rather than as a crime
against individuals. Abuse is seen as the theft of innocence. And who knows
more about theft, or initiation of the young into the world of erotic desire,
than the homosexual? Living beyond the traditional family, homosexuals are
seen as placing themselves outside of the reproductive cycle, without respect
for the age-related boundaries defining the law of succession. Kitzinger argues that our assumptions about childhood innocence, passivity, and vulnerability help to perpetuate child abuse and are part of the political process
through which children are made an oppressed group. Placing the phenomenon of abuse in this context, she advocates a deconstruction of childhood
as we know it so as to clarify the way that power circulates among adults
and children and to recognize the forms of active resistance through which
children defy their oppression and fend off abusive adults.

In his explication of Victorian fiction and scientific texts, Kincaid (1992)
helps us to see that the figure of the sinister, corrupting pedophile created
through our hysterical talk of child pornography and prostitution, incest and
abductions is an inevitable by-product of the pure and fragile child of our
imaginations:

If the child is desirable, then to desire it can hardly be freakish. To maintain
otherwise is to put into operation pretty hefty engines of denial and self-
deception. And that is what we have done. By insisting so loudly on the innocence, purity and asexuality of the child, we have created a subversive echo:
experience, corruption, eroticism. More than that, by attributing to the child
the central features of desirability in our culture—purity, innocence, emptiness,
Otherness—we have made absolutely essential figures who would enable this
desire. Such figures are certainly not us, we insist, insist so violently because
we must, so violently that we come to think that what we are is what these
figures are not. (p. 4)

The pedophile whom we demonize even as we construct, marginalize
as we normalize, distance as we bring closer has become a primary vehicle
for expressing/repressing our own erotic interests in children. The innocent
child is always ignorant, empty of knowledge, in need of protection: the

perfect receptacle for the adult's imaginings. The child/pedophile dyad emerges from the Foucaultian strategy of highlighting the normal through the abnormal, reading the text by deciphering the barely legible notes in the margins. The intensity with which we pursue the pedophile, the campaign to root out evil, tells the story of our own desires, not of a subversive sexuality located in others. The drive to obey the laws of the superego does not reflect an innate desire to do the right thing but the strength of Oedipal longings and the need to suppress them.

Indeed, centering the pedophile throws us off center, raising questions about two essential paradoxes: 1) the presence on the inside of one who is presumed only to exist on the outside, and 2) the violence committed against children—the denial of their sexuality—in our overly zealous attempts to protect them. Focusing on the corrupting power of the pedophile allows us to enjoy the role of defending the hapless child.

> When it comes to children, the first assumption is that their sexuality can never be directed towards an adult. Secondly they are deemed incapable of self-expression. Thus no one ever believes them. They are believed to be immune to sexuality, and unable to discuss it. (Foucault, 1980b, p. 41)

Kitzinger proposes that we would be more effective advocates for children if we empowered them to come to their own defense, to realize their own strategies and skills of protection, to imagine them as strong rather than as weak, sexual rather than without desire. Kincaid also recognizes the complexity of child/adult relations in which the former may in fact make unrecognized emotional claims on the latter. However, Kincaid's approach is to shift the play of child/adult relations entirely off the turf of power and onto fields of affinity/communication, play/inconsequence. The cultural equation of power and sex makes it impossible to think of relationships between children and adults in any terms other than hierarchy and consequence, masking the potential for common interests explored on more level ground. Decentering power would open less protected spaces but ones in which new and non-threatening relational qualities might be valued.

While the nineteenth-century interest in pedophilia is expressed through literary and scientific texts, in the twentieth century our desires are expressed and produced through a multiplicity of vehicles including movies, television, schools, athletic fields, playgrounds, day-care centers, and courtrooms. It is in the last that Kincaid patiently situates himself, as a recorder and witness to the second part of the "McMartin Pre-School Case." The longest court trial in U.S. history, it originated in over 200 counts of child molesting involving 42 children, 4 members of the Buckey family, and 3 additional teachers. After exhaustively reviewing the history of the improbable—at times fantastic and salacious—accusations, Kincaid concludes that the trial cannot in any way be construed as a search for truth or closure. Rather it serves a totally other function: the multiplication of narratives and texts that will continuously engage us with the idea of childhood innocence and its violation. It is the strength of our denial, the eight-year duration of the trial itself, that signals our desire.

> We keep the story alive and before us, being told over and over. At the same time, we find ways to deny emphatically that we are authoring this story, much less serving as its leading players. By creating gothic melodramas, monster stories of child-molesting and playing them out periodically (often), we provide not just titillation but assurances of righteousness. Demonizing the child-molester ... we can connect to a pedophile drama while pretending to shut down the theater. (Kincaid, 1992, p. 341)

Considering the relationship between childhood innocence and adult sexuality in the context of child-loving, the issue is posed as one of age, not gender. Although the gender of the object of desire is a matter of relative indifference—the delicate, vulnerable child is desexed—the desiring subject is inevitably imagined as male, reflecting the ongoing association of sex with social power. But from the perspective of homosexual stereotypes, rather than pedophilia per se, the belief in the older man preying on the younger boy continues. In fact, with a wider public acceptance of homosexual relationships among adults, a conservative minority would intensify the association of pedophilia with homosexuality, rekindling homophobic attitudes and reinforcing socioeconomic prohibitions to men caring for young children. This remapping of pedophilia onto homosexuality occurs despite statistics indicating that ... in 82% of child abuse cases the alleged offender is a heterosexual partner of a close relative and in only 0.7% of cases can the offender be identified as potentially homosexual (Jenny, Roesler, & Poyer, 1994).

Educational Pederasty

Ironically, in classical cultures the prototypical and only sanctioned sexual relationship between men was one in which difference in age was celebrated. The pederastic model encourages the older partner, the one who is presumed to know and able to act, to fill the younger, passive partner with his own desire. The youth, who is without intentionality, is made a desiring and knowledgeable adult when penetrated by wisdom and age. He is not substantially different from his teacher as he awaits the introduction of the latter's knowledge. The teacher is a unique phallic presence; students are many empty receptacles.

But have our biblical morality, laws of consent, and new psychosexual categories proscribed the pederastic relationship, or has it in fact become so fundamental to our way of socializing children that we have lost sight of its pervasive presence? Have we been blinded by the preponderance of female teachers in the early grades and the academic successes of young girls, not to see the degree to which our classrooms, with their teacher-centered methods, preplanned curricula, and high teacher/pupil ratios, replicate ancient pedagogical models? Perhaps it is not a matter of blindness. After all, contemporary educational critics have been eager to point out the passive role assigned to students in our schools, the assumption that the adult must motivate the child, and the focus on quantitative rather than qualitative assessments of progress. They have also indicated their preference for less personally threatening metaphors to be extracted from the economic arena (Freire, 1986). Yet to talk of the banking model of education is to sanitize the pedagogical discourse, transforming the sexual economics of adult/child interactions into the political economics of capital accumulation. While in either model there is only one source of knowledge/desire and multiple accounts into which it may be placed, it would be a mistake to assume that they are the same.

What the banking model does not allow us to talk about, and the pederastic model forces us to grapple with, are the assumptions of innocence or guilt, protection and control that form the boundaries of the childhood closet. For with our gaze we enclose children in a space not so very different from the closet of the homosexual. In both instances we construe definitions of a particular time and place as having universal validity. Qualities that might be used to explore alternative ways of being in the world are instead employed to measure developmental maturity, to separate rather than to connect us in a common project.

As we have seen, the naming of the homosexual, and the medical discourse it engendered, sprang from the same source as the labeling of the psychological child and the proliferation of developmental specialists. Both are part of a larger nineteenth-century movement of reterritorialization, an attempt to assert order in a world of unmanageable complexity and disorder. The space children and homosexuals have come to occupy together is that of the undeveloped, egocentric, and impulse-ridden members of society. For although desire itself might best be described as emergent—neither homosexual nor heterosexual by design, its components only discernible *a posteriori*—it is the homosexual who is described in the psychiatric literature as caught in a matrix of unresolved fixations, pre-Oedipal fantasies, and undifferentiated desires that have been unsatisfactorily repressed. By failing to accomplish the work of the Oedipal stage, the homosexual does not achieve the socially sanctioned level of genital sexuality that leads to a heterosexual orientation. The homosexual is one who does not reproduce, who lives out-side of the generative family, who subverts his or her own family drama and therefore does not know the law of succession.

Until the symbolic order asserts itself through the social organization of phallic desire, the child's polymorphous perversity is greeted with vary-ing degrees of anxiety and control on the part of the adult. But once past childhood, any indications of homosexual desire, literally and figuratively represented by interest in seeking pleasure from the anus, an organ associ-ated with waste and pre-Oedipal erotic satisfactions, is not tolerated. For the anus has been characterized in our phallocentric world as that which is private, interiorized, and therefore antisocial (Hocquenghem, 1978). As it poses the possibility of multiple sites of pleasure and organizing principles, anal eroticism threatens our entire system of binary oppositions: male/female, adult/child, heterosexual/homosexual. The possibility of homosexual desire, of the expression of childhood's polymorphous perversity, undercuts the edifice upon which our reproductive arrangements have been built, in turn threatening the gendered nature of our economic system.

Perhaps it is not surprising that a culture that works so hard to believe that children are innocent, devoid of the corrupting desires of sexuality once past the Oedipal crisis, would choose to talk of pedagogical economics so as to mask the measured but relentless way that children are objectified in schools, filled with the desires of others. Even as we try to protect our chil-dren from the touch of strangers, the invasive explorations of professionals, and the social ills they are presumed unready to manage, we all too readily expose them to institutions that cripple their sense of agency, replacing the knowledges with which they arrive by the canonical knowledges of teacher and text. To treat the student as knowing subject is to subvert the traditional notion of pedagogical authority, throwing into question the phallic economy of the classroom on which it is based. A multiplicity of desiring actors sug-gests that there are multiple zones from which to receive satisfaction and toward which to direct one's attention. By legitimizing the engagement of students with one another, we promote a return to a polymorphous perver-sity in which pleasure/knowledge potentially emanates from and circulates among all the actors in the classroom drama.

I do not mean to imply that educators ignore age-related differences, or that our current institutional arrangements are so constructed as to deny the possibility of individual resistance, although resistance is inevitably a response to and shaped by the existing social context. However, I do want to argue that the working assumptions undergirding these arrangements need to be more carefully articulated and examined for the way that they deny the sexu-ality of both adults and children.

As long as education is imagined to be entirely nonsexual, the actual erotics of the pedagogic situation can be displaced away in the imaginary likeness of the evil pervert, "promoting" his or her sexuality with "innocent" children. The question is *not* whether or not children are sexual beings, but how adults respond to children's sexuality, in ways that range from total denial to an untroubled acceptance. (Watney, 1991, p. 398)

WHAT'S POLITICS GOT TO DO WITH IT?

This chapter began with questions about how sexuality became central to our conceptions of identity. I sought answers in changing notions of the public and private, the constitution of sexuality as a discrete domain of human behavior, and the construction of a power–knowledge axis for the surveillance of human populations in the nineteenth century. The silence pervading the memorial services I attended became readily understandable both in terms of the significance afforded to sexuality in our culture and of the stereotypes informing popular ideas about homosexuality. In other contexts, including radio, television, and the tabloids, the incessant talk of sexual perverts and childhood innocence confirms the link between the child and the homosexual. This previously unimaginable couple serves to regulate civil society and produce a discourse of "normal" desire. But what of all my own talk: from the impulse to interrupt the sanctity of the dead, to engagement in gay politics, to the writing of these chapters? Doesn't my own verbal production only reinforce a categorical system that limits everyone's possibilities? At times, especially in classrooms filled with young adults who seem to take a special pleasure in simplification, I have been reluctant to identify myself as gay. In part this is a reflection of not wanting to bear the discomfort of being "out" in potentially hostile terrain. It is also a recognition that sexual identity is a double-edged sword. Labels have the potential to reinforce the status quo as well as to become the rallying point for change.

Although Foucault's volumes of political philosophy can hardly be construed as an activist's handbook, they do make clear that resistance to dominant modes of knowing and speaking is always problematic, always in doubt. If the expanding scientific discourse of the nineteenth century created the homosexual species, it also "made possible the formation of a 'reverse' discourse: homosexuality began to speak in its own behalf, to demand that its legitimacy or 'naturality' be acknowledged" (Foucault, 1978, p. 101). However, in using the same vocabulary, the same categories by which it had been medically disqualified, the reverse discourse becomes part of the field of power it would ostensibly oppose.

Mapping the contemporary political landscape, Sullivan (1993) confirms that today everyone has a theory of sexual identity. For example, extreme conservatives and radicals share a constructivist perspective, leading the former to a politics of punishment and cure and the latter to one of liberation and expansion. In between, moderates and modern liberals accept some essentialist elements, while assuming that the majority of gay people are persuaded by others or freely choose their sexual orientation. Where moderates tolerate without approval, modern liberals proactively seek to protect homosexuals through a legislative agenda banning private discrimination in housing, employment, public accommodations, and so on. In contrast, Sullivan advocates a classic liberal politics that respects the public/private distinction by eschewing direct state intervention in the lives of individuals and the framing of gays as a victimized group similar to racial minorities. Classic liberals would instead focus on assuring civil equality in order to create a state that models rather than mandates tolerance for its citizens. Most immediately, this would mean unlimited participation in the military, an organization at the heart of the state, and the right to marry, an act symbolizing full membership in civil society.

Within gay/lesbian politics, constructivism has without a doubt had the upper hand (Halley, 1989). Unfortunately, it still leaves activists unable to account for the possibility of a core of differentiating elements that bind gay people together by something more than their shared oppression. When individual life is left open to constant revision and transformation, as in the constructivist model, then sexuality becomes only a matter of choice, a mere preference. Essentialists for their part have always left the individual trapped in a history of constraint and unable to theorize social change. Sexuality is a given, an immutable orientation.

Cohen (1991) identifies two additional problems with our reliance on socially constructed categories in political life. First, they often lead to unwarranted assumptions about similarities among those who live within their boundaries. Complexity and contradiction resulting from our multiple positionings in society are erased as we unwittingly subscribe to the coherence embedded in notions of sexual and/or gender identity. "Our" history, too, has often been written to exclude nonwhite, nonmale and nonurban gay people (Bravmann, 1990). Living, working, and socializing in the newly formed communities of identity can be empowering and exhilarating; it can also be confining and exhausting.

The drive for certainty makes us individually vulnerable to destabalizing crises as we become aware of contradictory aspects of our lived experience. The reification of categories also weakens the ability of political and cultural institutions to act in an inclusive rather than exclusive manner, making them less mobile in response to the changing social situation. But identity politics is not easily fixed or adjusted. At its core is the very denial of difference among group members that allows them to claim a unique identity, membership in this group rather than that. Fuss (1989) says this best: "to the extent that identity always contains the specter of non-identity within it, the subject is always divided and identity is always purchased at the price of the exclusion of the Other, the repression or repudiation of non-identity" (p. 103).

The second difficulty with social constructivism, especially as it is realized in academic discourse analysis, is that it can deprive individuals of agency. The subject is left to drown in the powerful swirl of social determinations, unable to grasp hold of transformational possibilities inherent to this perspective. When our minds are seduced and captured by discourse theory, we run the risk of losing our bodies as they are designated a conceptual problem, merely the "effect" of how others talk. In recent years much of this talk has been conducted by academics, literary critics, and expert rhetoricians, thus ensuring their own power—by moving the conversation out of the realm of scientists speaking of biological determinism, or sociologists looking to the regularities of our daily interactions, and into the world of textual hermeneutics. Cohen (1991) becomes an advocate for understanding political movements as embodied processes, asserting that "bodies do make a (political) difference and that difference is often a matter of (e)motion" (p. 85). Indeed, it is this sense of difference, these (e)motions that I have tried to represent in the stories that shape the preceding chapters.

The tenacity of the debates, the way in which they echo discussions among feminists about gender differences and among educators about the nature of childhood, seems to confirm Foucault's belief that it is virtually impossible to escape the fields of power in which they are at play. But in more existential moments, Foucault (1981) suggests the possibility of resisting determinism and fixity with choice and futurity:

> We must be aware of . . . the tendency to reduce being gay to the questions: "Who am I?" and "What is the secret of my desire?" Might it not be better if we asked ourselves what sort of relationships we can set up, invent, multiply or modify through our homosexuality? The problem is not trying to find out the truth of one's sexuality within oneself, but rather, nowadays, trying to use our sexuality to achieve a variety of different types of relationships. And this is why homosexuality is probably not a form of desire, but something to be desired. We must therefore insist on *becoming* gay, rather than persist in defining ourselves as such. (p. 4)

In this book I have not only wanted to explore becoming gay before the epidemic, and living as a gay man during its reign, but also becoming an adult who mourns the loss of a generation of peers even as he cares for the living, and becoming a teacher who recognizes the difficult realities of childhood even while holding open future possibilities. At times, these projects have seemed oppositional, reflecting irreconcilable differences, contradictions, and issues that would not allow themselves to be discussed together. At others, they seemed to be one and the same project, theoretically and practically linked through the lived experiences I have narrated. In the end, I am convinced that it is only such a journey through the borderlands, the spaces where our diverse identities abut, bisect, and overlap, that permits the elusive truth of our coherent subjectivity to emerge.

Postscript

As I rush to visit classrooms of young children born during the second decade of the HIV/AIDS epidemic, scramble to prepare notes for classes of graduate students, themselves only young children when HIV first appeared, conscientiously edit drafts of this volume begun well after HIV irrevocably changed my world, I realize how difficult it has been for me to find a way forward. Burdened with a history that is at once social and personal, public and private, political and professional, I have tried to manage the responsibility through textual production. At times I have been like an astronaut forced to jettison canisters of used materials while in orbit, leaving behind many of the emotions that have powered my journey in the past in order to move into the future. At others, I have been a more earthbound backpacker—shifting, rearranging, and organizing the load to make it more bearable. The painful, sometimes mundane work of unpacking and repacking can have surprising consequences. The load is suddenly lighter, a new balance has been established, and the drudgery of the miles to come transformed.

The transformative potential of art is like the successful work of mourning individual instances of suffering leading to more general laws of existence (Kristeva, 1993). In writing I have tried to capture moments of emotional recognition and make clear the pathways from my personal history to the larger themes that inform our pedagogical efforts, realizing the truth of Proust's assertion that "ideas come to us as the successors to griefs." Grief develops the powers of the mind. Indeed, grief that does not lead to ideas ends up by killing us.

But my efforts have been plagued by a nagging sense of disloyalty. Have I falsified another's life in the service of my own art? Is my survival itself a silent rebuke to those who have died? How does writing fulfill my commitment to ending an endless epidemic?

Once again, I find myself better able to answer these questions through navigating the unpredictable waters of academic life. Accepting an invitation to join a symposium on advocacy for young children, I confront the irony of being one who is fascinated by silence and obsessed with ignorance, while

208

suggesting to others how they might speak out, make public arguments, assume the position of one who knows. As the date approaches, I rifle through my files searching for clues about how to enter a conversation on advocacy. Among the folders filled with overworked lectures, drafts of unpublished papers, yellowed newspaper clippings and the like, is an unmarked, forgotten envelope. I open it hesitantly . . . photographs.

Photographs of Michael, photographs I did not want to find so soon again. Can four years still be too soon? Freud is right. Under the sway of primary processes, the unconscious does not know about time. All the rational modes of the ego, all the logical, sequential, cognitive processes, cannot protect us from yesterday's pain. Placed in this innocuous manila envelope, the photographs have found a home between "obituaries"—what others have said about friends and loved ones, and "remembrances"—the eulogies that I myself have been called upon to deliver. The photographs are both obituary and remembrance, texts that another has created and I am now about to read. But I do not want to remember, not in the way that photographs make you remember.

I resist the verisimilitude of the photograph in favor of the emotions, stories, and ongoing dialogues that are part of my inner life. My own memories of Michael are not visual. They are encoded in the objects with which I surround myself: a statuette of an Indian goddess he gave me at Christmas 1985, which sits on my desk as I write; the audiotape of a radio interview he gave a year before his death, to which I have never listened but which I always dust off some time during the morning; the card of a stranger with whom I shared a lunch break during a hospital visit, now worn and blackened with years pressed between dollar bills in my wallet.

In the photographs he looks so young, so handsome. He is young, barely 35 I suppose. His gaze is direct, unnerving. Photographs offer an unexpected confrontation with temporality, and I am unsettled. The unconscious does not know time, does not know who is aging and who can no longer age. We live in and at the same time. In the photographs he does not change either. Yet they mock the unconscious, begging comparison with my own mirrored reflection that tells daily of how I grow older. Preserving a unique image, photographs are cruel reminders of his absence. They have the power to evoke feelings I both want to forget and am afraid of forgetting.

And what was it like then, nine years ago, when these photographs were taken and we struggled to make a life together? In one picture he is sitting on the floor, cross-legged in jeans, dress shirt, with a broad, open smile. Now my heart opens to that smile the way it did thirteen years ago as we sat across the aisle from one another in the university auditorium, along with other gay activists from around the country, in what was planned as the inaugural meeting of a radical new political organization. He listens intently to the speakers, caucuses frequently with his friends, and eyes me shyly, distractedly.

We meet at the break. I do not remember who spoke first but the connection is electric. We spend much of the afternoon walking through the campus, holding hands, talking about the politics of gay liberation and the future of the movement. Our meeting is consummated there and then. He kneels before me and I before him. We worship one another. And this is how our story begins—directly, physically, rebelliously, in an academic institution, at a political conference, our backs against the wall of a bathroom stall. These first hours contain all the elements that will shape our relationship in the years to come—a commitment to activism, a rich play of intellect, an appreciation of the body and its dangers. It is only six months before the first article about GRID will appear in *The New York Times*, nine years till his death from that same disease, thirteen years till I recover the photographs that tell me so vividly that I resist remembering, that I am remembering. Is there a relationship between these private memories and public policy? How can writing about the connections that bind us to others be considered research, let alone activism?

In this book I have argued that research should involve speaking and writing from a responsibly identified position. In naming the experiences of loss and attachment, separation and nurture that frame my work, I name the sources of my passions even as I struggle to understand how these passions inform my thinking about children, childhood, and the classrooms we share. I also speak as an early childhood educator, addressing a field that does not easily support such direct, unmediated explorations of personal experience. These explorations would appear to contradict the official messages about what we can know, what we allow ourselves to know, and how this knowing can affect our life with children.

Disloyalty? Silent rebuke? The only disloyalty is silence. The only rebuke is resignation. I understand testimony as a form of advocacy (Murphy, 1993). In bearing witness to the suffering of others, to the painful presence of absence in my own life, I act as guarantor. The failure to testify would be a betrayal of self and other. To inscribe the merit and worth of those who can no longer speak for themselves is to convince others, an indifferent world, that someone was here and, death notwithstanding, a presence remains. At the same time this affirmation of his life and the willingness to face disbelief signal my own return to a concern with human temporality, to a concern for living. Heidegger (1924/1992) reminds us that speaking is fundamental to our being-in-the-world. As we speak *out*, we speak *with* others *about* something. In testimony I do not attempt to overcome death but rather to claim the last word, to prevent it from undermining the meaning of my continued existence.

As a teacher–author, I speak and write, living in the tension between thought and action, work and the word so ably described by Paul Ricoeur (1965). I once believed that the work of advocacy was the work of picket lines and protests, sit-ins and street theater, public hearings and private lobby efforts. Now I realize that the work of advocacy is also the work of the word—our talking and teaching, our writing and witnessing, our texts and testimonies. It is true that work aims at useful effect and words at intersubjective understanding. There is certainty about work, visible accomplishments to be admired, a changed world to appreciate. The word is more often gratuitous, its usefulness never certain, its effects problematic. But the word is also gesture and action. People are mobilized by its power and caught in its consequences. Through the word we incite others to act, set forth our meanings, indicate what is to be done.

Work and the word are an essential dialectic; the efficacious products of the former need to be framed by the critical and poetic function of the latter. It is the tension between them that drives civilization forward. The uncertainty and risk that come with the word are the price we pay for the services it renders. The word is corrective to the deadly routine and depersonalization of modern work, endowing our efforts with social meaning. It compensates for work by offering the possibility of a spiritually fulfilling leisure. The word is foundational, too, allowing for theory to emerge through the disinterested play of ideas. In language we can imagine the new, we can create the unrehearsed, construct the worlds in which we would live.

My words are imperative, the words of one who, seeing only confusion, comes to decision and takes a position. I want to move others to action. My words are also dubitative. They bring decision into question. They ask about meaning and wait for response. The dubitative word captures us in an ironic, reflective mode, assuming an interrogative stance toward being, while the imperative word defines us as worker and actor. Finally, my words are invocation. I have given up rational argument. We declare ourselves in poetry and song, elegy and lyric. By chanting the names of those I have lost, invoking the lives of children who are deprived of their childhoods, publicly mourning the legions of unrealized lives, I turn toward the world and ask how we can make it better. What does our work mean? Does it have value? At the same time, I turn toward spiritual sources to accomplish this work and toward others to exclaim, to entreat them to join in the task of bearing witness to suffering. Cornell West (quoted in Anderson, 1994) names this responsibility:

> The quest for truth, the quest for the good, the quest for the beautiful, for me, presupposes allowing suffering to speak, allowing victims to be visible, and allowing social misery to be put on the agenda of those with power. (p. 40)

Words have always been my work. I declare my position now. I engage in dialogue. I beseech others for assistance. I try to stay close to first-person knowing, so long excluded from the official domains of professional discourse. To advocate is to take up a position, and I find mine among those whom I know and love—children, people with HIV/AIDS, gay men and lesbians. I want similar things for them all: equity, social justice, and respect for the integrity of their lives. Together they teach me about the rejection of difference, the paralyzing anxiety about sex and death, and the overwhelming fear of the stranger that permeate our culture. Separately they help me to recognize what Audre Lorde (1988) has long known: "I learn my most lasting lessons about difference by closely attending to the ways in which the differences inside me lie down together" (p. 117).

References

Abelove, H., Barale, M., & Halperin, D. (Eds.). (1993). *The lesbian and gay studies reader*. New York: Routledge.

Adan, J. (1991). *The children in our lives: Knowing and teaching them*. Albany: State University of New York Press.

Ade, W. (1982). Professionalism and its implications for the field of early childhood education. *Young Children, 37*(3), 25–32.

Albert, E. (1986). Illness and deviance: The response of the press to AIDS. In D. Feldman & T. Johnson (Eds.), *The social dimensions of AIDS* (pp. 163–178). New York: Praeger.

Alcoff, L. (1988). Cultural feminism versus post-structuralism: The identity crisis in feminist theory. *Signs, 13,* 405–436.

Alexander, R. J. (1984). *Primary teaching*. London: Holt, Rinehart & Winston.

Almy, M. (1975). *The early childhood educator at work*. New York: McGraw-Hill.

Almy, M. (1982, November). *An early childhood education/care research agenda*. Paper presented at the annual conference of the National Association for the Education of Young Children, Washington, DC.

Alston, K. (1991). Teaching, philosophy, and eros: Love as relation to truth. *Educational Theory, 41*(4), 385–395.

Altman, L. (1993a, June 15). Conference ends with little hope for AIDS cure. *The New York Times*, p. C1,3.

Altman, L. (1993b, June 8). World health official says AIDS spread could be controlled. *The New York Times*, p. C6.

Alves, R. (1972). *Tomorrow's child*. New York: Harper & Row.

Anderson, J. (1994, January 14). The public intellectual. *The New Yorker*, pp. 39–48.

Antler, J. (1982). Progressive education and the scientific study of the child. *Teachers College Record, 83,* 559–593.

Aoki, T. T. (1992). Layered voices of teaching: The uncannily correct and the elusively true. In W. F. Pinar & W. M. Reynolds (Eds.), *Understanding curriculum as phenomenological and text* (pp. 17–27). New York: Teachers College Press.

Apple, M. W. (1979). *Ideology and curriculum*. London: Routledge & Kegan Paul.

Apple, M. W. (Ed.). (1982). *Cultural and economic reproduction in education*. Boston: Routledge & Kegan Paul.

Apple, M. W., & Weiss, L. (Eds.). (1983). *Ideology and practice in schooling.* Philadelphia: Temple University Press.

Arendt, H. (1958). *The human condition.* Chicago: University of Chicago Press.

Arendt, H. (1961). *Between past and future.* New York: Viking.

Aries, P. (1962). *Centuries of childhood—A social history of family life.* New York: Knopf.

Aronowitz, S., & Giroux, H. (1991). *Postmodern education.* Minneapolis: University of Minnesota Press.

Ashton-Warner, S. (1963). *Teacher.* New York: Bantam Books.

Ball, S. J. (Ed.). (1990). *Foucault and education.* New York: Routledge.

Banks, J. (1993). Multicultural education: Historical development, dimensions, and practice. In L. Darling-Hammond (Ed.), *Review of research in education 1993* (pp. 3–51). Washington, DC: American Educational Research Association.

Baratz, S. S., & Baratz, J. C. (1970). Early childhood intervention: The social science base of institutional racism. *Harvard Educational Review, 83,* 1170–1186.

Barritt, L., Beekman, T., Bleeker, H., & Mulderij, K. (1985). *Researching educational practice.* Grand Forks: University of North Dakota Press.

Barthes, R. (1982). *A Barthes reader* (S. Sontag, Ed.; R. Miller, Trans.). London: Jonathan Cape.

Basch, C. E. (1989). Preventing AIDS through education: Concepts, strategies, and research priorities. *Journal of School Health, 59,* 296–300.

Beauchamp, D. E. (1985, December). Community: The neglected tradition of public health. *Hastings Center Report, 15,* 28–35.

Beck, E. T. (1988, June). *The search for language, voice and "home."* Paper presented at symposium, "Encounter with Austrian-born scholars of German literature: 1938–1988," Vienna, Austria.

Bell, N. Z. (1991). Ethical issues in AIDS education. In F. G. Reimer (Ed.), *AIDS and ethics* (pp. 128–154). New York: Columbia University Press.

Bellah, R. N., Madsen, R., Sullivan, W. M., Swidler, A., & Tipton, S. D. (1985). *Habits of the heart.* Berkeley: University of California Press.

Ben-Peretz, M., & Bromme, R. (1990). *The nature of time in schools.* New York: Teachers College Press.

Bensimon, E. M. (1992). Lesbian existence and the challenge to normative constructions of the academy. *Journal of Education, 174*(3), 98–114.

Bereiter, C., & Englemann, S. (1966). *Teaching disadvantaged children in the preschool.* Englewood Cliffs, NJ: Prentice-Hall.

Berger, L., & Luckmann, P. (1967). *The social construction of reality.* Garden City, NY: Doubleday.

Bergman, D. (1991). *Gaiety transfigured: Gay self-representation in American literature.* Madison: University of Wisconsin Press.

Berliner, D. (1986). In pursuit of the expert pedagogue. *Educational Research, 15*(7), 5–13.

Bernstein, B. (1975). *Class, codes and control* (Vol. 3). London: Routledge & Kegan Paul.

Bersani, L. (1988). Is the rectum a grave? In D. Crimp (Ed.), *AIDS: Cultural analysis/Cultural activism* (pp. 197–222). Cambridge: MIT Press.

Best, J. (1990). *Threatened children: Rhetoric and concern about child-victims.* Chicago: University of Chicago Press.

Beyer, L. (1986). Schooling for moral and democratic communities. *Issues in Education, 1*(12), 371–393.

Beyer, L., & Liston, D. (1992). Discourse or moral action: A critique of postmodernism. *Educational Theory, 42*(4), 371–395.

Biber, B., Shapiro, E., & Wickens, D. (1971). *Promoting cognitive growth: A developmental-interaction point of view.* Washington, DC: National Association for the Education of Young Children.

Bloch, M. N. (1992). Critical perspectives on the historical relationship between child development and early childhood education research. In S. Kessler & B. B. Swadener (Eds.), *Reconceptualizing the early childhood curriculum* (pp. 3–20). New York: Teachers College Press.

Bloom, B. (1964). *Stability and change in human characteristics.* New York: Wiley.

Bloom, B., Davis, A., & Hess, R. (1965). *Compensatory education for cultural deprivation.* New York: Holt.

Boone, J. A., & Cadden, M. (Eds.). (1990). *Engendering men: The question of male feminist criticism.* New York: Routledge.

Boswell, J. (1988). *The kindness of strangers.* New York: Pantheon.

Bowen, P. M. (1993). AIDS 101. In T. F. Murphy & S. Poirier (Eds.), *Writing AIDS: Gay literature, language and analysis* (pp. 140–160). New York: Columbia University Press.

Bowles, S., & Gintis, H. (1976). *Schooling in capitalist America.* New York: Basic Books.

Bowman, B. (1993). Early childhood education. In L. Darling-Hammond (Ed.), *Review of research in education 1993* (pp. 101–135). Washington, DC: American Educational Research Association.

Brandt, A. M. (1987). *No magic bullet: A social history of venereal disease in the United States since 1800.* New York: Oxford University Press.

Bravmann, S. (1990). Telling hi(stories): Rethinking the lesbian and gay historical imagination. *OutLook, 2*(4), 68–74.

Breckinridge, S. P. (1912). *The child in the city.* Chicago: Hollister Press.

Bredekamp, S. (1987). *Developmentally appropriate practices in early childhood programs serving children from birth through age 8.* Washington, DC: National Association for the Education of Young Children.

Bredekamp, S. (1991). Redeveloping early childhood education: A response to Keller. *Early Childhood Research Quarterly, 6*, 199–209.

Brick, P. (1989). *Teaching safer sex.* Hackensack, NJ: Planned Parenthood of Bergen County.

Bronski, M. (1988, July 24). Death, AIDS, and the transfiguration of grief. *Gay Community News,* p. 20.

Bronski, M. (1989). Death and the erotic imagination. In E. Carter & S. Watney (Eds.), *Taking Liberties* (pp. 219–228). London: Serpent's Tail.

Brooks-Gunn, J., Boyer, C. B., & Hein, K. (1988). Preventing HIV infection and AIDS in children and adolescents: Behavioral research and intervention strategies. *American Psychologist, 43*, 958–965.

Bruner, J. (1980). *Under five in Britain.* London: Grant McIntyre.

Bruner, J. (1990). *Acts of meaning.* Cambridge: Harvard University Press.

Brunner, D. D. (1992). Discussing sexuality in the language arts classroom: Alternative meaning making and meaning making as an alternative. In J. T. Sears (Ed.), *Sexuality and the curriculum* (pp. 226–242). New York: Teachers College Press.

Buber, M. (1966). *The way of response* (N. Glatzer, Ed.). New York: Schocken.

Bullough, R. V., Goldstein, S. L. & Holt, L. (1984). *Human interests in the curriculum: Teaching and learning in a technological society.* New York: Teachers College Press.

Butler, J. (1990). *Gender trouble: Feminism and the subversion of identity.* New York: Routledge.

Butler, J. (1991). Imitation and gender insubordination. In D. Fuss (Ed.), *Inside-out: Lesbian theories, gay theories* (pp. 13–32). New York: Routledge.

Cady, J. (1993). Immersive and counterimmersive writing about AIDS: The achievement of Paul Monette's *Love alone.* In T. F. Murphy & S. Poirier (Eds.), *Writing AIDS: Gay literature, language and analysis* (pp. 244–264). New York: Columbia University Press.

Caldwell, B. (1984). Growth and development. *Young Children, 39*(6), 53–56.

Callen, M. (1989, March). AIDS is a gay disease! *PWA Coalition Newsline, 40.*

Callen, M. (1991). *Surviving AIDS.* New York: HarperCollins.

Carter, E., & Watney, S. (1989). *Taking liberties: AIDS and cultural politics.* London: Serpent's Tail.

Casper, V., Schultz, S., & Wickens, E. (1992). Breaking the silences: Lesbian and gay parents and the schools. *Teachers College Record, 94*(1), 109–138.

CDC AIDS Weekly. (1986, December 15). p. 9.

Center for Population Options (1989). *Adolescents, AIDS and HIV: A community wide responsibility.* [Available from Center for Population Options, 1012 14th Street, N.W., Washington, DC.]

Chamboredon, J. C., & Prevort, J. (1975). Changes in the social definition of early childhood. *Theory and Society, 3,* 331–350.

Chapman, S. (1992). *The power of children's literature: A rationale for using books on gay and lesbian headed families.* Unpublished master's thesis, Bank Street College, New York.

Charest, P., Gwinn, T., Reinisch, N., Terrien, J., & Strawbridge, C. (1987). *Project Charlie.* [Available from Storefront/Youth Action, 4570 West 77th Street, Edina, MN 55435.]

Chodorow, N. (1978). *The reproduction of mothering.* Berkeley: University of California Press.

Chodorow, N. (1992). Heterosexuality as a compromise formation: Reflections on the psychanalytic theory of sexual development. *Psychoanalysis and Contemporary Thought, 15*(3), 267–304.

Chronic disease and health promotion reprints from the mmwr: 1990 youth risk behavior surveillance system. (1990). [Available from U.S. Department of Health and Human Services, Centers for Disease Control, Atlanta, GA 30333.]

Cleverley, J., & Phillips, D. C. (1986). *Visions of childhood: Influential models from Locke to Spock.* New York: Teachers College Press.

Cochran-Smith, M., & Lytle, S. (1990). Research on teaching and teacher research: the issues that divide. *Educational Researcher, 19*(2), 2–11.

Code, L. (1991). *What can she know? Feminist theory and the construction of knowledge.* Ithaca, NY: Cornell University Press.

Coe, R. N. (1984). *When the grass was taller: Autobiography and the experience of childhood.* New Haven, CT: Yale University Press.

Cohen, E. (1991). Who are "we"? Gay "identity" as political (e)motion (a theoretical rumination). In D. Fuss (Ed.), *Inside/out: Lesbian theories, gay theories* (pp. 71–92). New York: Routledge.

Coles, R. (1989). Moral energy in the lives of impoverished children. In T. F. Duggan & R. Coles (Eds.), *The child in our times: Studies in the development of resiliency* (pp. 45–55). New York: Brunner/Mazel.

Collins, C. (1974). The multiple realities of schooling. In D. Denton (Ed.), *Existentialism and phenomenology in education: Collected essays* (pp. 139–155). New York: Teachers College Press.

Counts, G. (1932). *Dare the school build a new social order?* Carbondale: Southern Illinois University Press.

Coveney, P. (1967). *The image of childhood: The individual and society: A study of the theme in English literature.* Baltimore: Penguin.

Cranston, K. (1992). HIV education for gay, lesbian, and bisexual youth: Personal risk, personal power, and the community of conscience. In K. Harbeck (Ed.), *Coming out of the classroom closet* (pp. 247–259). New York: Haworth.

Crimp, D. (Ed.). (1988). *AIDS: Cultural analysis/cultural activism.* Cambridge, MA: MIT Press.

Crimp, D. (1990a). *AIDS demographics.* Seattle: Bay Press.

Crimp, D. (1990b). Mourning and militancy. *October, 51* (Winter 1989), 3–18.

Crimp, D. (1992). Right on, girlfriend! *Social Text, 33,* 2–18.

Crites, S. (1986). Storytime: Recollecting the past and projecting the future. In T. R. Sarbin (Ed.), *Narrative psychology: The storied nature of human conduct* (pp. 152–171). New York: Praeger.

Croteau, J. M., & Morgan, S. (1989). Combating homophobia in AIDS education. *Journal of Counseling & Development, 68,* 86–91.

Cruikshank, M. (Ed.). (1982). *Lesbian studies: Present and future.* New York: Feminist Press.

Cuban, L. (1989). The "at risk" label and the problem of urban school reform. *Phi delta kappan, 70,* 780–801.

Cuffaro, H. (1991). A view of materials as the texts of the early childhood curriculum. In B. Spodek & O. Saracho (Eds.), *Issues in early childhood curriculum* (pp. 64–85). New York: Teachers College Press.

Cuffaro, H. K. (1995). *Experimenting with the world: John Dewey and the early childhood classroom.* New York: Teachers College Press.

Damon, W. (1977). *The social world of the child.* San Francisco, CA: Jossey-Bass.

Danzelot, J. (1979). *The policing of families* (R. Hurley, Trans.). New York: Pantheon. (Original work published 1977)

Darling-Hammond, L. (1985). Valuing teachers: The making of a profession. *Teachers College Record, 87*(2), 205–218.

Darwin, C. (1859). *The origin of species.* New York: Doubleday.

de Beauvoir, S. (1972). *The second sex* (H. M. Parshley, Trans.). New York: Vintage.

Delaporte, F. (1986). *Disease and civilization: The cholera in Paris, 1832* (A. Goldhammer, Trans.). Cambridge, MA: MIT Press.

Delpit, L. D. (1988). The silenced dialogue: Power and pedagogy in educating other people's children. *Harvard Educational Review, 58,* 280–298.

The demand side of the health care crisis. (1993). *Harvard Magazine, 95*(4), 30–32.

DeMause, L. (Ed.). (1974). *The history of childhood.* New York: Psychohistory Press.

D'Emilio, J., & Freedman, E. B. (1988). *Intimate matters: A history of sexuality in America.* New York: Harper & Row.

Denton, D. (1970). *The language of ordinary experience.* New York: Philosophical Library.

Derman-Sparks, L., & the A.B.C. Task Force (1989). *Anti-bias curriculum: Tools for empowering young children.* Washington, DC: National Association for the Education of Young Children.

Desforges, C. (1986). Developmental psychology applied to teacher training. In J. Harris (Ed.), *Child psychology in action: Linking research and practice* (pp. 208–219). Cambridge, MA: Brookline Books.

Des Jarlais, D. C., Padian, N. S., & Winkelstein, W. (1994, February). *Targeted and generalized strategies for preventing transmission of HIV.* Paper presented at the annual meeting of the American Association for the Advancement of Science, San Francisco, CA.

De Tocqueville, A. (1945). *Democracy in America* (B. Philips, Ed.). New York: Knopf. (Original work published 1838)

Dewey, J. (1916). *Democracy and education.* New York: Macmillan.

Dewey, J. (1938). *Experience and education.* New York: Macmillan.

Dewey, J. (1956). *The child and the curriculum/The school and society.* Chicago: University of Chicago Press. (Original works published 1902 and 1900).

Dewey, J. (1959). The school and society. In M. S. Dworkin (Ed.), *Dewey on education* (pp. 33–90). New York: Teachers College Press. (Original work published 1899)

Dews, P. (Ed.). (1986). *Habermas: Autonomy & solidarity.* New York: Schocken.

DiClemente, R. J., Boyer, C. B., & Morales, E. D. (1988). Minorities and AIDS: Knowledge, attitudes and misconceptions among black and Latino adolescents. *American Journal of Public Health, 78,* 55–57.

Diorio, J. (1985). Contraception, copulation, domination, and the theoretical barrenness of sex education literature. *Educational Theory, 35,* 239–255.

Donaldson, M. (1978). *Children's minds.* New York: Norton.

Dreeben, R. (1970). *The nature of teaching.* Glenview, IL: Scott, Foresman.

Eckland, J. D. (1989). Policy choices for AIDS education in the public schools. *Education Evaluation and Policy Analysis, 11,* 377–387.

Egan, K. (1983). *Education and psychology.* New York: Teachers College Press.

Egan, K. (1988). Education and the mental life of young children. In L. Williams & D. Fromberg (Eds.), *The proceedings of "Defining the field of early childhood education: An invitational symposium"* (pp. 41–77). New York: Teachers College, Columbia University.

Elbaz, F. (1983). *Teacher thinking: A study of practical knowledge.* New York: Nichols.

Elbaz, M., & Murbach, R. (1992). Fear of the other, condemned and damned: AIDS, epidemics and exclusions. In A. Klusacek & K. Morrison (Eds.), *Leap in the dark: AIDS, art & contemporary culture* (pp. 1–9). Montreal: Véhicule Press.

Elkind, D. (1981a). *Children and adolescents.* New York: Oxford University Press.

Elkind, D. (1981b). *The hurried child: Growing up too fast, too soon.* Reading, MA: Addison-Wesley.

Elkind, D. (1987). The child yesterday, today, and tomorrow. *Young Children, 42*(4), 6–11.

Elsbree, W. (1939). *The American teacher: Evolution of a profession in a democracy.* New York: American Book Company.

Engels, F. (1971). *The condition of the working class in England.* Oxford: Basil Blackwell. (Original work published in 1845).

Engler, R. K. (1988, October). *Safe sex and dangerous poems: AIDS, literature and the gay and lesbian community college student.* Paper presented at the Annual National Literature Conference, Chicago.

Epstein, S. (1987). Gay politics, ethnic identity: The limits of social constructionism. *Socialist Review, 17*(93–94), 9–54.

Epstein, S. (1990, October). *AIDS and the experts: Science, activism and the politics of knowledge.* Paper presented at the Lesbian, Bisexual & Gay Studies Conference, Cambridge, MA.

Evans, E. (1982). Curriculum models and early childhood education. In B. Spodek (Ed.), *Handbook of research in early childhood education* (pp. 117–134). New York: Free Press.

Family in AIDS case quits town after house fire. (1987, August 30). *The New York Times,* pp. 1, 20.

Farmer, P. (1992). *AIDS and accusation: Haiti and the geography of blame.* Berkeley: University of California Press.

Farquhar, C. (1990a). *Answering children's questions about HIV/AIDS in the primary school: Are teachers prepared?* Unpublished manuscript, University of London, Institute of Education, Thomas Coram Research Unit, London.

Farquhar, C. (1990b). *What do primary school children know about AIDS?* (Working Paper No. 1). London: University of London, Institute of Education Thomas Coram Research Unit.

Fee, E., & Fox, D. M. (1988). *AIDS: The burdens of history.* Berkeley: University of California Press.

Fein, G., & Schwartz, P. (1982). Developmental theories in early education. In B. Spodek (Ed.), *Handbook of research in early childhood education* (pp. 82–104). New York: Free Press.

Felman, S. (1982). Psychoanalysis and education: teaching terminable and interminable. In B. Johnson (Ed.), *The pedagogical imperative: Teaching as a literary genre* (pp. 21–45). New Haven, CT: Yale University Press.

Felsman, J. K. (1989). Risk and resiliency in childhood: The lives of street children. In T. F. Duggan & R. Coles (Eds.), *The child in our times: Studies in the development of resiliency* (pp. 56–80). New York: Brunner/Mazel.

Fine, M. (1988). Sexuality, schooling, and adolescent females: The missing discourse of desire. *Harvard Educational Review, 58*(1), 29–53.

Flora, J. A., & Thoresen, C. E. (1988). Reducing the risk of AIDS in adolescents. *American Psychologist, 43*, 965–971.

Forrest, J. D., & Silverman, J. (1989). What public school teachers teach about preventing pregnancy, AIDS and sexually transmitted diseases. *Family Planning Perspectives, 21*(2), 65–72.

Forster, E. M. (1908). *Howards end.* New York: Vintage Books.

Foucault, M. (1965). *Madness and civilization: A history of insanity in the age of reason* (R. Howard, Trans.). New York: Pantheon.

Foucault, M. (1973). *The birth of the clinic: An archaeology of medical perception* (A. M. Smith, Trans.). New York: Pantheon.

Foucault, M. (1974). *The archaeology of knowledge.* London: Tavistock.

Foucault, M. (1977). *Discipline and punish: The birth of the prison* (A. Sheridan, Trans.). New York: Pantheon.

Foucault, M. (1978). *The history of sexuality: Vol. I. An introduction* (R. Hurley, Trans.). New York: Pantheon.

Foucault, M. (1980a). *Power/knowledge: Selected interviews and other writings 1972–1977* (C. Gordon, Ed.; C. Gordon, L. Marshall, J. Mepham, & K. Soper, Trans.). New York: Pantheon Books.

Foucault, M (1980b, Summer). *Semiotext(e) Special Intervention Series 2: Loving children,* 41–42.

Foucault, M. (1981). Friendship as a lifestyle: An interview with Michel Foucault. *Gay Information 7.*

Foucault, M. (1984). *The Foucault reader* (P. Rabinow, Ed.). New York: Pantheon Books.

Fraser, K. (1989). *Someone at school has AIDS.* Alexandria, VA: National Association of State Boards of Education.

Freire, P. (1986). *Pedagogy of the oppressed* (M. B. Ramos, Trans.). New York: Seabury Press.

French, J., & Adams, L. (1986). From analysis to synthesis. *Health Education Journal, 45*(2), 71–74.

Furth, H. G. (1979). Young children's understanding of society. In H. McGurk (Ed.), *Issues in childhood social development* (pp. 228–256). London: Methuen.

Fuss, D. (1989). *Essentially speaking: Feminism, nature and difference.* New York: Routledge.

Fuss, D. (1991a). Inside/out. In D. Fuss (Ed.), *Inside/out: Lesbian theories, gay theories* (pp. 1–10). New York: Routledge.

Fuss, D. (Ed.). (1991b). *Inside-out: Lesbian theories, gay theories.* New York: Routledge.

Gage, L. N. (1989). The paradigm wars and their aftermath. *Educational Researcher,* *18*(7), 4–10.

Gagnon, J. H., & Simon, W. (1973). *Sexual conduct: The social sources of human sexuality.* London: Hutchinson.

Gagnon, M., & Folland, T. (1992). The spectacular ruse. In A. Klusacek & K. Morrison (Eds.), *Leap in the dark: AIDS, art & contemporary cultures* (pp. 96–105). Montreal: Véhicule Press.

Gallagher, J. (1993, June 15). Why Johnny can't be safe. *The Advocate, 631,* 46–47.

Gallop, J. (1982). *The daughter's seduction: Feminism and psychoanalysis.* Ithaca, NY: Cornell University Press.

Garbarino, T. (1992). *Children in danger.* San Francisco: Jossey-Bass.

Garber, L. (Ed.). (1994). *Tilting the tower.* New York: Routledge.

Gardner, W., & Wilcox, B. L. (1993). Political intervention in scientific peer review: Research on adolescent sexual behavior. *American Psychologist, 48*(9), 972–983.

Gasch, H., Poulson, M., Fullilove, R., & Fullilove, M. (1991). Shaping AIDS education and prevention programs for African Americans amidst community decline. *Journal of Negro Education, 60*(1), 85–96.

Geertz, C. (1983). *Local knowledge: Further essays in interpretive anthropology.* New York: Basic Books.

Gesell, A. (1940). *The first five years of life: A guide to the study of the preschool child.* New York: Harper & Bros.

Giddings, P. (1984). *When and where I enter: The impact of black women on race and sex in America.* New York: William Morrow.

Gilbert, P. (1989). Personally (and passively) yours: Girls, literacy and education. *Oxford Review of Education, 15,* 257–265.

Gilligan, C. (1982). *In a different voice: Psychological theory and woman's development.* Cambridge, MA: Harvard University Press.

Giroux, H. (1980). Crtical theory and rationality in citizenship education. *Curriculum Inquiry, 10,* 329–367.

Glauser, B. (1990). Street children: Deconstructing a construct. In A. James & A. Prout (Eds.), *Constructing and reconstucting childhood* (pp. 138–156). New York: Falmer Press.

Glück, R. (1991). *My community.* Unpublished manuscript.

Gordon, L. (1988). *Heroes of their own lives: The politics of family violence.* New York: Penguin Books.

Gould, S. J. (1981). *The mismeasure of man.* New York: Norton.

Graham, R. J. (1991). *Reading and writing the self: Autobiography in education and the curriculum.* New York: Teachers College Press.

Gramsci, A. (1971). *Selections from the prison notebooks* (Q. Hoare & G. Nowell-Smith, Eds.). London: Lawrence & Wishart.

Greene, M. (1978). *Landscapes of learning.* New York: Teachers College Press.

Greene, M. (1984). Excellence: Meanings and multiplicity. *Teachers College Record, 86*(2), 283–299.

Grumet, M. (1980). Autobiography and reconceptualization. *Journal of Curriculum Theorizing, 2*(2), 155–158.

Grumet, M. (1985). Bodyreading. *Teachers College Record, 87*(2), 175–195.

Grumet, M. (1988). *Bitter milk*. Amherst: University of Massachusetts Press.

Habermas, J. (1968). *Knowledge and human interests*. Boston: Beacon.

Halley, J. E. (1989). The politics of the closet: Towards equal protection for gay, lesbian, and bisexual identity. *UCLA Law Review, 36*, 915–976.

Halperin, D. (1990). *One hundred years of homosexuality*. New York: Routledge.

Hanson, E. (1991). Undead. In D. Fuss (Ed.), *Inside/out: Lesbian theories, gay theories* (pp. 324–340). New York: Routledge.

Harbeck, K., & Woods, S. (1992). Living in two worlds. In K. Harbeck (Ed.), *Coming out of the classroom closet* (pp. 247–261). New York: Haworth.

Hartley, E. E., Rosenbaum, M., & Schwartz, S. (1948). Children's perception of ethnic group membership. *Journal of Psychology, 26*, 387–397.

Hatch, J. A., & Freeman, E. B. (1988). Kindergarten philosophies and practices: Perspectives of teachers, principals, and supervisors. *Early Childhood Research Quarterly, 3*, 151–166.

Heath, S. (1987). Male feminism. In A. Jardine & P. Smith (Eds.), *Men in feminism* (pp. 1–32). New York: Methuen.

Heidegger, M. (1962). *Being and time* (J. Macquarrie & E. Robinson, Trans.). New York: Harper & Row.

Heidegger, M. (1992). *The concept of time* (W. McNeill, Trans.). Cambridge, MA: Blackwell. (Original work published 1924)

Hendrick, H. (1990). Constructions and reconstructions of British childhood: An interpretative survey, 1800 to the present. In A. James & A. Prout (Eds.), *Constructing and reconstructing childhood: Contemporary issues in the sociological study of childhood* (pp. 35–59). New York: Falmer.

Henig, R. M. (1982, February 6). AIDS: A new disease's odyssey. *The New York Times Magazine*, p. 36.

Henriquez, J., Hollway, W., Urwin, C., Venn, C., & Walkerdine, V. (1984). *Changing the subject: Psychology, social regulation and subjectivity*. New York: Methuen.

Hermans, H., Kempen, J., & van Loon, R. (1992). The dialogical self: Beyond individualism and rationalism. *American Psychologist, 47*(1), 23–33.

Herron, R., & Sutton-Smith, B. (1971). *Child's play*. New York: Wiley.

Hingson, R., & Strunin, L. (1989). *Summary of results: Boston schools baseline surveys, spring 1988, 1989*. Unpublished manuscript, Boston University, School of Public Health.

Hirschfeld, M. (1946). *Sexual anomalies and perversions*. London: Torch Publishing.

Hocquenghem, G. (1978). *Homosexual desire*. London: Allison & Busby.

Hoffman, N. (1981). *Woman's "true" profession*. Old Westbury, NY: Feminist Press.

Holdstock, T. (1990, August). *The African self: An holistic cosmology*. Paper presented at the William James Principles Congress, Amsterdam, the Netherlands.

Holt, J. (1964). *How children fail*. New York: Dell.

Homans, H., & Aggleton, P. (1988). Health education, HIV infection and AIDS. In P. Aggleton & H. Homans (Eds.), *Social aspects of AIDS* (pp. 154–176). London: Falmer Press.

Horowitz, E. L. (1965). Development of attitudes towards Negroes. In H. Proschansky & B. Seidenberg (Eds.), *Basic studies in social psychology*. New York: Holt, Rinehart & Winston. (Original work published 1936)

Hsu, F. (1985). The self in cross-cultural perspective. In A. Marsella, G. de Vos, & F. Hsu (Eds.), *Culture and self: Asian and western perspectives* (pp. 24–55). New York: Tavistock.

Hubbard, R. (1993, Spring). Viewpoint. *The AIDS Report* [The Harvard AIDS Institute], pp. 13–14.

Huebner, D. (1975a). Curricular language and classroom meanings. In W. Pinar (Ed.), *Curriculum theorizing: The reconceptualists* (pp. 217–236). Berkeley: McCutchan.

Huebner, D. (1975b). Curriculum as concern for man's temporality. In W. Pinar (Ed.), *Curriculum theorizing: The reconceptualists* (pp. 237–249). Berkeley: McCutchan.

Hunt, J. (1961). *Intelligence and experience*. New York: Ronald.

Illich, I. (1970). *Deschooling society*. New York: Harper & Row.

Illich, I. (1976). *Medical nemesis: The expropriation of health*. New York: Pantheon.

Illich. I. (1979). Vernacular values and education. *Teachers College Record, 81*(1), 31–75.

Irigaray, L. (1977). *Ce sexe qui n'en est pas une*. Paris: Editions de Minuit.

Irigaray, L. (1984). *Ethique de la difference sexuelle*. Paris: Minuit.

Isaacs, S. (1930). *Intellectual growth in young children*. London: Routledge & Kegan Paul.

Jackson, E. (1991). Scandalous subjects: Robert Glück's embodied subjects. *Differences, 3*(2), 112–135.

Jackson, P. (1968). *Life in classrooms*. New York: Holt.

Jahoda, G. (1963). The development of children's ideas about country and nationality. Part I: The conceptual framework. *British Journal of Educational Psychology, 33*, 47–60.

James, A., & Prout, A. (1990a). *Constructing and reconstructing childhood: Contemporary issues in the sociological study of childhood*. New York: Falmer.

James, A., & Prout, A. (1990b). A new paradigm for the sociology of childhood? Provenance, promise and problems. In A. James & A. Prout (Eds.), *Constructing and reconstructing childhood: Contemporary issues in the sociological study of childhood* (pp. 7–34). New York: Falmer.

James, A., & Prout, A. (1990c). Re-presenting childhood: Time and transition in the study of childhood. In A. James & A. Prout (Eds.), *Constructing and reconstructing childhood: Contemporary issues in the sociological study of childhood* (pp. 216–237). New York: Falmer.

Jeffcoate, R. (1977). Children's racial ideas and feelings. *English in Education, 11*(1), 32–46.

Jenny, A., Roesler, T. A., & Poyer, K. L. (1994). Are children at risk for sexual abuse by homosexuals? *Pediatrics, 94*(1), 41–44.

Jersild, A. (1946). *Child development and the curriculum*. New York: Teachers College.

Jipson, J. (1991). Developmentally appropriate practice: Culture, curriculum, connections. *Early Education and Development, 2,* 120–136.

Jipson, J. (1992). The emergent curriculum: Contextualizing a feminist perspective. In S. Kessler & B. B. Swadener (Eds.), *Reconceptualizing the early childhood curriculum* (pp. 149–164). New York: Teachers College Press.

Joffe, C. (1977). *Friendly intruders.* Berkeley: University of California Press.

Johnston, R. (1987). AIDS and "otherness." In J. Griggs (Ed.), *AIDS: Public policy dimensions* (pp. 77–83). New York: United Hospital Fund.

Jones, E. (1991). Do ECE people really agree? Or are we just agreeable? *Young Children, 46*(4), 59–61.

Jonson, A. R., & Stryker, J. (Eds.). (1993). *The social impact of AIDS in the United States.* Washington, DC: National Academy Press.

Kahn, A. D. (1993). *AIDS: The winter war.* Philadelphia: Temple University Press.

Katz, J. (1990). The invention of heterosexuality. *Socialist Review, 21*(1), 7–34.

Katz, L. (1977). *Talks with teachers.* Washington, DC: National Association for the Education of Young Children.

Katz, L. (1989). *Engaging children's minds: The project approach.* Norwood, NJ: Ablex.

Katz, M. (1971). *Class, bureaucracy and the schools.* New York: Praeger.

Katz, P. A. (1983). Developmental foundations of gender and racial attitudes. In R. L. Leahy (Ed.), *The child's construction of social inequality.* New York: Academic Press.

Kayal, P. M. (1993). *Bearing witness: Gay Men's Health Crisis and the politics of AIDS.* Boulder, CO: Westview.

Keeling, R. P. (Ed.). (1989). *AIDS on the college campus.* Rockville, MD: Amercian College Health Association.

Kelly, G. A. (1955). *The psychology of personal constructs.* New York: Norton.

Kendler, H. H. (1993). Psychology and the ethics of social policy. *American Psychologist, 48*(10), 1046–1053.

Kennedy, H. (1988). *Ulrichs: The life and works of Karl Heinrich Ulrichs.* Boston: Alyson Publications.

Kenney, A. M., Guardado, S., & Brown, L. (1989). Sex education and AIDS education in the schools: What states and large school districts are doing. *Family Planning Perspectives, 21*(2), 56–64.

Kerr, D. L., Allensworth, D. D., & Gayle, J. A. (1989). The ASHA national HIV education needs assessment of health and education professionals. *Journal of School Health, 59,* 301–305.

Kessler, S. (1991). Alternative perspectives on early childhood education. *Early Childhood Research Quarterly, 6,* 183–197.

Kessler, S. (1992). The social context of the early childhood curriculum. In S. Kessler & B. B. Swadender (Eds.), *Reconceptualizing the early childhood curriculum* (pp. 21–42). New York: Teachers College Press.

Khayatt, M. D. (1992). *Lesbian teachers: An invisible presence.* Albany: State University of New York Press.

Kincaid, J. (1992). *Child-loving: The erotic child and Victorian culture.* New York: Routledge.

King, E. (1993). *Safety in numbers.* New York: Routledge.

King, J. R. (1993, April). *Is it crossteaching?: Gay men, feminist theory, and teaching.* Paper presented at the annual meeting of the American Educational Research Association, Atlanta, GA.

King, J. R. (1994, February). *Uncommon caring: Primary males and implicit judgements.* Paper presented at Ethnography and Education Forum, Philadelphia.

King, N. (1983). Play in the workplace. In M. Apple & L Weis (Eds.), *Ideology and practice in schooling* (pp. 262–280). Philadelphia: Temple University Press.

King, R. (1978). *All things bright and beautiful: A sociological study of infants'classrooms.* Chichester: Wiley.

Kinsey, A. C., Pomeroy, W. P., & Martin, C. E. (1948). *Sexual behavior in the human male.* Philadelphia: Saunders.

Kirp, D. (1989). *Learning by heart: AIDS and schoolchildren in America's communities.* New Brunswick, NJ: Rutgers University Press.

Kitzinger, J. (1990). Who are you kidding? Children, power and the struggle against sexual abuse. In A. James & A. Prout (Eds.), *Constructing and reconstructing childhood: Contemporary issues in the sociological study of childhood* (pp. 157–183). New York: Falmer.

Klein, M. (1989). *Poets for life: Seventy-six poets respond to AIDS.* New York: Crown.

Klein-Davis, J. (1993). Jump-starting masculinity: Queer artists expand an arrested development. *Afterimage, 21*(3), 4–7.

Klusacek, A., & Morrison, K. (1992). *Leap in the dark: AIDS, art & contemporary cultures.* Montreal: Véhicule Press.

Kohl, H. (1967). *36 children.* New York: New American Library.

Kohlberg, L. (1981). *The philosophy of moral development.* San Francisco: Harper & Row.

Kohlberg, L., & Mayer, R. (1972). Development as the aim of education. *Harvard Educational Review, 43,* 449–496.

Koopman, C., Rotheram-Borus, M., Henderson, R., Bradley, J., & Hunter, J. (1990). Assessment of knowledge of AIDS and beliefs about prevention among adolescents. *AIDS Education and Prevention, 2*(1), 58–70.

Krafft-Ebing, R. (1931). *Psychopathia sexualis.* New York: Physicians and Surgeons Book Co.

Kristeva, J. (1980). *Desire in language: A semiotic approach to literature and art* (T. Gora, A. Jardine, & L. S. Roudiez, Trans.). New York: Columbia University Press.

Kristeva, J. (1993). *Proust and the sense of time* (S. Bann, Trans.). New York: Columbia University Press.

Kuhn, D., Nash, S. C., & Brucken, L. (1978). Sex role concepts of two- and three-year-olds. *Child Development, 49,* 445–451.

Kummel, F. (1965). Time as succession and the problem of duration. In J. T. Fraser (Ed.), *The voices of time* (pp. 31–55). New York: Braziller.

Kwitny, J. (1992). *Acceptable risks.* New York: Posidon Press.

Lacan, J. (1975). *Le seminaire: Livre xx. Encore.* Paris: Seuil.

Lazerson, M. (1971). Social reform and early childhood education: Some historical perspectives. In R. Anderson & H. Shane (Eds.), *As the twig is bent* (pp. 22–33). Boston: Houghton Mifflin.

Leahy, R. L. (1983). The development of the conception of social class. In R. L. Leahy (Ed.), *The construction of social inequality* (pp. 79–109). New York: Academic Press.

LeVay, S. (1993). *The sexual brain.* Cambridge, MA: MIT Press.

Levin, D. (1982). Moral education: The body's felt sense of value. *Teachers College Record, 84,* 283–301.

Lightfoot, S. (1978). *Worlds apart.* New York: Basic Books.

Livesley, W., & Bromley, D. (1973). *Person and perception in childhood and adolescence.* London: Wiley.

Lorde, A. (1982). *Zami: A new spelling of my name.* Trumansburg, NY: Crossing Press.

Lorde, A. (1988). *A burst of light.* Ithaca, NY: Firebrand Books.

Lortie, D. (1975). *Schoolteacher.* Chicago: University of Chicago Press.

Lynch, M. (1989). *These waves of dying friends.* New York: Contact II Publications.

Lynch, M. (1990, October). *Last onsets—Teaching with AIDS.* Paper presented at the 4th annual Lesbian, Bisexual and Gay Studies Conference, Cambridge, MA.

Maccoby, E., & Zellner, M. (1970). *Experiments in primary education: Aspects of project follow through.* New York: Harcourt Brace Jovanovich.

Macdonald, J. (1975). Curriculum and human interests. In W. Pinar (Ed.), *Curriculum theorizing: The reconceptualists* (pp. 283–294). Berkeley, CA: McCutchan.

Mann, J., Tarantola, D., & Netter, T. W. (Eds.). (1992). *AIDS in the world.* Cambridge, MA: Harvard University Press.

Markus, H., & Nurius, P. (1986). Possible selves. *American Psychologist, 41,* 954–969.

Martin, J. R. (1986). Redefining the educated person: Rethinking the significance of gender. *Educational Researcher, 15*(6), 6–10.

Martin, L., Gutman, H., & Hutton, P. (Eds.). (1988). *Technologies of the self.* London: Tavistock

Martusewicz, R. A. (1992). Mapping the terrain of the post-modern subject: Poststructuralism and the educated woman. In W. F. Pinar & W. M. Reynolds (Eds.), *Understanding curriculum as phenomenological and deconstructed text* (pp. 131–158). New York: Teachers College Press.

Matthews, G. (1980). *Philosophy and the young child.* Cambridge, MA: Harvard University Press.

McIntosh, M. (1981). The homosexual role. In K. Plummer (Ed.), *The making of the modern homosexual.* London: Hutchinson.

Mead, G. H. (1934). *Mind, self and society.* Chicago: University of Chicago Press.

Merleau-Ponty, M. (1962). *Phenomenology of perception* (C. Smith, Trans.). New York: Humanities Press.

Merleau-Ponty, M. (1964). *The primacy of perception.* Evanston, IL: Northwestern University Press.

Mickler, S. E. (1993). Perceptions of vulnerability: Impact on AIDS-preventive behavior among college adolescents. *AIDS Education and Prevention, 5*(1), 43–53.

Miller, D. A. (1988). *The novel and the police.* Berkeley: University of California Press.

Miller, J. (Ed.). (1992). *Fluid exchanges: Artists and critics in the AIDS crisis.* Toronto: University of Toronto Press.

Minuchin, P. (1990). Social change and social reality: Some implications for social studies. *Thought and Practice, 2*(2), 3–16.

Moger, A. (1982). The obscure object of narrative. *Yale French Studies, 63,* 129–139.

Mohr, R. D. (1992). *Gay ideas: Outing and other controversies.* Boston: Beacon.

Monette, P. (1988). *Love alone: Eighteen elegies for Rog.* New York: St. Martin's Press.

Montessori, M. (1912). *The Montessori method* (A. Geroge, Trans.). New York: Federick A. Stokes.

Munro, P. (1992, April). *Teaching as "women's work": A century of resistant voices.* Paper presented at the Annual Meeting, American Educational Research Association, San Francisco.

Murphy, T. F. (1993). Testimony. In T. F. Murphy & S. Poirier (Eds.), *Writing AIDS: Gay literature, language and analysis* (pp. 306–320). New York: Columbia University Press.

Murphy, T. F., & Poirier, S. (Eds.). (1993). *Writing AIDS: Gay literature, language and analysis.* New York: Columbia University Press.

Nais, J. (1989). *Primary teachers talking.* New York: Routledge.

Natanson, M. (1972). The nature of social man. In H. Y. Jung (Ed.), *Existential phenomenology and political theory: A reader* (pp. 160–188). Chicago: Henry Regnery Company.

National Academy of Sciences. (1988). *Confronting AIDS: Update 1988.* Washington, DC: National Academy of Sciences.

National Association for the Education of Young Children. (1990). *Guidelines for appropriate curriculum content and assessment in programs serving children ages 3 through 8: A position statement of the National Association for the Education of Young Children and the National Association of Early Childhood Specialists in State Departments of Education.* Washington, DC: Author.

National Center for Health Education. (1985). *Growing healthy.* (Available from the National Center for Health Education, 30 East 29th Street, New York, NY 10016.)

National Commission on Excellence in Education. (1984). *A nation at risk: The full account.* Cambridge, MA: USA Research.

Navarre, M. (1987). Fighting the victim label. *October, 43,* 143–147.

Navarro, V. (1988). Professional Dominance or Proletarianization?: Neither. *The Millbank Quarterly, 66*(2), 57–75.

Nelson, E. S. (1992). *AIDS the literary response.* New York: Twayne Publishers.

Nettles, S. M., & Scott-Jones, D. (1989). The role of sexuality and sex equity in the education of minority adolescents. *Peabody Journal of Education, 64*(4), 183–198.

New York City Board of Education, Office of Research, Evaluation, and Assessment. (1990). *AIDS education project: Evaluation section report*. New York: Author.

New York State Education Department (1987). *AIDS Instructional Guide*. Albany, NY: Author.

Noddings, N. (1991). Stories in dialogue: Caring and interpersonal reasoning. In C. Witherell & N. Noddings (Eds.), *Stories lives tell: Narrative and dialogue in education* (pp. 157–170). New York: Teachers College Press.

Noddings, N. (1992). *The challenge to care in schools: An alternative approach to education*. New York: Teachers College Press.

Nunokawa, J. (1991). "All the sad young men": AIDS and the work of mourning. In D. Fuss (Ed.), *Inside/out: Lesbian theories, gay theories* (pp. 311–324). New York: Routledge.

Nye, A. (1987). Woman clothed with the sun: Julia Kristeva and the escape from/to language. *Signs, 12*(4), 664–687.

Oakes, J., Hare, S., & Sirotnik, K. (1986). Collaborative inquiry: A congenial paradigm in a cantankerous world. *Teachers College Record, 87*, 545–563.

Odets, W. (1990). *The psychological epidemic: The impact of AIDS on uninfected gay and bisexual men*. (Available from: Walt Odets, 3865 Howe Street, Oakland, CA 94611).

Odets, W. (1994). AIDS education and harm reduction for gay men: Psychological approaches for the 21st century. *AIDS and Public Policy Journal, 9*(1), 3–15.

Owen, G. (1920). *Nursery school education*. New York: Dutton.

Owens, C. (1987). Outlaws: Gay men in feminism. In A. Jardine & P. Smith (Eds.), *Men in feminism* (219–233). New York: Methuen.

Oyemade, U. J., & Washington, V. (1989). Drug abuse prevention begins in early childhood. *Young Children, 44*(5), 6–12.

Ozga, J., & Lawn, M. (1981). *Teachers, professionalism and class*. London: Falmer.

Pagano, J. (1990). *Exiles and communities: Teaching in the patriarchal wilderness*. Albany: State University of New York Press.

Paley, V. G. (1990). *The boy who would be a helicopter*. Cambridge, MA: Harvard University Press.

Paley, V. G. (1991). The heart and soul of the matter: Teaching as a moral act. *The Educational Forum, 55*(2), 155–166.

Pastore, J. (1992). *Confronting AIDS through literature*. Champaign: University of Illinois Press.

Pattison, R. (1978). *The child figure in English literature*. Athens: University of Georgia Press.

Patton, C. (1985). *Sex and germs: The politics of AIDS*. Boston: South End Press.

Patton, C. (1990). *Inventing AIDS*. New York: Routledge.

Pestalozzi, J. (1907). *Leonard and Gertrude* (E. Channing, Trans.). Boston, MA: D. C. Heath.

Piaget, J. (1950). *The psychology of intelligence*. London: Routledge & Kegan Paul.

Piaget, J. (1954). *The construction of reality in childhood*. New York: Basic Books.

Piaget, J. (1962). *Play dreams and imitation in childhood*. New York: Norton.

Pinar, W. (1980). Life history and educational experience [Parts 1 & 2]. *Journal of Curriculum Theorizing, 2*(2), 159–212; *3*(1), 259–286.

Pinar, W., & Reynolds, W. (Eds.). (1992). *Understanding curriculum as phenomenological and deconstructed text.* New York: Teachers College Press.

Plumb, J. H. (1972). Children: The victims of time. In J. H. Plumb, *In the light of history.* London: Allen Lane.

Plummer, K. (1975). *Sexual stigma: An interactionist account.* New York: Routledge & Kegan Paul.

Plummer, K. (1992). Speaking its name: Inventing a lesbian and gay studies. In K. Plummer (Ed.), *Modern homosexualities: Fragments of lesbian and gay experience* (pp. 3–25). New York: Routledge.

Polakow, V. (1982). *The erosion of childhood.* Chicago: University of Chicago Press.

Polakow, V. (1989). Deconstructing development. *Journal of Education, 171*(2), 75–87.

Porter, C. (1981). *Voices from the preschool: Perspectives on early childhood educators.* Unpublished doctoral dissertation, State University of New York at Buffalo.

Postman, N. (1982). *The disappearance of childhood.* New York: Delacorte.

Presidential Commission on the Human Immunodeficiency Virus Epidemic. (1988). *Report of the Presidential Commission on the Human Immunodeficiency Virus Epidemic.* Washington, DC: U.S. Government Printing Office.

Preston, J. (1989). *Dispatches.* Boston: Alyson Press.

Proust, M. (1985). *Remembrance of things past* (3 vols.; T. Kilmartin, Trans.). Harmondsworth: Penguin Classics.

Pynchon, T. (1984). *Slow learner: Early stories.* Boston: Little Brown.

Quackenbush, M., & Villarreal, S. (1988). *"Does AIDS hurt?" Educating young children about AIDS.* Santa Cruz, CA: Network Publications.

Ramirez, M., & Castaneda, A. (1974). *Cultural democracy, biocognitive development, and education.* New York: Academic Press.

Raymond, S. (1990). "Let's all say we've got it": AIDS and schoolchildren in the United States. *Harvard Educational Review, 60*(1), 125–138.

Reuben, C. (1986, September). AIDS: The promise of alternative treatments. *EastWest.*

Rich, A. (1980). Compulsory heterosexuality and lesbian existence. *Signs, 5,* 631–660.

Richardson, V. (1990). Significant and worthwhile change in teaching practice. *Educational Researcher, 19*(7), 10–18.

Ricoeur, P. (1965). *History and truth* (A. Kelbley, Trans.). Evanston: Northwestern Univeristy Press.

Riessman, F. (1962). *The culturally deprived child.* New York: Harper & Row.

Rodham, H. (1973). Children under the law. *Harvard Educational Review, 43,* 487–514.

Rofes, E. (1989). Opening up the classroom closet: Responding to the educational needs of gay and lesbian youth. *Harvard Educational Review, 59*(4), 444–452.

Rogoff, B. (1987). Specifying the development of cognitive skill in its cultural context. *Monographs of the Society for Research in child development, 52*(2).

Rogoff, B., & Wertsch, J. (1984). *Children's learning in the zone of proximal development*. San Francisco: Jossey-Bass.

Rose, J. (1983). Femininity and its discontents. *Feminist Review, 14,* 5–21.

Rose, N. (1990). *Governing the soul: The shaping of the private self.* New York: Routledge.

Rosenberg, C. E. (1987). *The care of strangers: The rise of America's hospital system.* New York: Basic Books.

Rothman, D. (1987). AIDS and the public schools. In J. Griggs (Ed.), *AIDS: Public policy dimensions* (pp. 57–69). New York: United Hospital Fund.

Rubin, G. (1984). Thinking sex: Notes for a radical theory of the politics of sexuality. In C. S. Vance (Ed.), *Pleasure and danger: Exploring female sexuality* (pp. 267–320). Boston: Routledge & Kegan Paul.

Sadker, M., Sadker, D., & Klein, S. (1991). The issues of gender in elementary and secondary education. In G. Grant (Ed.), *Review of research in education* (pp. 269–335). Washington, DC: American Educational Research Association.

Sanders, P., & Farquhar, C. (1991). *Positively primary: Strategies for approaching HIV/AIDS, with primary school children.* West Sussex, England: The AIDS Education & Research Trust.

Sarason, S. B. (1982). *The culture of the school and the problem of change.* Boston: Allyn & Bacon.

Sarbin, R. (1986). The narrative as a root metaphor for psychology. In T. R. Sarbin (Ed.), *Narrative psychology: The storied nature of human conduct* (pp. 3–21). New York: Praeger.

Sartre, J-P. (1964). *The words.* New York: George Braziller.

Scarr, S. (1992). Development theories fo the 1990s. *Child Development, 63,* 1–19.

Schleifer, R. (1990). *Rhetoric and death: The language of modernism and postmodern discourse theory.* Urbana: University of Illinois Press.

Schmidt, W. E. (1993, May 9). British health officials alter AIDS strategy. *The New York Times,* p. 8.

Schrader, G. (1972). Responsibility and existence. In H. Jung (Ed.), *Existential phenomenology and political theory: A reader* (pp. 265–294). Chicago: Henry Regnery Company.

Schubert, W. H. (1991). Teacher lore: A basis for understanding praxis. In C. Witherell & N. Noddings (Eds.). *Stories lives tell: Narrative and dialogue in education* (pp. 207–233). New York: Teachers College Press.

Schultz, S. (October, 1993). *Reconceptualizing gender in the early childhood curriculum.* Paper presented at Third Annual Conference, Reconceptualizing Early Childhood Education: Theory, Research & Practice, Ann Arbor, MI.

Schvaneveldt, J. D., Lindauer, S., & Young, M. H. (1990). Children's understanding of AIDS: A developmental viewpoint. *Family Relations, 38,* 330–335.

Seaver, J., & Cartwright, C. (1977). A pluralistic foundation for training early childhood professionals. *Curriculum Inquiry, 7,* 310–329.

Sedgwick, E. (1990). *Epistemology of the closet.* Berkeley: University of California Press.

Selman, R. L. (1980). *The growth of interpersonal understanding.* New York: Academic Press.

Sergios, P. A. (1993). *One boy at war: My life in the AIDS underground.* New York: Knopf.

Sergiovanni, T. (1985). Landscapes, mindscapes and reflective practice in supervision. *Journal of Curriculum and Supervision, 1*(1), 5–18.

Shabatay, V. (1991). The stranger's story: Who calls and who answers? In C. Witherell & N. Noddings (Eds.), *Stories lives tell* (pp. 136–152). New York: Teachers College Press.

Shakeshaft, C. (1986). Methodological issues in researching women in educational research: The legacy of a century. *Educational Researcher, 15*(6), 13–15.

Sharp, R., & Green, A. (1975). *Education and social control: A study in progressive primary education.* London: Routledge & Kegan Paul.

Sherry, M. S. (1993). The language of war in AIDS discourse. In T. F. Murphy & S. Poirier (Eds.), *Writing AIDS: Gay literature, language, and analysis* (pp. 39–54). New York: Columbia University Press.

Shilts, R. (1987). *And the band played on.* New York: St. Martin's Press.

Short, G. (1991). Children's grasp of controversial issues. In M. Woodhead, P. Light, & R. Carr (Eds), *Growing up in a changing society* (pp. 333–351). New York: Routledge.

Short, G., & Carrington, B. (1987). Towards an anti-racist initiative in the all white primary school. In A. Pollard (Ed.), *Children and their primary schools: A new Perspective* (pp. 220–235). Lewes: Falmer Press.

Shorter, E. (1977). *The making of the modern family.* New York: Basic Books.

Silin, J. (1982). *Protection and control: Early childhood teachers talk about authority.* Unpublished doctoral dissertation, Teachers College, Columbia University, New York.

Silin, J. (1987a). Dangerous knowledge. *Christopher Street, 10*(5), 34–42.

Silin, J. (1987b). The early childhood educator's knowledge base: A reconsideration. In L. Katz (Ed.), *Current topics in early childhood education: Volume 7* (pp. 17–31). Norwood, NJ: Ablex.

Silin, J. (1988). Becoming knowledgeable professionals. In B. Spodek, O. Saracho, & D. Peters (Eds.), *Professionalism and the early childhood practitioner* (pp. 117–134). New York: Teachers College Press.

Silverman, K. (1992). *Male subjectivity at the margins.* New York: Routledge.

Sinclaire, C. (1992, June). *Remembrances for teaching.* Paper presented at 11th International Human Science Research Conference, Rochester, MI.

Sinclaire, C. (1994). *Looking for home: A phenomenological study of home in the classroom.* Albany: State University of New York Press.

Singer, E. (1992). *Child-care and the psychology of development* (A. Porcelijn, Trans.). New York: Routledge.

Skeen, P., & Hudson, D. (1987). What we should and should not tell our children about AIDS. *Young Children, 42*(4), 65–71.

Sloane, D. C., & Sloane, B. C. (1990). AIDS in schools: A comprehensive initiative. *McGill Journal of Education, 25*(2), 205–227.

Smith, S. J. (1991). Remembrances of childhood as a source of pedagogical understanding. *Phenomenology + Pedagogy, 9*, 158–171.

Snyder, A. (1972). *Dauntless women in childhood education.* Washington, DC:
Association for Childhood Education.

Society for Adolescent Medicine. (1994). HIV infection and AIDS in adolescents:
A position paper for the Society for Adolescent Medicine. *Journal of Adolescent Health, 15*(5), 427–434.

Sontag, S. (1977). *Illness as metaphor.* New York: Farrar, Straus & Giroux.

Sontag, S. (1988). *AIDS and its metaphors.* New York: Farrar, Straus & Giroux.

Sorenson, R. C. (1973). *Adolescent sexuality in contemporary America.* New York:
World Publishing.

Speier, M. (1976). The adult ideological viewpoint in studies of childhood. In A.
Skolnick (Ed.), *Rethinking childhood* (pp. 168–186). Boston: Little, Brown.

Spodek, B. (1970). What are the sources of early childhood curriculum? *Young
Children, 26*(1), 48–58.

Spodek, B. (1984, April). The past as prologue: Exploring the historic roots of present
day concerns in early childhood education. Paper presented at the annual
meeting of the American Educational Research Association, New Orleans.

Spodek, B. (1991). Early childhood curriculum and cultural definitions of knowledge. In B. Spodek & O. Saracho (Eds.). *Issues in early childhood curriculum:
Yearbook in Early Childhood Education, Vol. 2* (pp. 1–21). New York: Teachers College Press.

Spodek, B., & Saracho, O. (1982). The preparation and certification of early childhood personnel. In B. Spodek (Ed.), *Handbook of research in early childhood
education* (pp. 399–425). New York: Free Press.

Steinberg, C. (1990, February 18). How "magic circles" build self-esteem. *The New
York Times,* sec. 12, p. 1.

Stevens, O. (1982). *Children talking politics: Political learning in childhood.* Oxford: Martin Robertson.

Sullivan, A. (1993, May 10). The politics of homosexuality. *The New Republic,*
No. 4,086, 24–37.

Surgeon General's report on acquired immune deficiency syndrome (1986). Washington, DC: Public Health Service.

Sutton-Smith, B. (1988). Radicalizing childhood: The multivocal mind. In L. Williams & D. Fromberg (Eds.), *The proceedings of "Defining the field of early
childhood education: An invitational symposium"* (pp. 77–153). New York:
Teachers College, Columbia University.

Sylva, K. (1986). Developmental psychology and the pre-school curriculum. In
J. Harris (Ed.), *Child psychology in action: Linking research and practice*
(pp. 127–142). Cambridge, MA: Brookline Books.

Takanishi, R. (1978). Childhood as a social issue: Historical roots of contemporary child advocacy movements. *Journal of Social Issues, 34*(2), 8–28.

Takanishi, R. (1981). Early childhood education and research: The changing relationship. *Theory and Practice, 20*, 86–93.

Tasker, M. (1992). *How can I tell you?* Bethesda, MD: Association for the Care of
Children's Health.

Taubman, P. (1990). Achieving the right distance. *Educational Theory, 40* (1), 121–133.

Tetreault, M., & Schmuck, P. (1985). Equity, educational reform, and gender. *Issues in Education, 3*(1), 45–68.

Traver, R. (1987). Autobiography, feminism, and the study of teaching. *Teachers College Record, 88*(3), 443–452.

Treichler, P. A. (1988a). AIDS, gender and biomedical discourse: current contests for meaning. In E. Fee & D. M. Fox (Eds.), *AIDS: The burdens of history* (pp. 190–266). Berkeley: University of California Press.

Treichler, P. A. (1988b). AIDS, homophobia, and biomedical discourse: An epidemic of signification. *October, 43*, 31–71.

Treichler, P. A. (1993). AIDS narratives on television: Whose story? In T. F. Murphy & S. Poirer (Eds.), *Writing AIDS: Gay literature, language, and analysis* (pp. 161–199). New York: Columbia University Press.

Troutner, L. (1974). Time and education. In D. Denton (Ed.), *Existentialism and phenomenology in education: Collected essays* (pp. 159–183). New York: Teachers College Press.

Trudell, B. K. (1992). Inside a ninth-grade sexuality classroom: The process of knowledge construction. In J. T. Sears (Ed.), *Sexuality and the curriculum* (pp. 203–226). New York: Teachers College Press.

Tyack, D. (1974). *The one best system*. Cambridge, MA: Harvard University Press.

Update: Acquired immunedeficiency syndrome US 1992. (1993, July 23). *Morbidity and Mortality Weekly Report, 42*, 547–557.

Urwin, C. (1984). Power relations and the emergence of language. In J. Henriquez et al., *Changing the subject* (pp. 264–322). New York: Methuen.

Vaihinger, H. (1935). *The philosophy of "as if."* London: Kegan Paul, Trench, & Trubner.

Vance, C. S. (1984). Pleasure and danger: Toward a politics of sexuality. In C. S. Vance (Ed.), *Pleasure and danger: Exploring female sexuality* (pp. 1–27). Boston: Routlege & Kegan Paul.

Vandenberg, D. (1971). *Being and education: An essay in existential phenomenology*. Englewood Cliffs, NJ: Prentice Hall.

van Manen, M. (1986). *The tone of teaching*. Richmond Hill, Ont.: Scholastic-Tab.

van Manen, M. (1990). *Researching lived experience: Human science for an action sensitive pedagogy*. Albany: State University of New York Press.

Vascellaro, S., & Genishi, C. (1994). All things that mattered: Stories written by teachers for children. In A. H. Dyson & C. Genishi (Eds.), *The need for story: Cultural diversity in the classroom and community*. Urbana, IL: National Council of Teachers of English.

Vygotsky, L. (1956). *Selected psychological research*. Moscow: Academy of Pedagogic Sciences of USSR.

Wagner, J. (1993). Ignorance in educational research: Or how can you not know that. *Educational Researcher, 22*(5), 15–23.

Waksler, F. C. (1991a). The hard times of childhood and children's strategies for dealing with them. In F. C. Waksler (Ed.), *Studying the social worlds of children: Sociological readings* (pp. 216–234). New York: Falmer.

Waksler, F. C. (1991b). Studying children: Phenomenological insights. In F. C. Waksler (Ed.), *Studying the social worlds of children: Sociological readings* (pp. 60–69). New York: Falmer.

Walkerdine, V. (1984). Developmental psychology and the child-centered pedagogy: The insertion of Piaget into early education. In J. Henriquez et al., *Changing the subject* (pp. 153–202). New York: Methuen.

Walkerdine, V. (1990). *School girl fictions*. London: Verso.

Waller, W. (1932). *The sociology of teaching*. New York: Russell & Russell.

Walsh, D. J. (1991). Extending the discourse on developmental appropriateness: A developmental perspective. *Early Education and Development, 2,* 109–118.

Walsh, W. (1959). *The use of the imagination*. London: Chatto & Windus.

Ward, J. V., & Taylor, J. M. (1992). Sexuality education for immigrant and minority students: Developing culturally appropriate curriculum. In J. T. Sears (Ed.), *Sexuality and the curriculum* (pp. 183–203). New York: Teachers College Press.

Watney, S. (1987). *Policing desire: Pornography, AIDS and the media*. Minneapolis: University of Minnesota Press.

Watney, S. (1991). School's out. In D. Fuss (Ed.), *Inside/out: Lesbian theories, gay theories* (pp. 387–401). New York: Routledge.

Watney, S. (1992). Short-term companions: AIDS as popular entertainment. In A. Klusacek & K. Morrison (Eds.), *A leap in the dark* (pp. 152–166). Montreal: Véhicule Press.

Weber, E. (1984). *Ideas influencing early childhood education*. New York: Teachers College Press.

Weeks, J. (1981). *Sex, politics and society: The regulation of sexuality since 1800.* New York: Longman.

Weeks, J. (1991). *Against nature: Essays on history, sexuality and identity*. London: Rivers Oram Press.

Weikart, D. (1988). Quality in early education. In C. Warger (Ed.), *A resource guide to public school early childhood programs* (pp. 63–72). Alexandria, VA: Association for Supervision and Curriculum Development.

Wexler, M. N. (1990). Conjectures on the future of ignorance. *Phenomenology + Pedagogy, 8,* 75–85.

What high school students want from an HIV education program and how it can be delivered effectively: A report to the Bureau of School Health Education Services, New York State Education Department. (1990). (Available from MAGI Educational Services, Inc., Larchmont, NY)

White, R., & Cunningham, A. M. (1991). *Ryan White: My own story*. New York: NAL Dutton.

Wickens, E. (1993). Penny's question: "I will have a child in my class with two moms—What do you know about this?" *Young Children, 48,* 3, 25–28.

Wilde, O. (1966). *A woman of no importance*. In *The complete works of Oscar Wilde*. London: Collins.

Wilde, O. (1985). *The picture of Dorian Gray*. New York: Random. (Original work published 1891)

Williams, L. (1990, March 28). Using self-esteem to fix society's ills. *The New York Times*, pp. C1,10.

Williams, W. L. (1986). *The spirit and the flesh: Sexual diversity in American Indian culture.* Boston: Beacon.

Willis, P. (1977). *Learning to labour.* Westmead, UK: Saxon House.

Wirth, A. G. (1989). The violation of people at work in schools. *Teachers College Record, 90*(4), 535–549.

Wishy, B. (1968). *The child and the republic.* Philadelphia: University of Pennsylvania Press.

Women and HIV: The research response. (1993, Spring). *The AIDS Report* (Harvard AIDS Institute), pp. 6–9.

Woodhead, M. (1990). Psychology and the cultural construction of children's needs. In A. James & A. Prout (Eds.), *Constructing and reconstructing childhood* (pp. 60–78). New York: Falmer.

Woodhead, M., Light, P., & Carr, R. (1991). *Growing up in a changing society.* New York: Routledge.

Woodruff, G. (1993). The invisible epidemic's littlest victims. *Reading, 8*(2), 18–23.

Yingling, T. (1993, March). AIDS, confession, and theory: The pedagogical dilemma. *Lesbian and Gay Studies Newsletter,* Department of English, Duke University.

Young, R. (1990). *A critical theory of education.* New York: Teachers College Press.

Young-Bruehl, E. (1989). *Mind and the body politic.* New York: Routledge.

Zelizer, V. A. (1985). *Pricing the priceless child: The changing social value of children.* New York: Basic Books.

Zimiles, H. (1991). Diversity and change in young children: Some educational implications. In B. Spodek & O. Saracho (Eds.), *Issues in early childhood curriculum* (pp. 21–45). New York: Teachers College Press.

Index

237

About the Author

Jonathan Silin is a member of the graduate faculty at the Bank Street College of Education, where he pursues research interests in contemporary childhood and gay/lesbian studies and supervises teachers. Formerly the Director of Public Information Services and Development for the Long Island Association for AIDS Care, he has been a consultant to numerous HIV/AIDS education and policy projects across the country. Before receiving his doctorate in Curriculum and Teaching from Teachers College, Columbia University, he was a classroom teacher and taught in a variety of early childhood settings.